W9-CTF-535

AT HOME
with the WORD
1 9 9 8

Sunday Scriptures and Reflections

Susan E. Myers

Kathleen K. Kane
Fabian C. Lochner
Jack Real

LTP
LITURGY
TRAINING
PUBLICATIONS

Reprinting from *At Home with the Word 1998*

A parish or an institution may purchase a license to reprint the Reflections (and their discussion questions), the Practices of Faith, Hope and Charity, the Prayer of the Season or the holy day boxes from *At Home with the Word 1998*. Please see page 156 for details.

If a parish or institution wishes to reproduce some or all of the scripture texts, a license must be acquired from the copyright owners (see below). When writing to copyright owners, state clearly which texts you wish to use, the number of copies to be made, and how often you'll be using the copies. There may be a license fee.

Acknowledgments

The Sunday scripture pericopes contained herein are from the *New Revised Standard Version of the Bible*, copyright © 1989, by the Division of Christian Education of the National Council of the Churches of Christ in the U.S.A. All rights reserved. Used by permission. Text emendations © 1996, Augsburg-Fortress. Used by permission.

Most Roman Catholic parishes proclaim the Sunday scriptures using the *New American Bible* readings from the *Lectionary for Mass*, copyright © 1970 by the Confraternity of Christian Doctrine. For information on reprint permission, write: Confraternity of Christian Doctrine, 1312 Massachusetts Avenue NW, Washington DC 20005.

The translations of the psalms used herein are from the *Liturgical Psalter*, copyright © 1993 by the International Committee on English in the Liturgy, Inc. (ICEL); the English translation of the gospel canticles ("Canticle of Zechariah," "Canticle of Mary" and "Canticle of Simeon") are copyright © 1993 by ICEL; the "Salve Regina" from *A Book of Prayers*, copyright © 1982 by ICEL. Used with permission. All rights reserved. For reprint permission, write: ICEL, 1522 K Street NW, Suite 1000, Washington DC 20005-1202.

The Prayers of the Season were written by Gabe Huck.

The holy day commentaries were written by Peter Mazar and Martin Connell.

The art in this book is by Nina Morlan. The design is by Jill Smith. Martin Connell was the editor, and Deborah Bogaert was the production editor. Typesetting was by Karen Mitchell, in Palatino and Universe. The book was printed and bound by Danner Press, Canton, Ohio.

At Home with the Word 1998, copyright © 1997, Archdiocese of Chicago: Liturgy Training Publications, 1800 North Hermitage Avenue, Chicago IL 60622-1101; 1-800-933-1800; fax 1-800-933-7094; e-mail: orders@ltp.org. All rights reserved.

ISBN 1-56854-193-7
CODE: AHW98

How to Use At Home with the Word

This book invites you to be at home *with* God's word, to live with the Sunday scriptures in order to live *by* them.

SCRIPTURE READINGS You may want to read the scriptures before going to church. Or, better yet, use this book to return to the Sunday scriptures again and again throughout the week.

Because the Sunday readings of many other Christian churches are the same as those proclaimed in Catholic communities, *At Home with the Word* has highlighted the scriptures we share. There are two minor changes that result. First, there may be a few more verses in the readings here than you will hear proclaimed in the Sunday assembly. Also, when Roman Catholic churches observe a particular feast on a given Sunday that is not celebrated by other Christian communities, there will be two sets of readings. Recognizing the steps that have already been taken will further the unity not yet realized.

REFLECTION Susan E. Myers is a PHD candidate in New Testament and Early Christianity at the University of Notre Dame. Her writing reveals her lifelong commitment to issues of peace and justice.

The reflections can be read to learn more background information on the scriptures and to consider things never considered before. One can also keep a journal of thoughts and discoveries. Households or small groups can meet weekly to share the readings and the reflection.

This is Year C, the year of the gospel according to Luke. Throughout Ordinary Time we will be reading most often from this gospel. See Susan Myers's introduction to the Gospel of Luke on pages 8 – 11.

PRACTICE OF FAITH Kathleen K. Kane, mother of five and preparer of candidates for initiation, brings her theological education and the experience of her family's sacramental life to this year's Practices of Faith.

PRACTICE OF HOPE Fabian C. Lochner, PHD, is a church musician and college music teacher. Awed by the gospel, he has connected with the stories of Jesus through creative intuition.

PRACTICE OF CHARITY Jack Real is a director of education and advocacy at the Colorado Coalition for the Homeless. He lobbies for the homeless in the state legislature.

WEEKDAY READINGS Some people may want to read more than the Sunday scriptures. We've listed the chapters of the book of the Bible from which the first readings for daily Mass are taken each week.

At Home with the Word also includes:

MORNING, EVENING AND NIGHT PRAYER These simple patterns of prayer can enrich the life of an individual Christian or of a household. The prayers take five or ten minutes and are meant to be repeated every day. Don't be afraid of repetition. After all, that's one way to learn.

SEASONAL PSALMS AND PRAYERS Each season is introduced by a special page that includes an acclamation, a psalm and a short prayer. Repeating a single psalm throughout a season is a fine way to learn the psalms by heart.

SUNDAY AND FRIDAY PSALMS AND PRAYERS Sunday is our day of feasting, Friday our day of fasting. Both days need extra prayer and acts of discipleship. Here are psalms, a Lord's Day poem by Henry Baker and a prayer for Fridays from the bishops' letter *The Challenge of Peace*.

CALENDAR
TABLE OF CONTENTS

The Lectionary and At Home with the Word

by Martin F. Connell

WHAT IS A LECTIONARY? A lectionary is an ordered selection of readings, chosen from both Testaments of the Bible, for proclamation in the assembly gathered for worship. Lectionaries have been used in Christian worship since about the fourth century. At different times and in different places the order of the readings has varied a bit, reflecting religious issues of importance to local communities.

Until Vatican II, the readings in Catholic churches were the same from year to year; and they were proclaimed in Latin, an ancient language that many Catholics did not understand. The use of the language of the people in the liturgy and the revision of the lectionary after the Council have had tremendous effects on the accessibility of the Bible for Catholics. The Bible is now a vibrant source of our faith and tradition.

SOME BACKGROUND: THE THREE-YEAR LEC-TIONARY The lectionary issued by the church after the Second Vatican Council appeared in 1970. The most exciting feature of the new lectionary was its basic three-year plan, which incorporated a fuller selection from the books of the Bible.

Each of the first three gospels — Matthew, Mark and Luke — corresponds with one year: Matthew for Year A, Mark for Year B and Luke for Year C. This liturgical year, 1998, is Year C.

YEAR C: THE GOSPEL OF LUKE You will find that most of the gospel readings proclaimed in your Sunday assembly this year and printed in *At Home with the Word* for 1998 will be from the Gospel of Luke. This gospel will be proclaimed on most Sundays from the first Sunday of Advent, November 30, 1997, to the celebration of Christ the King, November 22, 1998.

THE GOSPEL OF JOHN You might ask: What about the Gospel of John? The Fourth Gospel is not excluded from proclamation during the three-year cycle. Although there is not a year during which it is highlighted, the Gospel of John punctuates certain seasons and times of the year. The readings from Year A on the third, fourth and fifth Sundays of Lent, for example, are proclaimed every year in parishes celebrating the Rite of Christian Initiation of Adults (RCIA); these three wonderful stories from the Gospel of John — the woman at the well, the man born blind and the raising of Lazarus — are important texts to accompany the celebration of the scrutinies in the process of Christian initiation. You will find two sets of readings on these Sundays: one set for churches celebrating the scrutinies of the RCIA, and one set for parishes not celebrating the initiation process during that particular liturgical year.

The Gospel of John also appears for the Mass of the Lord's Supper on Holy Thursday and for the long passion reading on Good Friday. And on most of the Sundays of Eastertime — the Fifty Days from Easter Sunday until Pentecost — the Gospel of John is proclaimed.

THE DIFFERENCE BETWEEN THE BIBLE AND THE LECTIONARY The shape of the lectionary comes from the ancient church practice of *lectio continua*, a Latin term which describes the successive reading through books of the Bible from Sunday to Sunday. You can see *lectio continua* in practice if you open up this book and consider the gospel texts assigned, for example, to the Sundays from the feast of the Body and Blood of Christ, June 14, to the Twentieth Sunday in Ordinary Time, August 16. Readings will be proclaimed from the Gospel of Luke in the order that they are in the gospel itself. Though not every verse from that part of the gospel is included, you will notice that these particular Sundays concentrate on chapters 9 through 12 of the gospel.

You will find, moreover, that the first readings will often echo some image, character or idea of the gospel, as is the church's intention. The second reading often stands on its own and is chosen from a letter of Paul or another letter of the New Testament. These readings appear in the same order that they do in the Bible; you will notice, for example, that readings from the first and second letters to Timothy are proclaimed as the second readings from the Twenty-fourth Sunday until the Thirtieth Sunday in Ordinary Time.

UNITY WITH OTHER CHRISTIAN CHURCHES IN THE WORD OF GOD The basic plan of the lectionary for Catholics is universal. The readings proclaimed in your church on a particular Sunday are the same as those proclaimed in Catholic churches all over the globe. The lectionary is one of the main things that makes our liturgy so "catholic," or universal.

Not only are the readings the same as those in other Catholic churches, but the revision of the Roman Catholic lectionary was so well received that other churches began to follow the three-year lectionary cycle. So not only are the readings the same in Catholic churches, but as time has passed, other Christian churches have adopted the Catholic lectionary.

Catholics and their neighbors who attend other Christian churches often hear the same word of God proclaimed and preached in the Sunday gathering. Even though you may not talk about the Sunday readings with your neighbors and therefore haven't realized that your readers read the same lections and your preachers preach on the same scriptural texts, this is really a remarkable change when you consider how very far apart from one another Catholic and non-Catholic churches were before the Second Vatican Council.

The slight differences you'll find between the readings in *At Home with the Word* and what is proclaimed on Sundays is a result of our efforts to highlight the scriptures shared by many Christian churches. The major parts of the readings will be secure, but there might be a few verses tacked on in *At Home with the Word* at the beginning or end of a reading to match those in the Revised Common Lectionary, which is used in many non-Catholic Christian churches. As always, when the page with the readings is short on space, we will give a shorter version of a reading or two and provide the full citation at the end so that you can check out the fuller text in your Bible.

Have a wonderful liturgical year being "at home with the word" of God.

An Introduction to the Gospel of Luke

by Susan E. Myers

The Gospel of Luke was written in order to give an "orderly account" (1:3) of the birth, ministry, death and resurrection of Jesus, who is proclaimed as the Christ. The events described in the gospel and in its sequel, the Acts of the Apostles, are set squarely within world (that is, Roman) history, and the God who has been working among the people Israel continues to guide the Christian church. Throughout the two-volume work of Luke and Acts, the Holy Spirit is active, guiding Jesus and empowering the nascent church while transforming all of history. Jesus is presented as a teacher, as one who instructs his listeners on what is necessary in the life of one who professes to follow him, especially as they travel together to Jerusalem. The lessons he teaches regarding concern for the poor and the marginalized are lessons he also lives.

AUTHORSHIP, STYLE AND PURPOSE The author of this two-part work is anonymous. The appellation "Luke," recalling a companion of Paul, was assigned a century after the work was written in order to give it greater authority. We do know a great deal about the author, though, thanks to the prefaces of both the gospel (1:1–4) and Acts (1:1–5). Unlike the other gospels and, in fact, most anonymous works, this gospel can be said with certainty to have been written by a man, a conclusion based on the masculine participle used in the preface. Luke-Acts is written to a Gentile audience, as evidenced by the recipient's Greek name, Theophilus ("lover of God").

The author writes in the tradition of the Greek historians, seeking to provide a carefully constructed account of events. This does not mean that the author is telling history as we know it. He was not himself an eyewitness to the events but recognizes their significance and wants to convey "the truth" to others. The gospel provides a carefully crafted, unified narrative of stories that the author learned from other sources. The author is quite creative, striving to make the account as interesting as possible, as evidenced especially by Acts, which reads much like an adventure novel. Indeed, the best modern analogy that might be made to this two-volume work is that of a historical novel in which facts are recounted but details of speech and action are created to provide for greater interest. Most important, the author provides a faith account, proclaiming that Jesus is risen and exalted with God, and recounts the foundational events that formed the Christian church. As a faith account, Luke-Acts does not claim to be unbiased; it is written precisely in order to move its readers to belief.

SOURCES, DATING AND RELATION TO JUDAISM The Gospel of Luke was written several decades after the events recounted in it. The words and deeds of Jesus were not recorded at the time they occurred, and the earliest witnesses to his triumph over death did not find it necessary to put their experiences in writing (Jesus' followers expected him to return in glory in the near future). Instead, the earliest traditions about Jesus were transmitted orally, his passion and death being remembered in especially clear detail. Eventually, some of the sayings of Jesus were recorded, and later, organized accounts of his life were written as gospels.

The author of Luke-Acts made use of an earlier account, the Gospel of Mark, following its general scheme but expanding it in significant ways. The author also used a source for sayings — usually designated as Q — known also to the author of the Gospel of Matthew, and a special source or sources that contained information about the infancy of Jesus and a number of unique stories. All of this information was skillfully interwoven, providing the reader with a compelling account of Jesus' life, an account that draws the reader into it as a disciple of Jesus.

The Gospel of Luke probably was written in the last decades of the first century (perhaps around 80). The author knows about the destruction of the holy city of Jerusalem and the Jewish Temple in the year 70. The community is settled, and the author seeks to present it as an integral part of the Roman empire. At the same time, the "salvation history" begun with the Hebrew people is continued in the Christian community. Jerusalem appears as the center of the world and the goal of both Jesus and the reader throughout much of the gospel. In Acts, Jerusalem is the starting point of the proclamation, taken even to the "ends of the earth," regarding the decisive events that occurred there. The author may have been one of, or may have written to a community of, "God-fearers," those attracted to the ethical demands of Judaism but not fully converted. The Judaism of Jesus and his first followers is central; this author suggests that it was only after the Jews rejected the gospel that it was preached to the Gentiles, eventually transforming the world.

THEMES OF THE GOSPEL The Gospel of Luke contains within it many of the best-loved stories of Jesus' life. It begins with the infancy of Jesus, recounting the story of Mary and Elizabeth and providing us with hymns (such as the Magnificat and the Canticles of Zechariah and of Simeon) that have formed part of the prayer life of Christians for centuries. Only in Luke-Acts do we read of the child Jesus in the Temple or of the ascension of Jesus. Several of Jesus' parables, such as the stories of the Prodigal Son and the Good Samaritan, are unique to this gospel as well.

Women figure prominently in the Gospel of Luke, beginning with the infancy account and continuing throughout the text. From this gospel we know that there were many women among Jesus' band of followers. Jesus visits his friends Martha and Mary, and, as in the other gospels, women are the first to find the empty tomb and to recognize that Jesus has vanquished death. Although we learn interesting information about women from this gospel (they financially support Jesus' itinerant ministry), it cannot be said that the gospel transforms the lot of women. In fact, women generally appear in precisely the traditional role of domestic caretakers.

PORTRAIT OF JESUS Throughout the gospel, Jesus is a person of prayer. He often takes himself away from his followers to pray by himself, an act which usually signals that a decisive event is about to occur. The Holy Spirit, by whom Mary conceives Jesus, descends upon him at his baptism and guides him throughout his ministry until he bestows the holy spirit upon his disciples after his exaltation with God. In Acts, it is the Spirit who inspires the first apostles and Paul to proclaim their faith in the risen Jesus to all and to perform many of the same deeds of healing and exorcism that Jesus had performed.

Jesus is portrayed in the Gospel of Luke as a man on a journey. Although his ministry begins in his home region of Galilee, he sets forth on a path to the religious, social and political capital city of Jerusalem. On the long path to Jerusalem and to his death, Jesus teaches his followers, both those in his inner circle and those who join him along the way. What Jesus teaches is precisely what it means to be his disciple, his student.

DISCIPLESHIP Although the gospel is set within human history (note the historical figures mentioned in the beginning of chapters 2 and 3), there is proclaimed also a certain detachment from the world in the theme of discipleship, which governs the journey of Jesus to Jerusalem. Jesus' teachings in this section are demanding. What is required to follow him is a life of total commitment, total faithfulness. Daily the disciple of Jesus is to shoulder the cross, not as a weapon of torture and execution, and not as an inconvenience or burden in life, but as a part of the Christian journey. To follow the one who carried his cross to death requires unwavering commitment. Nothing else can be more important than walking in his footsteps.

CONCERN FOR THE DISENFRANCHISED The road of discipleship has an ethical component to it that involves commitment to those on the fringes of society. This gospel is exceedingly uncomfortable with capitalism, viewing as abhorrent the concentration of wealth in the hands of a few while others have need. It is, however, not only the contemporary economic system that is challenged. All might and prestige are illusory; in the kingdom of God, those who are outside the power structures will be rewarded and exalted, while the powerful will be humbled. Justice is not simply a worthy goal or a lofty ideal but a demand of all who would follow Jesus.

To convey this concern for the poor and downtrodden, the author includes a number of stories that appear only in this gospel and in which care and compassion are central. Jesus does not only preach compassion in stories such as those of the Good Samaritan, the Prodigal Son and the Rich Man and Lazarus. Indeed, in his own life, he lives the ideal, comforting the weeping women who follow his final path to death, forgiving the "good thief" on the cross and asking forgiveness for his persecutors. Being a disciple of Jesus involves living and loving as he did.

SUGGESTED READING

Danker, Frederick W. *Luke.* Proclamation Commentaries, 2d ed. Philadelphia: Fortress, 1987.

LaVerdiere, Eugene. *Luke.* New Testament Message 5. Wilmington, DE: Michael Glazier, 1980.

Ringe, Sharon H. *Luke.* Westminster Bible Companion. Louisville, KY: Westminster John Knox, 1995.

M O R N I N G
p r a y e r

This order of prayer may be said upon waking
or before or during breakfast.

O Lord, open my lips,
and my mouth shall declare your praise.

The Sign of the Cross

In the name of the Father
and of the Son
and of the Holy Spirit.

Psalm 63

God, my God, you I crave;
my soul thirsts for you,
my body aches for you
like a dry and weary land.
Let me gaze on you in your temple:
a vision of strength and glory.

Your love is better than life,
my speech is full of praise.
I give you a lifetime of worship,
my hands raised in your name.
I feast at a rich table,
my lips sing of your glory.

On my bed I lie awake,
your memory fills the night.
You have been my help,
I rejoice beneath your wings.
Yes, I cling to you,
your right hand holds me fast.

Let those who want me dead
end up deep in the grave!
They will die by the sword,
their bodies food for jackals.
But let the king find joy in God.
All who swear by truth be praised,
every lying mouth be shut.

*One of the seasonal psalms throughout this book
may be prayed instead of Psalm 63.*

The Canticle of Zechariah

Praise the Lord, the God of Israel,
who shepherds the people and sets them free.

God raises from David's house
a child with power to save.
Through the holy prophets
God promised in ages past
to save us from enemy hands,
from the grip of all who hate us.

The Lord favored our ancestors
recalling the sacred covenant,
the pledge to our ancestor Abraham,
to free us from our enemies,
so we might worship without fear
and be holy and just all our days.

And you, child, will be called
Prophet of the Most High,
for you will come to prepare
a pathway for the Lord
by teaching the people salvation
through forgiveness of their sin.

Out of God's deepest mercy
a dawn will come from on high,
light for those shadowed by death,
a guide for our feet on the way to peace.

The Lord's Prayer

*You may join hands with others or hold your
hands with palms facing upward while praying the
Lord's Prayer.*

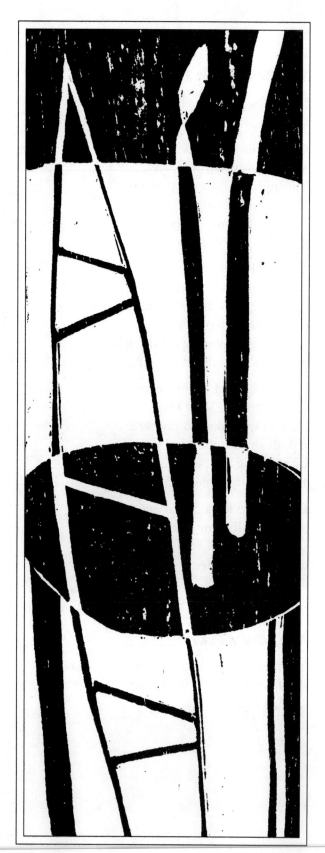

E V E N I N G
prayer

This order of prayer may be said before or after dinner.

O God, come to my assistance.
O Lord, make haste to help me.

The Lighting of a Candle

A candle may be lit to welcome the evening while saying:

Jesus Christ is the light of the world,
a light no darkness can overcome.

Psalm 141:1–5, 8

Hurry, Lord! I call and call!
Listen! I plead with you.
Let my prayer rise like incense,
my upraised hands, like an evening sacrifice.

Lord, guard my lips,
watch my every word.
Let me never speak evil
or consider hateful deeds,
let me never join the wicked
to eat their lavish meals.

If the just correct me,
I take their rebuke as kindness,
but the unction of the wicked
will never touch my head.
I pray and pray
against their hateful ways.

Lord my God, I turn to you,
in you I find safety.
Do not strip me of life.

The Canticle of Mary

I acclaim the greatness of the Lord,
I delight in God my savior,
who regarded my humble state.
Truly from this day on
all ages will call me blest.

For God, wonderful in power,
has used that strength for me.
Holy the name of the Lord!
whose mercy embraces the faithful,
one generation to the next.

The mighty arm of God
scatters the proud in their conceit,
pulls tyrants from their thrones,
and raises up the humble.
The Lord fills the starving,
and lets the rich go hungry.

God rescues lowly Israel,
recalling the promise of mercy,
the promise made to our ancestors,
to Abraham's heirs for ever.

Intercession and Lord's Prayer

*At day's end we offer our petitions in Jesus' name.
We make intercession for our church, our world,
our parish, our neighbors, our family and friends
and ourselves. We seal all our prayers with the
Lord's Prayer. In conclusion, all may exchange the
sign of peace.*

N I G H T
p r a y e r

This order of prayer may be said before going to sleep.

May Almighty God give us a restful night and a peaceful death.

Psalm 131

Lord, I am not proud,
holding my head too high,
reaching beyond my grasp.

No, I am calm and tranquil
like a weaned child
resting in its mother's arms:
my whole being at rest.
Let Israel rest in the Lord,
now and for ever.

The Canticle of Simeon

Lord, let your servant
now die in peace,
for you kept your promise.

With my own eyes
I see the salvation
you prepared for all peoples:

a light of revelation for the Gentiles
and glory to your people Israel.

Invocation to Mary

The final prayer of the day is customarily to Mary.

Hail, holy Queen, Mother of mercy,
our life, our sweetness, and our hope!
To you we cry, the children of Eve;
to you we send up our sighs,
mourning and weeping in this land of exile.
Turn, then, most gracious advocate,
your eyes of mercy toward us;
lead us home at last
and show us the blessed fruit of your
womb, Jesus:
O clement, O loving, O sweet Virgin Mary.

The Sign of the Cross

We end the day the way we began it,
with the sign of the cross.

May the almighty and merciful Lord,
the Father and the Son and the Holy Spirit,
bless and keep us. Amen.

SUNDAY
prayer

Sunday is our weekly feast day, our celebration of creation, liberation and resurrection.

The wedding feast of the Lamb has begun, and his bride is prepared to welcome him.

Psalm 100

Shout joy to the Lord, all earth,
serve the Lord with gladness,
enter God's presence with joy!

Know that the Lord is God,
our maker to whom we belong,
our shepherd, and we the flock.

Enter the temple gates,
the courtyard with thanks and praise;
give thanks and bless God's name.

Indeed the Lord is good!
God's love is for ever,
faithful from age to age.

Prayer of the Day

On this day, the first of days,
God the Father's name we praise;
Who, creation's Lord and spring,
Did the world from darkness bring.

On this day the eternal Son
Over death the triumph won;
On this day the Spirit came
With the gift of living flame.

God, the blessed Three in One,
May thy holy will be done;
In thy word our souls are free.
And we rest this day with thee.

Lord, by your cross and resurrection
    you have set us free.
You are the savior of the world.

Psalm 51:3-6, 12-13

Have mercy, tender God,
forget that I defied you.
Wash away my sin,
cleanse me from my guilt.

I know my evil well,
it stares me in the face,
evil done to you alone
before your very eyes.

Creator, reshape my heart,
God, steady my spirit.
Do not cast me aside
stripped of your holy spirit.

Prayer of the Day

All praise be yours, God our Creator,
as we wait in joyful hope
for the flowering of justice
and the fullness of peace.

All praise for this day, this Friday.
By our weekly fasting and prayer,
cast out the spirit of war, of fear and mistrust,
and make us grow hungry
    for human kindness,
thirsty for solidarity
    with all the people of your dear earth.

May all our prayers, our fasting and our deeds
be done in the name of Jesus. Amen.

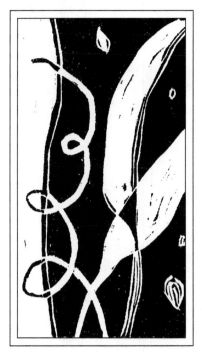

Friday is our weekly fast day, our day of special prayer, fasting and almsgiving.

ADVENT

Maranatha! Come, Lord Jesus!

God owns this planet
and all its riches.
The earth and every creature
belong to God.

God set the land on top of the seas
and anchored it in the deep.

Who is fit to climb God's mountain
and stand in his holy place?

Whoever has integrity:
not chasing shadows,
not living lies.

God will bless them,
their savior will bring justice.
These people long to see the Lord,
they seek the face of Jacob's God.

Stretch toward heaven, you gates,
open high and wide.
Let the glorious sovereign enter.

Who is this splendid ruler?
The Lord of power and might,
the conqueror of chaos.

Stretch toward heaven, you gates,
open high and wide.
Let the glorious sovereign enter.

Who is this splendid ruler?
The Lord of heaven's might,
this splendid ruler is God.

In the long nights of December,
we call you God of Jacob
because our ancestor Jacob
   wrestled all night long with you
and won your blessing
   and the name Israel.
Remember Jacob
who saw the ladder in the sky
and all your angels going up and down,
Jacob, who was the child
of Rebekah and Isaac,
the husband of Leah and Rachel,
the father of Joseph and Judah
and of all the tribes.
These are the tribes
that climb your mountain,
seek your face.
These are the tribes of Joseph and Mary
with whom we stand and reach up
like high, open gates
that wait for you to enter, God of Jacob,
wait for your gentleness and justice
to save us.

— Prayer of the Season

— Psalm 24

READING I *Jeremiah 33:14–16*

The days are surely coming, says the LORD, when I will fulfill the promise I made to the house of Israel and the house of Judah. In those days and at that time I will cause a righteous Branch to spring up for David, who shall execute justice and righteousness in the land. In those days Judah will be saved and Jerusalem will live in safety. And this is the name by which it will be called: "The LORD is our righteousness."

READING II *1 Thessalonians 3:9–13, 4:1–2*

How can we thank God enough for you in return for all the joy that we feel before our God because of you? Night and day we pray most earnestly that we may see you face to face and restore whatever is lacking in your faith.

Now may that very God, our Father, and our Lord Jesus direct our way to you. And may the Lord make you increase and abound in love for one another and for all, just as we abound in love for you. And may the Lord so strengthen your hearts in holiness that you may be blameless before our God and Father at the coming of our Lord Jesus with all his saints.

Finally, brothers and sisters, we ask and urge you in the Lord Jesus that, as you learned from us how you ought to live and to please God, as, in fact, you are doing, you should do so more and more. For you know what instructions we gave you through the Lord Jesus.

GOSPEL *Luke 21:25–36*

Jesus said:

"There will be signs in the sun, the moon, and the stars, and on the earth distress among nations confused by the roaring of the sea and the waves. People will faint from fear and foreboding of what is coming upon the world, for the powers of the heavens will be shaken. Then they will see 'the Son-of-Man coming in a cloud' with power and great glory. Now when these things begin to take place, stand up and raise your heads, because your redemption is drawing near."

Then Jesus told them a parable: "Look at the fig tree and all the trees; as soon as they sprout leaves you can see for yourselves and know that summer is already near. So also, when you see these things taking place, you know that the dominion of God is near. Truly I tell you, this generation will not pass away until all things have taken place. Heaven and earth will pass away, but my words will not pass away.

"Be on guard so that your hearts are not weighed down with dissipation and drunkenness and the worries of this life, and that day does not catch you unexpectedly, like a trap. For it will come upon all who live on the face of the whole earth. Be alert at all times, praying that you may have the strength to escape all these things that will take place, and to stand before the Son-of-Man."

REFLECTION

Many of the Jewish people of Jesus' time expected great things to happen in their day. Some hoped for a messenger of God to "come in a cloud" and intervene to bring about justice and judgment. The earliest hope of Christians was that Jesus was this promised one of God and would soon return to judge the world with righteousness. The passage of time has tempered hope in an imminent parousia, but we continue to look forward to the day when Christ's reign will be complete, and justice and peace will flourish.

In this season, we celebrate three advents of Christ: his coming to the world in a particular time and place as a human being with all the same concerns that we experience; his coming to dwell in our hearts and to work through us to establish the reign of God on earth; and his future coming as judge to execute justice and righteousness.

The words of Jesus in today's gospel warn us always to be Advent people: expectant, hope-filled and watchful, attentively looking for the signs indicating that the day of judgment is approaching. Most of us go through life knowing that we will die someday but not expecting it to happen anytime soon. We make plans; we find ourselves preoccupied with the cares of day-to-day life and of this season; we think that *someday* we will put more time and energy into eating well, exercising, spending time in prayer. But today's gospel makes it clear that we must be prepared for the end at all times. We do not always have the leisure of waiting until tomorrow; we may not be here to live out the plans we have made.

We must live always in ways that are "unblamable in holiness" and pleasing to God so that we will be prepared for Christ's coming, whether at Christmas, in the quiet darkness of prayer, or on the Day of the Lord, when we stand humbly before God.

■ **This Advent, take time daily to sit in quiet darkness. Allow God to touch you, to speak to you. Listen.**

■ **Reflect on your life. Reflect especially on your death. The day may come unexpectedly, as a thief in the night. Are you ready? How might you be more prepared?**

PRACTICE OF FAITH

PROMISE. The people of the readings of Advent inspire and lead us to receive and believe promises. In the weeks ahead we will hear stories of response to God's promises. The powerful witness of Mary, Joseph, Elizabeth and Zechariah embodies the recognition and response that fills the story of promise. The fullness of response to the promise of incarnation comes in the response to the cross.

The wood of the crib promises the wood of the cross. Celebrate the promises of Advent by using real branches in the Advent wreath, real candles (yes, with real wax drippings) and real wood for the empty crib that awaits the birth of the Christ child.

Celebrate Saint Nicholas on December 6 with candy canes for the bishop's crosier and chocolate coins for Nicholas' rescue of young people from poverty.

PRACTICE OF HOPE

ENDTIME. If the sun, moon and stars, and the earth, wind and water, resound in my body, soul and spirit, then how, in turn, does my every thought, feeling and action resound in the elements? If the sweltering heat of summer can blissfully dissolve my soul into the universe, and if the cold of winter can squeeze me back into my body and enkindle memory and fellowship by the fireside, then what tectonic plate will quiver at the unending drunkenness and dissipation of my soul? What slumbering volcano will begin to rumble at my relentless care of life? How much envy will it take to form a killer tornado? How much hatred is needed to arouse a tidal wave? And how much love and wakefulness will be needed to build a shelter on the day the stars come falling down?

PRACTICE OF CHARITY

PLEASING TO GOD. A married couple in counseling mentioned that writing down each other's complaints could curb their anger toward each other. When the counselor asked them where that good idea came from, the woman said that her brother, who was in grade school, told her about the technique. He had learned it in a conflict resolution program at school. Many programs now teach how to resolve arguments in a nonviolent manner. Prepare for Christ's new year of peace by learning about interpersonal and international peace processes. Contact Pax Christi USA, 348 E. 10th St., Erie PA 16503; 814-452-4784.

WEEKDAY READINGS (Mo) Isaiah 2:1 – 5; (Tu) 11:1 – 10; (We) 25:6 – 10; (Th) 26:1 – 6; (Fr) 29:17 – 24; (Sa) 30:19 – 26

READING I *Baruch 5:1–9*

Take off the garment of your sorrow and affliction,
    O Jerusalem,
and put on forever the beauty of the glory from God.
Put on the robe of the righteousness
    that comes from God;
put on your head the diadem of the glory
    of the Everlasting;
for God will show your splendor
    everywhere under heaven.
For God will give you evermore the name,
"Righteous Peace, Godly Glory."
Arise, O Jerusalem, stand upon the height;
    look toward the east,
and see your children gathered from west and east
    at the word of the Holy One,
    rejoicing that God has remembered them.
For they went out from you on foot,
    led away by their enemies;
but God will bring them back to you,
carried in glory, as on a royal throne.
For God has ordered that every high mountain
    and the everlasting hills be made low
    and the valleys filled up, to make level ground,
    so that Israel may walk safely in the glory of God.
The woods and every fragrant tree
    have shaded Israel at God's command.
For God will lead Israel with joy,
    in the light of divine glory,
    with the mercy and righteousness
    that come from God.

READING II *Philippians 1:3–5, 8–11*

I thank my God every time I remember you, constantly praying with joy in every one of my prayers for all of you, because of your sharing in the gospel from the first day until now. I am confident of this, that the one who began a good work among you will bring it to completion by the day of Jesus Christ. For God is my witness, how I long for all of you with the compassion of Christ Jesus.

And this is my prayer, that your love may overflow more and more with knowledge and full insight to help you to determine what is best, so that in the day of Christ you may be pure and blameless, having produced the harvest of righteousness that comes through Jesus Christ for the glory and praise of God.
[Complete reading: Philippians 1:3–11]

GOSPEL *Luke 3:1–6*

In the fifteenth year of the reign of Emperor Tiberius, when Pontius Pilate was governor of Judea, and Herod was ruler of Galilee, and his brother Philip ruler of the region of Ituraea and Trachonitis, and Lysanias ruler of Abilene, during the high priesthood of Annas and Caiaphas, the word of God came to John son of Zechariah in the wilderness. And John went into all the region around the Jordan, proclaiming a baptism of repentance for the forgiveness of sins, as it is written in the book of the words of the prophet Isaiah,

"The voice of one crying out in the wilderness:
    'Prepare the way of the Lord,
        make straight the paths of the Lord.'
    'Every valley shall be filled,
        and every mountain and hill shall be made low,
    and the crooked shall be made straight,
        and the rough ways made smooth;
    and all flesh shall see the salvation of God.'"

Monday, December 8, 1997

IMMACULATE CONCEPTION OF THE VIRGIN MARY

Genesis 3:9–15, 20 *Eve is "the mother of the living."*

Ephesians 1:3–6, 11–12 *God chose us before the world began.*

Luke 1:26–38 *I am the servant of the Lord.*

Sin means separation from God. We believe Mary was never separated from God, from the moment of her conception in her mother's womb. On this Advent feast of Mary, her "yes" undoes Eve's "no." Mary, the mother of the living God, is our new Eve.

R E F L E C T I O N

The Gospel of Luke, according to its author, is an "orderly account of events" of Jesus' life, recorded only after careful investigation. Jesus lived in a particular time and place. Although not strictly a history, the gospel is concerned with placing this Jesus, this savior, squarely in the middle of human history, active during the reign of the emporer Tiberius.

During Advent, we continue to prepare for the celebration of Christmas, when we rejoice that God has become so much a part of our lives as to become incarnate, to become one of us. We have hope in a God who is not only magnificent and splendid, beyond full human comprehension, but also intimate, a God who shares in our hopes and joys, our sorrows and sufferings. As a result, all of life is transformed. All of history, all time, is made holy.

Irenaeus, the second-century bishop of Lyons, France, said it this way: God became human so that we might become divine. By deigning to share in human life through the person of Jesus, God bridges the gulf between the divine world of eternal life, of completion, of holiness, and the earthly reality of death and failure. By being willing to undergo the very human reality of dying, Jesus opens for us the possibility of life. Through baptism, Christians have the opportunity to be divinized, to be transformed and united with God. Baptismal garments are white as a symbol of this reality: We "put on forever the beauty of the glory from God," the "robe of righteousness."

In order to keep pure these garments, God sends prophets into our midst, people who, like John the Baptizer, look at the present reality and see its implications for the future. Prophets are not afraid to announce the coming of God and to prepare God's way, figuratively leveling mountains and raising valleys in the process, calling us to an ever greater commitment to the one who loves us enough to share in our life.

■ Who are the prophets of our time who call us to be mindful of God in our midst?

■ What does it mean to be divinized?

PRACTICE OF FAITH

BEGINNINGS. "Let me start at the beginning . . ." "I was born into poverty . . ." "It all began when . . ." How often the truth of a story, event or person lies at the beginning. How often the end of a story only makes sense by going back to the beginning. Neither beginnings nor endings stand alone well.

Mary's whole life was a gracious patience with beginnings and endings. The Feast of the Immaculate Conception on December 8 reveals, in the heart of Advent, how important a blessed beginning is in pointing to a holy ending.

The feast of the Immaculate Conception is a day to tell household stories of beginning. Tell stories of pregnancies, new friendships, new loves. Thank God for forming us in beginnings.

PRACTICE OF HOPE

THE STRAIGHT AND THE CROOKED. Where I live, there are too many highways. They cut through the land like giant razors. Valleys have been filled and hills have been brought low to make straight the paths of aggression. Let me then, O prophet, sing a new song for our restless time, the voice of one crying at the mall, at the subway station and in every corporate office: Remember the ways of the Lord. Follow the winding paths of his inscrutable wisdom. Rejoice in every valley that leads you down into shady groves. Honor every mountain that leads you up into the vastness of the sky. Embrace the crooked with love, for every angle holds a new mystery. Then you shall see indeed the salvation of God.

PRACTICE OF CHARITY

YOUR CHILDREN GATHERED. A villager spotted a baby floating down the river in a basket. He immediately rescued the baby, and the villagers began caring for the child. A day later, another basket and baby were seen. Again the village cared for the child. A third, then a fourth baby were discovered and cared for. In this story, caring for the baby is charity, an indisputable, noble act. But when the villagers ask, "What is happening upstream where the infants are being abandoned?," that is the beginning of social justice. *Why* are unfair, evil things happening? Be aware. Ask what causes racism, poverty, domestic violence and substance abuse. Think through possible solutions. Link together with others who seek solutions.

WEEKDAY READINGS (Mo) Immaculate Conception, see box; (Tu) Isaiah 40:1 – 11; (We) 40:25 – 31; (Th) 41:13 – 20; (Fr) Zechariah 2:14 – 17; (Sa) Sirach 48:1 – 4, 9 – 11

READING I *Zephaniah 3:14–20*

Sing aloud, O daughter Zion;
  shout, O Israel!
Rejoice and exult with all your heart,
  O daughter Jerusalem!
The LORD has taken away
    the judgments against you,
  and has turned away your enemies.
The Sovereign of Israel, the LORD, is in your midst;
  you shall fear disaster no more.
On that day it shall be said to Jerusalem:
Do not fear, O Zion;
  do not let your hands grow weak.
The LORD, your God, is in your midst,
  a warrior who gives victory;
the LORD will rejoice over you with gladness,
  and will renew you with love;
the LORD will exult over you with loud singing
  as on a day of festival.
I will remove disaster from you,
  so that you will not bear reproach for it.
I will deal with all your oppressors at that time.
And I will save the lame
  and gather the outcast,
and I will change their shame into praise
  and renown in all the earth.
At that time I will bring you home,
  at the time when I gather you;
for I will make you renowned and praised
  among all the peoples of the earth,
when I restore your fortunes
  before your eyes, says the LORD.

READING II *Philippians 4:4–7*

Rejoice in the Lord always; again I will say, Rejoice. Let your gentleness be known to everyone. The Lord is near. Do not worry about anything, but in everything by prayer and supplication with thanksgiving let your requests be made known to God. And the peace of God, which surpasses all understanding, will guard your hearts and your minds in Christ Jesus.

GOSPEL *Luke 3:7–18*

John said to the crowds that came out to be baptized by him, "You brood of vipers! Who warned you to flee from the wrath to come? Bear fruits worthy of repentance. Do not begin to say to yourselves, 'We have Abraham as our ancestor'; for I tell you, God is able from these stones to raise up children to Abraham. Even now the ax is lying at the root of the trees; every tree therefore that does not bear good fruit is cut down and thrown into the fire."

And the crowds asked John, "What then should we do?" In reply he said to them, "Whoever has two coats must share with anyone who has none; and whoever has food must do likewise." Even tax collectors came to be baptized, and they asked him, "Teacher, what should we do?" John said to them, "Collect no more than the amount prescribed for you." Soldiers also asked him, "And we, what should we do?" He said to them, "Do not extort money from anyone by threats or false accusation, and be satisfied with your wages."

As the people were filled with expectation, and all were questioning in their hearts concerning John, whether he might be the Messiah, John answered all of them by saying, "I baptize you with water; but one who is more powerful than I is coming, the thong of whose sandals I am not worthy to untie. He will baptize you with the Holy Spirit and fire. With a winnowing fork in hand, he will clear the threshing floor and gather the wheat into his granary, burning the chaff with unquenchable fire."

So, with many other exhortations, John proclaimed the good news to the people.

REFLECTION

The days are getting shorter. The darkness outside is more penetrating. But the Advent wreath grows brighter as we move forward in this season of joyful expectation. Today is Gaudete Sunday, the day on which we pause in our Advent preparation to rejoice at the promises of God in Christ Jesus.

It is also a time when the busyness that accompanies this season can begin to get overwhelming. Only by rooting ourselves in quiet reflection can we really live without anxiety, as Paul enjoins us, and dwell in the peace of God. Today's gospel reminds us that part of that reflection is a recognition of our own sinfulness and a sincere repentance.

The prophetic voice of John speaks loudly here that true repentance takes the form of action. Earlier, the words of Isaiah were used to describe John as one who would demand a level roadway for the Lord so that all might be able to see the salvation of God. In today's gospel, John tells his listeners concrete ways to prepare for God's coming: Share with those who are less fortunate; strive to be fair; do not take advantage of positions of authority and power. Then, as now, the mountains of life were economic and social.

John's portrait of the Messiah is a harsh one: He will gather all the usable grain but will burn the rest. This righteous judge will consider how well each person has worked to make straight the paths for others. John, in the tradition of the prophets of Israel, demands justice for the oppressed and compassion for the needy.

■ **How often do you make use of "connections" — whether familial, social or economic — to help yourself or someone else? What can you do to help someone who has no connections, who is struggling alone? Contact your local urban youth center, YMCA or YWCA, or a similar program to offer your services to assist in the development of all members of the community.**

■ **Reflect on how much you and your family spend on gifts. Resolve to do with less this Christmas. Remember: Jesus was born poor.**

PRACTICE OF FAITH

LODGING. The search for shelter — safe lodging, a place to call home — and the journey back home are deep human longings. Longing for a resting place in God echoes through the poetry of the Psalms. The church celebrates John of the Cross on December 14. John was a poet who went on an uncertain, perilous journey in prayer to find lodging with God.

December 16 is the first day of *Las Posadas,* or lodgings, for many Mexican families. The journey of Mary and Joseph to Bethlehem will be celebrated for nine days. In your own home, begin or continue the journey of the crèche figures of Mary and Joseph through the rooms of the house. The empty crib awaits them.

PRACTICE OF HOPE

EXPECTATION. John, wild man, caller in the wilderness! For the strain of your voice I left behind the lights of the city. I shared your bed of stone, your shirt of hair and your abject meals. I waded with you into the chill of the Jordan, where you dunked me until I almost drowned. Then, with barely a glimmer in your eye, you sent me away. I have followed your instructions well. My accounts are settled, I have given away half my clothes, and I share my food with strangers. So tell me, then, great Baptizer: Why is my heart still restless? Why are my days still unfulfilled? What is that strange longing in my soul to be consumed by a fire yet unknown, to conceive and to be conceived, to bear a child and to be born a child again?

PRACTICE OF CHARITY

GATHER THE OUTCAST. He was called "Funky" by the other men who lived under the bridge. Two days before Christmas, the outreach workers found him. He was indistinguishable from the debris around the bridge supports. Funky was so cold that he overcame his paranoia and went willingly to the clinic. After frostbite surgery and psychiatric medication, Funky could return to his family in Texas. Had the services not been available, Funky probably would have frozen to death in a schizophrenic haze. Only the process of social justice brought him help — outreach, clinic, hospital and mental health services. Find out about the needs of the homeless from the National Coalition for the Homeless, 1612 K St. NW #1004, Washington DC 20006; 202-775-1322. Offer a monthly contribution, or find out where you can volunteer.

WEEKDAY READINGS (Mo) Numbers 24:2 – 17a; (Tu) Zephaniah 3:1 – 13; (We) Genesis 49:2, 8 – 10; (Th) Jeremiah 23:5 – 8; (Fr) Judges 13:2 – 7, 24 – 25; (Sa) Isaiah 7:10 – 14

READING I *Micah 5:2 – 5*

But you, O Bethlehem of Ephrathah,
   who are one of the little clans of Judah,
from you shall come forth for me
   one who is to rule in Israel,
whose origin is from of old,
   from ancient days.
Therefore they shall be given up until the time
   when she who is in labor has brought forth;
then the rest of the ruler's kindred shall return
   to the people of Israel.
And the ruler shall stand and feed his flock
   in the strength of the LORD,
   in the majesty of the name of the LORD his God.
And they shall live secure, for now the ruler
   shall be great
   to the ends of the earth;
and he shall be the one of peace.

READING II *Hebrews 10:5 – 10*

Consequently, when Christ came into the world, he said,
   "Sacrifices and offerings you have not desired,
     but a body you have prepared for me;
   in burnt offerings and sin offerings
     you have taken no pleasure.
   Then I said, 'See, God, I have come to do
     your will, O God'
   (in the scroll of the book it is written of me)."
When Christ said above, "You have neither desired nor taken pleasure in sacrifices and offerings and burnt offerings and sin offerings" (these are offered according to the law), then he added, "See, I have come to do your will." Christ abolishes the first in order to establish the second. And it is by God's will that we have been sanctified through the offering of the body of Jesus Christ once for all.

GOSPEL *Luke 1:39 – 55*

In those days Mary set out and went with haste to a Judean town in the hill country, where she entered the house of Zechariah and greeted Elizabeth. When Elizabeth heard Mary's greeting, the child leaped in her womb. And Elizabeth was filled with the Holy Spirit and exclaimed with a loud cry, "Blessed are you among women, and blessed is the fruit of your womb. And why has this happened to me, that the mother of my Lord comes to me? For as soon as I heard the sound of your greeting, the child in my womb leaped for joy. And blessed is she who believed that there would be a fulfillment of what was spoken to her by the Lord."
And Mary said,
   "My soul magnifies the Lord,
   and my spirit rejoices in God my Savior,
   who has looked with favor on me, a lowly servant.
   Surely, from now on all generations
     will call me blessed;
for the Mighty One has done great things for me:
holy is the name of the Lord,
whose mercy is for the God-fearing
from generation to generation.
The arm of the Lord is filled with strength,
scattering the proud in the thoughts
   of their hearts.
God has brought down the powerful
   from their thrones,
and lifted up the lowly;
God has filled the hungry with good things,
and sent the rich away empty.
God has helped Israel, the Lord's servant,
in remembrance of mercy,
according to the promise God made
   to our ancestors,
to Abraham and to his descendants forever."

REFLECTION

The Gospel of Luke begins by describing two visits by the angel Gabriel to announce pregnancies: First the angel appears to Zechariah, Elizabeth's husband and the father of John the Baptist. Then Gabriel appears to Mary, who is engaged to Joseph. In today's reading, these two strands are brought together as we read of the meeting of these two women and of Elizabeth's insight into the conditions of Mary's pregnancy.

Nowhere is the issue addressed that a young, unmarried girl has left her home, her neighbors and her betrothed in order to spend three months with an older female relative. We are not told the reason for the visit or the situation Mary had left. Was she fleeing the gossip and raised eyebrows of her neighbors? We are not told if Mary assisted at the birth of John. Instead, the author creates a setting for these two pregnant women to share in the joy of the life within them.

Although women are prominent in the Gospel of Luke, the present story is unique: Only the voices of these women are heard. Indeed, no men are present. Pregnancy is something that bonds women together; no man can ever completely comprehend this experience. Often a woman, considering the new life growing within her, becomes more reflective, contemplative, open. Elizabeth's child teaches her about Mary's pregnancy, and Elizabeth warmly greets the young girl. Mary will respond with the Magnificat (1:46–55), a song celebrating the justice of God, who assists the lowly by overturning oppressive powers and inverting the socioeconomic reality. There is excitement and anticipation in the air. Something wondrous is about to happen.

■ **Think about what it must have been like for Mary, an unwed, pregnant teenager. What implications does her situation have for our response to young women in our lives who find themselves in similar situations?**

■ **The Advent readings and the Magnificat, which is part of today's gospel reading and is an integral part of the prayer life of Christians, have consistently stressed the importance of correcting injustices and upsetting the status quo. This is part of our preparation for God's manifestation in our lives. How does your community respond to the needs of the powerless and those less fortunate?**

PRACTICE OF FAITH

RECEPTION. "Please join us for a reception honoring . . ." What gives rise to our formal reception of one another? We receive others in beginnings, new relationships and new associations.

What does it mean to receive another, to celebrate a new identity and a promise made? Mary and Elizabeth received promise, identity and God into their very beings. They proclaimed new identity in new relationship, redefinition in God and joyfully expanding families.

As we pray throughout these final days of Advent, let us take special care in listening and proclaiming the reception of Mary by Elizabeth ("Hail Mary, full of grace") and the reception of the angel Gabriel by Mary ("I acclaim the greatness of the Lord").

PRACTICE OF HOPE

LORD OF THE DANCE. "Come, dance with me!" cried the baby in Elizabeth's womb. "My arms and legs are twitching at the drumbeat of my mother's heart. She calls you blessed, and blessed you are. Our meeting exceeds all joy! So let us dance, my Lord, let us dance!"

"I gladly dance with you," replied the baby in Mary's womb. "Before the beginning of time I pulsed through the womb of creation. I lit the first stars on the firmament. I taught the ocean to dance with the moon, and I led the round of the kids and the lions in paradise. Now I have come to earth for the most trying number of all. The piper death will pipe me all the way to the cross."

"But you will overcome!" cried Elizabeth's baby, "for you are the Lord of the Dance indeed."

PRACTICE OF CHARITY

SOUL MUSIC. A traveler in Prague sat quietly and let the music fill his soul. Prague is a 1000-year-old city miraculously undamaged by the bombs of war. Soprano, cello and organ touch a place in the spirit that longs for peace and serenity. It may be much like Mary's visit to the hill country. The practice of charity, the pursuit of justice, arises from a fullness of soul that is rare. It is fed by prayer, poetry and sometimes the glory of sound. Prepare for Christ today by feeding your soul with five minutes of your favorite music or ten minutes of your favorite reading.

WEEKDAY READINGS (Mo) 1 Samuel 1:24–28; (Tu) Malachi 3:1–4, 23–24; (We) 2 Samuel 7:1–16

CHRISTMASTIME

The Lord our God comes, comes to rule the earth!

Sing to the Lord a new song,
the Lord of wonderful deeds.
Right hand and holy arm
brought victory to God.

God made that victory known,
revealed justice to nations,
remembered a merciful love
loyal to the house of Israel.
The ends of the earth have seen
the victory of our God.

Shout to the Lord, you earth,
break into song, into praise!
Sing praise to God with a harp,
with a harp and sound of music.
With sound of trumpet and horn,
shout to the Lord, our king.

Let the sea roar with its creatures,
the world and all that live there!
Let rivers clap their hands,
the hills ring out their joy!

The Lord our God comes,
comes to rule the earth,
justly to rule the world,
to govern the peoples aright.

—Psalm 98

When people witness deeds like these—
mercy winning victories
and justice welcomed
        in the public places—
then the earth itself will be an orchestra
and all creatures a choir,
and we shall sing together a song
that announces you,
God of poor shepherds and stargazers.
Rehearse us now in that Christmas song:
Like those shepherds may we know where
        to look,
like the magi may we know
        when to listen to the powerful
and when to mere dreams.
Come, Lord, and lift us up in song.

—Prayer of the Season

READING I *Isaiah 9:1–6*

There will be no gloom for those who were in anguish. In the former time the Lord brought into contempt the land of Zebulun and the land of Napthali, but in the latter time the Lord will make glorious the way of the sea, the land beyond the Jordan, Galilee of the nations.

The people who walked in darkness
   have seen a great light;
those who lived in a land of deep darkness—
   on them light has shined.
You have multiplied the nation,
   you have increased its joy;
they rejoice before you
   as with joy at the harvest,
   as people exult when dividing plunder.
For the yoke of their burden,
   and the bar across their shoulders,
   the rod of their oppressor,
   you have broken as on the day of Midian.
For all the boots of the tramping warriors
   and all the garments rolled in blood
   shall be burned as fuel for the fire.
For a child has been born for us,
   a son given to us;
authority rests upon his shoulders;
   and he is named
     Wonderful Counselor, Mighty God,
     Everlasting Father, Prince of Peace.

READING II *Titus 2:11–14*

The grace of God has appeared, bringing salvation to all, training us to renounce impiety and worldly passions, and in the present age to live lives that are self-controlled, upright, and godly, while we wait for the blessed hope and the manifestation of the glory of our great God and Savior, Jesus Christ.

It is Jesus Christ who gave himself for us to might redeem us from all iniquity and purify for himself a people of his own who are zealous for good deeds.

GOSPEL *Luke 2:1–20*

In those days a decree went out from Emperor Augustus that all the world should be registered. This was the first registration and was taken while Quirinius was governor of Syria. All went to their own towns to be registered. Joseph also went from the town of Nazareth in Galilee to Judea, to the city of David called Bethlehem, because he was descended from the house and family of David. He went to be registered with Mary, to whom he was engaged and who was expecting a child. While they were there, the time came for her to deliver her child. And she gave birth to her firstborn son and wrapped him in bands of cloth, and laid him in a manger, because there was no place for them in the inn.

In that region there were shepherds living in the fields, keeping watch over their flock by night. Then an angel of the Lord stood before them, and the glory of the Lord shone around them, and they were terrified.

But the angel said to them, "Do not be afraid; for see—I am bringing you good news of great joy for all the people: to you is born this day in the city of David a Savior, who is the Messiah, the Lord. This will be a sign for you: you will find a child wrapped in bands of cloth and lying in a manger." And suddenly there was with the angel a multitude of the heavenly host, praising God and saying, "Glory to God in the highest heaven, and on earth peace among those whom God favors!"

When the angels had left them and gone into heaven, the shepherds said to one another, "Let us go now to Bethlehem and see this thing that has taken place, which the Lord has made known to us." So they went with haste and found Mary and Joseph, and the child lying in the manger. When they saw this, they made known what had been told them about this child; and all who heard it were amazed at what the shepherds told them. But Mary treasured all these words and pondered them in her heart.

The shepherds returned, glorifying and praising God for all they had heard and seen, as it had been told them.

REFLECTION

We have been awaiting the coming of the Lord, a coming that will establish justice and bring an end to oppression. In today's first reading, Isaiah tells us that now is the time for rejoicing. There is hope in a descendant of David who will bring about peace, establishing justice and righteousness forever. This Davidic king, so Christians proclaim, is actually the child born to Mary, born without benefit of midwife or fine linens to caress his tiny body, born without a palace in which to rest, born without even a building for shelter. All our expectations for a ruler, for the anointed one of God, for our Lord, are turned on their heads. As with so much that we have witnessed in this season, it is the poor and lowly who are glorified. It is for the helpless child lying in an animal food trough that the angels sing.

Children often have insights that adults miss. For the harried parent wondering how everything can possibly be accomplished this Christmas — can I make it from the kitchen to the living room without tripping, will the turkey be done on time, and where on earth will we seat all the guests — there is the wide-eyed child who gazes at the bright lights and wiggles with excitement. While adults are consumed with the hustle and bustle, children want attention, to be held and loved, to be joined in play and song.

On this dark night we proclaim that the light shines. Let us take time to be quiet, to sit in the darkness, to hold one another. Let us be as young children, in awe, unaware of the varying degrees of status, power and wealth that govern so much of life. Let us learn especially from the child who has nothing but through whom God speaks a message of love and comfort that is yet challenging and demanding.

■ **As we celebrate Christmas in the warmth of our homes, let us recall those who are alone or who are cold and hungry. Rather than simply giving to them at this time of year, let us resolve to work throughout the year to create just economic situations.**

PRACTICE OF FAITH

WITNESS. The gift of the incarnation is the witness of the cross. Jesus is born into humanity to redeem and save it on the cross. And yet the proximity of Christmas to Good Friday always seems to short-circuit what we want to know about Jesus' growth and development. The church celebrates others whose lives were ended for the cross.

December 26 is the feast of the martyr Saint Stephen. As was the custom in killing the stubborn witnesses of the crucifixion, a leafy wreath to represent the crown of thorns was placed on his head. The entryway and door wreathes of the season can become year-round witnesses to the victory of Christ. A wreath of plain wood vine can be hung in the entryway and decorated colorfully and appropriately for each liturgical season.

PRACTICE OF HOPE

THE TREE. O night of nights, you have glorified me in my most trying hour. I have grown in the dark of the forest, shooting up toward the sky, my boughs stretching wider every year. When they came to cut down the trees, I thought "This is the time. I will see the light of Christmas in the eyes of beautiful children, as foretold in the ancient lore of the forest." But I didn't grow straight enough, they said, and my branches were all crooked. They left me alone in the dark, and I despaired. But behold, you have come to me, brightest night of all. In the midst of my shadows, you have descended upon me. Your angels have surrounded my flagging treetop, singing, "Peace to the forest and all its creatures!" And my crooked branches are aglow with a hundred dancing flames.

PRACTICE OF CHARITY

NO ROOM IN THE INN. Bill and Becca had driven with their two kids from Memphis to Denver. Bill had a job waiting for him. His friend failed to tell him that the job might not begin for 6 to 8 weeks. Becca couldn't have prepared for more than two weeks of apartment hunting. When the emergency shelter swung into action, an array of services became available to carry the family through their crisis. The agency found emergency housing and the clinic provided physicals, vaccinations and asthma medicine. This is an example of social justice at work. Resources came together to offer jointly the services no single individual could provide. This Christmas, inquire about services your community offers for families in crisis. Offer to volunteer.

WEEKDAY READINGS (Fr) Acts 6:8 – 10, 7:54 – 59; (Sa) 1 John 1:1 – 4

READING I *1 Samuel 1:11, 20, 24–28*

Hannah, wife of Elkanah, had no children. She prayed to the Lord and made this vow: "O Lord of hosts, if only you will look on the misery of your servant, and remember me, and not forget your servant, but will give to your servant a male child, then I will set him before you as a nazirite until the day of his death. He shall drink neither wine nor intoxicants, and no razor shall touch his head." In due time Hannah conceived and bore a son. She named him Samuel, for she said, "I have asked him of the Lord."

When she had weaned him, she took him up with her, along with a three-year-old bull, an ephah of flour, and a skin of wine. She brought him to the house of the LORD at Shiloh; and the child was young. Then they slaughtered the bull, and they brought the child to Eli. And she said, "Oh, my lord! As you live, my lord, I am the woman who was standing here in your presence, praying to the LORD. For this child I prayed; and the LORD has granted me the petition that I made. Therefore I have lent him to the LORD; as long as he lives, he is given to the LORD." She left him there for the LORD.

[Complete reading: 1 Samuel 1:11, 20–22, 24–28]

READING II *Colossians 3:12–17*

As God's chosen ones, holy and beloved, clothe yourselves with compassion, kindness, humility, meekness, and patience. Bear with one another and, if anyone has a complaint against another, forgive each other; just as the Lord has forgiven you, so you also must forgive. Above all, clothe yourselves with love, which binds everything together in perfect harmony.

And let the peace of Christ rule in your hearts, to which indeed you were called in the one body. And be thankful. Let the word of Christ dwell in you richly; teach and admonish one another in all wisdom; and with gratitude in your hearts sing psalms, hymns, and spiritual songs to God. And whatever you do, in word or deed, do everything in the name of the Lord Jesus, giving thanks to God, the Father, through him.

[Complete reading: Colossians 3:12–21]

GOSPEL *Luke 2:41–52*

Now every year Jesus' parents went to Jerusalem for the festival of the Passover. And when he was twelve years old, they went up as usual for the festival. When the festival was ended and they started to return, the boy Jesus stayed behind in Jerusalem, but his parents did not know it. Assuming that he was in the group of travelers, they went a day's journey. Then they started to look for him among their relatives and friends. When they did not find him, they returned to Jerusalem to search for him.

After three days they found Jesus in the temple, sitting among the teachers, listening to them and asking them questions. And all who heard Jesus were amazed at his understanding and his answers. When his parents saw him they were astonished; and his mother said to him, "Child, why have you treated us like this? Look, your father and I have been searching for you in great anxiety." Jesus said to them, "Why were you searching for me? Did you not know that I must be in my Father's house?" But they did not understand what he said to them.

Then Jesus went down with them and came to Nazareth, and was obedient to them. His mother treasured all these things in her heart. And Jesus increased in wisdom and in years, and in divine and human favor.

Thursday, January 1, 1998

MARY, MOTHER OF GOD

Numbers 6:22–27 *The Lord let his face shine on you!*

Galatians 4:4–7 *You are no longer slaves but children of God.*

Luke 2:16–21 *Mary pondered these things in her heart.*

Our merry Christmastime unfolds with the blessing of the new year, with the astonishing good news of peace on earth, and with the treasures that Mary pondered within her heart.

REFLECTION

It is not easy to be a holy family. Some days everything goes wrong: The children are late for school, the baby is crabby, tempers flare, angry words are exchanged. The story of the child Jesus in the Temple, which is unique to the Gospel of Luke, indicates tensions within Jesus' own family. His parents reproach him for treating them poorly by running off without permission and causing them anxiety, and Jesus returns the sentiment.

As a child, Jesus, like any other child, must have needed correction, instruction and an occasional reprimand. Perhaps Mary, the model of patience, sometimes felt impatient and frustrated. If we truly believe in the full humanity of Jesus and the reality of his earthly life, we must allow for these possibilities. And when we reflect on the difficulties in Jesus' family, perhaps we can be more patient with ourselves in our struggles to balance work and family, to be loving, to be holy.

Whatever the makeup of our families, it is our task to create relationships that nurture growth for each member. Unfortunately, it is often the people we love the most whom we hurt and disappoint. Although it is not always easy to apologize or to acknowledge being hurt, it is through such honest, respectful communication that we create the families we want to be.

The complete text of the second reading, from Colossians, which continues to verve 3:21, has been used not to build relationships but to force others into submission. The household codes used in this letter, beginning in verse 18, were taken from the Greco-Roman rules for the household. There is nothing specifically Christian about them, and they clearly represent a different culture (complete with slaves in verse 22) than that which we know. Although the rules may have served to establish order within society when they were written, now they often cause strife within our families. The gospel is not a club with which to beat another; rather, the gospel demands mutual respect and love: "Bear with one another . . . forgive one another."

■ **Reflect on the communication habits in your family. What are some concrete ways in which you can strive to form a holy family?**

PRACTICE OF
FAITH

ABUNDANCE. The hospitality of God is resolute in its blessing, "May the Lord bless you and keep you. May the Lord let his face shine upon you and be gracious to you. May the Lord look upon you kindly and give you peace." The church hears this blessing on January 1, the feast of Mary, Mother of God.

As we continue to celebrate the fullness of the Christmas season, we are gifted with this blessing, which, along with the motherhood of Mary, speaks of grace, kindness and love in such *abundance* as to surpass the *amount* of food and drink and parties of these days of the new year.

Let us bless our children and families these days with the words of this blessing of God.

PRACTICE OF
HOPE

OUTING. Perhaps a few years after the episode in Jerusalem, the holy family went on a group outing in the mountains. When they returned from the hike, Mary and Joseph found that their son was missing. They had assumed he was in the group behind them. "Here we go again!" sighed Joseph. But he was concerned because the daylight was waning. So he climbed up the mountain again to search for his son. When he reached the wooded ridge, he found his son sitting under a tree among the mountain birds, listening to them and asking them questions. Joseph almost lost it: "Son, I know what you are going to say about your 'Father's house.' I still don't understand it. But will you please come with me now? You know how much your mother gets worried!"

PRACTICE OF
CHARITY

DECISIONS IN THE FAMILY. I once saw the notes that Anne Frank had jotted on the wallpaper above her bed in her family's hiding place in Amsterdam — the notes of a young, vibrant teenager. Her fate, death in a concentration camp, was the result of a diabolically evil philosophy. It was also the inevitable consequence of thousands of individual decisions to go along with the authorities. Her goodness resulted from her family's love and from the heroic actions of individuals who refused, at the risk of their lives, to accommodate an evil empire. Our daily decisions make a difference. Good or evil, usually not dramatic — that's our choice. Make a decision to spend extra time today with your family to clean a room, wash a car, write a letter.

WEEKDAY READINGS (Mo) 1 John 2:3 – 11; (Tu) 2:12 – 17; (We) 2:18 – 21; (Th) Mary, Mother of God, see box; (Fr) 1 John 2:22 – 28; (Sa) 2:29 — 3:6

READING I *Isaiah 60:1–6*

Arise, shine; for your light has come,
  and the glory of the LORD has risen upon you.
For darkness shall cover the earth,
  and thick darkness the peoples;
but the LORD will arise upon you,
  and the glory of the LORD will appear over you.
Nations shall come to your light,
  and rulers to the brightness of your dawn.
Lift up your eyes and look around;
  they all gather together, they come to you;
your sons shall come from far away,
  and your daughters shall be carried on their
    nurses' arms.
Then you shall see and be radiant;
  your heart shall thrill and rejoice,
because the abundance of the sea shall be brought
    to you,
  the wealth of the nations shall come to you.
A multitude of camels shall cover you,
  the young camels of Midian and Ephah;
  all those from Sheba shall come.
They shall bring gold and frankincense,
  and shall proclaim the praise of the LORD.

READING II *Ephesians 3:1–6*

This is the reason that I Paul am a prisoner for Christ Jesus for the sake of you Gentiles — for surely you have already heard of the commission of God's grace that was given me for you, and how the mystery was made known to me by revelation, as I wrote above in a few words, a reading of which will enable you to perceive my understanding of the mystery of Christ.

  In former generations this mystery was not made known to humankind, as it has now been revealed to his holy apostles and prophets by the Spirit: that is, the Gentiles have become heirs with us, members of the same body, and sharers in the promise in Christ Jesus through the gospel.
[Complete reading: Ephesians 3:1–12]

GOSPEL *Matthew 2:1–12*

In the time of King Herod, after Jesus was born in Bethlehem of Judea, magi from the East came to Jerusalem, asking, "Where is the child who has been born king of the Jews? For we observed his star at its rising, and have come to pay him homage."

  When King Herod heard this, he was frightened, and all Jerusalem with him; and calling together all the chief priests and scribes of the people, he inquired of them where the Messiah was to be born. They told him, "In Bethlehem of Judea; for so it has been written by the prophet:

  'And you, Bethlehem, in the land of Judah,
    are by no means least
    among the rulers of Judah;
  for from you shall come a ruler
    who is to shepherd my people Israel.'"

Then Herod secretly called for the magi and learned from them the exact time when the star had appeared. Then he sent them to Bethlehem, saying, "Go and search diligently for the child; and when you have found him, bring me word so that I may also go and pay him homage."

  When they had heard the king, they set out; and there, ahead of them, went the star that they had seen at its rising, until it stopped over the place where the child was. When they saw that the star had stopped, they were overwhelmed with joy. On entering the house, they saw the child with Mary his mother; and they knelt down and paid him homage. Then, opening their treasure chests, they offered him gifts of gold, frankincense, and myrrh.

  And having been warned in a dream not to return to Herod, they left for their own country by another road.

REFLECTION

The first major controversy of the early Christian church was a question of inclusiveness, of acceptance. Some held that the promises made to Israel were to be reserved for those of Jewish ancestry. Others, notably Paul, believed that the salvation offered in Christ extended beyond any national or ethnic boundaries and was available to all who had faith in Christ's resurrection. God had chosen the Hebrew people, teaching them, drawing them close and also expecting of them fidelity and holiness. God's blessings included great expectations; Israel was to be a "light for the nations." But followers of Jesus, Jew and Gentile alike, believed that in Jesus himself were the promises to Israel fulfilled; he was truly the "light for the nations."

Epiphany is a celebration of the manifestation of God in the world. Jesus was born into a Jewish family, was raised to abide by the law of Israel, and was a prophet and reformer of the chosen people. But the significance of his life and death, told symbolically in the visit of these foreigners from the East, applies to all people. In Jesus is God most fully present to all the world.

The story of the Magi visiting the child Jesus is a story for adults. It is a story of the barriers of race and class division being shattered forever by the God who came to earth as a young child. It is a story that, by picturing wealthy, educated adults paying homage to a poor, unknown infant, challenges assumptions about age and status. It is a story that exclaims that this Jesus transforms the world.

Since most of us who are Christians today are not of Jewish ancestry and do not keep the Jewish laws, but rather are Gentiles, we are direct recipients of this Epiphany message. Our challenge is to join the Magi, not only in worshiping the God incarnate but in returning to our homelands and living the message that hierarchies, racial divisions and inequities have no place in the lives of those who follow the one who draws all people to himself.

■ **Reflect on your circle of friends. How can you be more inclusive, more accepting of people from various social, economic and racial groups?**

PRACTICE OF FAITH

STARS. In Disney's *The Lion King,* Simba, the exiled future king, is asked what he knows of the "sparkling dots up there." Simba remembers being told, "The great kings of the past are up there . . . watching over us." His companion's mocking reply is, "You mean a bunch of royal dead guys are watching us?"

The Quantrantid Meteor Shower on January 3 and 4 draws us to the night sky. What is the role of the remembered dead in our lives? The week of January 4 begins with the Magi and continues to celebrate the stars of Elizabeth Ann Seton (January 4), John Neumann (January 5), Blessed Andre Besette (January 6) and Raymond of Penyafort (January 7). This is a week to look up and name the stars of our families and our faith.

PRACTICE OF HOPE

FOR A CHILD. When the Magi brought their presents to the newborn child, his parents were quite embarrassed. "How can we accept such costly gifts?" cried Mary. "We have nothing to give you in return!"

"O, but you do!" exclaimed the Magi. "This star above has guided us all the way to you. Would you give it to us to take to our home in the East?"

"Who has ever heard of giving away a star?" grumbled Joseph.

But lo, the child began to smile, and soon three golden threads of light descended from the star and rested on each of the Magi. And all the starlight came pouring down into their hearts. "O thank you!" cried the Magi. "Now we are truly happy." And when the Magi took their leave, they vanished into the dark like three dancing globes of light.

PRACTICE OF CHARITY

MAKING JUSTICE KNOWN. "Epiphany" means making known, manifestation. Today's letter to the Ephesians says that mysteries are waiting to be made known to humankind. Social justice seems to be a mystery awaiting revelation. Martin Luther King Jr. witnessed social justice in terms of racism and peace. Gandhi witnessed it in terms of nationhood and non-violence. Jesus addressed it when he did not ignore the Pharisees and the evils they wrought. He did not fail to cry out against prejudices that called for the stoning of the woman, but not the man, caught in adultery. We should be so aware and responsive. Foster social justice as an awakening in your life by reading the words of King or Gandhi — or Jesus.

WEEKDAY READINGS (Mo) 1 John 3:22 — 4:6; (Tu) 4:7 – 10; (We) 4:11 – 18; (Th) 4:19 — 5:4; (Fr) 5:5 – 13; (Sa) 5:14 – 21

JANUARY 11, 1998
Baptism of the Lord
First Sunday after the Epiphany

READING I *Isaiah 42:1–4, 6–7*

Here is my servant, whom I uphold,
  my chosen, in whom my soul delights,
upon whom I have put my spirit,
  to bring forth justice to the nations.
Not crying out, not lifting up his voice,
  not making it heard in the street,
a bruised reed my servant will not break,
  nor quench a dimly burning wick,
  but will faithfully bring forth justice.
My chosen one will not grow faint or be crushed
  until he has established justice in the earth;
  and the coastlands wait for his teaching.
I am the Lord, I have called you in righteousness,
  I have taken you by the hand and kept you;
I have given you as a covenant to the people,
  a light to the nations,
  to open the eyes that are blind,
to bring out the prisoners from the dungeon,
  from the prison those who sit in darkness.

READING II *Acts 10:34–38*

Peter began to speak to the people: "I truly understand that God shows no partiality, but in every nation anyone who is God-fearing and does what is right is acceptable to God.

"You know the message God sent to the people of Israel, preaching peace by Jesus Christ — who is Lord of all. That message spread throughout Judea, beginning in Galilee after the baptism that John announced: how God anointed Jesus of Nazareth with the Holy Spirit and with power; how Jesus went about doing good and healing all who were oppressed by the devil, for God was with him."

GOSPEL *Luke 3:15–16, 21–22*

As the people were filled with expectation, and all were questioning in their hearts concerning John, whether he might be the Messiah, John answered all of them by saying, "I baptize you with water; but one who is more powerful than I is coming, the thong of whose sandals I am not worthy to untie. He will baptize you with the Holy Spirit and fire."

Now when all the people were baptized, and when Jesus also had been baptized and was praying, the heaven was opened, and the Holy Spirit descended upon him in bodily form like a dove. And a voice came from heaven, "You are my Son, the Beloved; with you I am well pleased."

REFLECTION

We read that at Jesus' baptism, spectacular things happened to indicate that this was no ordinary person. The account in Luke differs somewhat from the accounts in Mark (1:9–11) and in Matthew (3:13–17), but all three include the story of Jesus' baptism by John. Apparently Jesus was a follower of John before he began his own ministry of preaching.

In the Lukan baptismal account, Jesus is praying when the Holy Spirit appears and the voice of God is heard. In this gospel, prayer is often a signal that something important is about to happen. Here, God speaks words of favor to a "son," one who serves God in righteousness. The first reading comes from the first "servant song" in Isaiah, in which is recounted what a servant of God does — establish justice and righteousness. Jesus will begin his ministry by reading this section from the scroll of Isaiah in the synagogue.

We too are called to be pleasing to God, to serve God and to allow God's spirit to move in our hearts. When we look at the people around us, we see those who make real in their lives the words of the servant song. Modern prophets, like those in the Hebrew tradition, sometimes spend much of their time in prison, reviled and impeded by those in power, perhaps even giving their lives, as did Jesus. One such prophet was Martin Luther King Jr., who dedicated his life to bringing forth justice to the nations. As we celebrate his birthday next week, let us examine in our own lives the call that we received in our own baptism: to live lives in faithfulness to God, who has called us in righteousness and asks us to establish justice in our land.

■ **What can you do to honor the remarkable Dr. King and to make real his dream of harmony among the races and equality for all? Resolve to participate in events commemorating his life and work, and plan "solidarity" events throughout the year.**

■ **Today is ecumenical Sunday, when we reflect on the many things we share with our Christian brothers and sisters of other denominations. What do you know of the faith of your friends and neighbors? How well do you understand your own tradition so that you can share it with others?**

PRACTICE OF FAITH

EXILE. For Jesus, the life of baptism begins with withdrawal, exile and the desert. The active ministry of witness comes after prayer and solitude. Some of the fruits of solitude are purification and clarification.

Saint Hilary (January 13) endured forced exile from his life and work at Poitiers. He spent his exile in cheerful prayer and in writing on the Trinity. In exile, he received the gifts of purification, clarification of faith and belief, and he sought to bring others to them in his writing. He was known to begin every conversation and act with prayer. Our prayer can include the desert prayer of solitude by setting aside a time for it each day, each week and each year.

PRACTICE OF HOPE

THE DOVE. In ancient times the birds had an argument about who was best at conjuring up the voice of the gods. So they gathered in the mountains to hold a contest. The eagle stirred his mighty pinions and caused a violent wind, breaking rocks and boulders. But the gods were not in the wind. The vulture knocked the ground with his beak until the earth rumbled and the mountains shook. But the gods remained silent. The heron flashed his eyes and unleashed a fire that traveled from peak to peak, torching the mountaintops. But the gods did not speak. Finally, the dove flew up through the gentle breeze with a light flap of her shining wings. And behold, a whisper arose from the air as of a thousand leaves: "This is my messenger, my beloved. With her I am well pleased."

PRACTICE OF CHARITY

BAPTISM OF FIRE. Alcohol and drug addictions are by no means limited to "drunks" on skid row. As many as one in ten Americans may suffer from drug or alcohol dependence, a nearly unquenchable fire. Alcoholics Anonymous, a 12-step program of recovery, is well known. Its derivatives — narcotics, cocaine and several other "anonymous" programs — have helped millions of people throughout the world face the sickness and take the steps toward recovery. The effects of addiction on personal lives, family life and society are devastating. Help is available because people who understand come together and dedicate themselves to finding a solution. Become acquainted with AA and similar programs. You can find them in the yellow pages.

WEEKDAY READINGS (Mo) 1 Samuel 1:1 – 8; (Tu) 1:9 – 20; (We) 3:1 – 10, 19 – 20; (Th) 4:1 – 11; (Fr) 8:4 – 22; (Sa) 9:1 – 4, 17 – 19; 10:1a

WINTER ORDINARY TIME

God speaks, the ice melts; God breathes, the streams flow.

Jerusalem, give glory!
Praise God with song, O Zion!
For the Lord strengthens your gates
guarding your children within.
The Lord fills your land with peace,
giving you golden wheat.

God speaks to the earth,
the word speeds forth.
The Lord sends heavy snow
and scatters frost like ashes.

The Lord hurls chunks of hail.
Who can stand such cold?
God speaks, the ice melts;
God breathes, the streams flow.

God speaks his word to Jacob,
to Israel, his laws and decrees.
God has not done this for others,
no others receive this wisdom.

Hallelujah!

—Psalm 147:12–20

Shall we praise you, hail-hurling God,
in winter's splendor,
in the grace of snow
that covers with brightness
and reshapes both your creation and ours?
Or shall we curse the fierce cold
that punishes homeless people
and shortens tempers?
Blessed are you
in the earth's tilt and course.
Blessed are you in the sleep of winter
and in the oncoming Lenten spring.
Now and then and always,
fill these lands with peace.

— Prayer of the Season

JANUARY 18, 1998
Second Sunday in Ordinary Time
Second Sunday after the Epiphany

READING I *Isaiah 62:1–5*

For Zion's sake I will not keep silent,
   and for Jerusalem's sake I will not rest,
until its vindication shines out like the dawn,
   and its salvation like a burning torch.
The nations shall see your vindication,
   and all the rulers your glory;
and you shall be called by a new name
   that the mouth of the LORD will give.

You shall be a crown of beauty in the hand
    of the LORD,
   and a royal diadem in the hand of your God.
You shall no more be termed Forsaken,
   and your land shall no more be termed Desolate;
but you shall be called My Delight,
   and your land Married;
for the LORD delights in you,
   and your land shall be married.
For as a young man marries a young woman,
   so shall your builder marry you,
and as one rejoices in marrying one's beloved,
   so shall your God rejoice over you.

READING II *1 Corinthians 12:1–11*

Now concerning spiritual gifts, brothers and sisters, I do not want you to be uninformed. You know that when you were pagans, you were enticed and led astray to idols that could not speak. Therefore I want you to understand that no one speaking by the Spirit of God ever says "Let Jesus be cursed!" and no one can say "Jesus is Lord" except by the Holy Spirit.

Now there are varieties of gifts, but the same Spirit; and there are varieties of services, but the same Lord; and there are varieties of activities, but it is the same God who activates all of them in everyone. To each is given the manifestation of the Spirit for the common good. To one is given through the Spirit the utterance of wisdom, and to another the utterance of knowledge according to the same Spirit, to another faith by the same Spirit, to another gifts of healing by the one Spirit, to another the working of miracles, to another prophecy, to another the discernment of spirits, to another various kinds of tongues, to another the interpretation of tongues. All these are activated by one and the same Spirit, who allots to each one individually just as the Spirit chooses.

GOSPEL *John 2:1–11*

On the third day there was a wedding in Cana of Galilee, and the mother of Jesus was there. Jesus and his disciples had also been invited to the wedding. When the wine gave out, the mother of Jesus said to him, "They have no wine." And Jesus said to her, "Woman, what concern is that to you and to me? My hour has not yet come." His mother said to the servants, "Do whatever he tells you."

Now standing there were six stone water jars for the Jewish rites of purification, each holding twenty or thirty gallons. Jesus said to them, "Fill the jars with water." And they filled them up to the brim. He said to them, "Now draw some out, and take it to the chief steward." So they took it. When the steward tasted the water that had become wine, and did not know where it came from (though the servants who had drawn the water knew), the steward called the bridegroom and said to him, "Everyone serves the good wine first, and then the inferior wine after the guests have become drunk. But you have kept the good wine until now."

Jesus did this, the first of his signs, in Cana of Galilee, and revealed his glory; and his disciples believed in him.

REFLECTION

The event at the wedding in Cana is said to have been the first of Jesus' signs, a sign that revealed his glory. It also revealed something about the relationship between Jesus and his mother. She was the one who initiated the event, alerting Jesus to the fact that the wine had run out. She was also the one who apparently had the authority to tell the servants to do whatever Jesus asked. And, significantly, she ignored Jesus' rebuke of her and knew that his time indeed had come. The young upstart who had abandoned his parents to spend time in the Temple, as the Gospel of Luke told us, has become an adult who challenges his mother's authority. But, as so often happens, mother really did know best.

The role of parents is to make decisions and take actions with regard to their children, even if those decisions and actions do not please the child. The perspective of age and maturity gives parents insight into what is really beneficial for their children. But it is not only parents, or even adults, who have something to offer their families and their communities. Paul's words to the church in Corinth emphasize the gifts given to every individual, gifts which all must be recognized and accepted for the Body of Christ to flourish. For it is one Spirit, active in all, which bestows these gifts and works to create harmony within communities so that each individual can use the strengths God has given to serve others.

For many of us, the cold winter has set in. Sometimes it is a struggle to continue with what once were considered daily activities. We have no choice but to change our plans and let go of these activities. This is a perfect time to curl up in a comfortable chair and spend some time in reflection.

■ **Think about the many ways in which God has blessed you. Concentrate especially on the skills you have and the insights you offer to others. It may help to consult friends and family members so that you may better recognize what you have to offer. Make a list of the things, great and small, in which you specialize. Thank God for these gifts.**

■ **Think about each member of your family or each person with whom you work or spend time. What gifts does each one have?**

PRACTICE OF FAITH

SAINTLINESS. Saint Francis de Sales (January 24) called us all to holiness when he said, "Saintliness is both desirable and possible." He further exhorted the so-called "ordinary" to sanctity in his *Introduction to the Devout Life.*

How proximate is the feeling of sanctity when rushing late to a soccer game or trying to plan dinner around Little League baseball? Saint Sebastian (January 20) is the patron saint of athletes. His story is of courage, perseverance and endurance. Left for dead because of his faith, he was saved by one who shared that faith.

Take an "ordinary" moment before sporting events to bless your young athletes. Ask for courage and endurance in the name of Saint Sebastian. Invite the possibility of sanctity in the athletic pursuit and in the people working for it.

PRACTICE OF HOPE

MOTHER'S MIRACLE. "Please, Mom, don't do this to me. I'm not ready yet, and you know it. I still haven't gotten those trills in the left hand down, and I always forget that long bridge passage before the coda of the finale. Do you really want to see me break down in front of all these people?"

"Hush, my son, and listen to your mother. This is the best audience you'll ever get for a first performance. It's a wedding, everybody's having a good time, and there's been a lot of drinking and singing. They'll love you, and they'll never forget that you first revealed your powers to save the show at a great party. So don't make a fuss, and get ready!"

"But Mom . . ."

"*Do whatever he tells you.* You're on, honey. Mother loves you. You're terrific!"

PRACTICE OF CHARITY

GIFTS OF THE SPIRIT. Weddings and celebrations are essential to true human life, but for today's Christian they can be problematic. On the one hand, there is the tendency toward mindless consumerism, which violates a spirit of simplicity. On the other hand, our Christian sacramentality, with its signs of love and meaning, calls us to give prominence to rituals and gifts. Concessions can be made with homemade and handmade gifts. Still other gifts benefit good causes, such as gifts and cards by local artists or by groups that assist children or the poor. Support your local potter, painter or poet.

WEEKDAY READINGS (Mo) 1 Samuel 15:16 – 23; (Tu) 16: 1 – 13; (We) 17:32 – 51; (Th) 18:6 – 9; 19:1 – 7; (Fr) 24:3 – 21; (Sa) 2 Samuel 1:1 – 27

JANUARY 25, 1998
Third Sunday in Ordinary Time
Third Sunday after the Epiphany

READING I *Nehemiah 8:1–3, 5–6, 8–10*

When the seventh month came—the people of Israel being settled in their towns—all the people gathered together into the square before the Water Gate. They told the scribe Ezra to bring the book of the law of Moses, which the LORD had given to Israel. Accordingly, the priest Ezra brought the law before the assembly, both men and women and all who could hear with understanding. This was on the first day of the seventh month. Ezra read from it facing the square before the Water Gate from early morning until midday, in the presence of the men and the women and those who could understand; and the ears of all the people were attentive to the book of the law.

And Ezra opened the book in the sight of all the people, for he was standing above all the people; and when he opened it, all the people stood up. Then Ezra blessed the LORD, the great God, and all the people answered, "Amen, Amen," lifting up their hands. Then they bowed their heads and worshiped the LORD with their faces to the ground. So the Levites read from the book, from the law of God, with interpretation. They gave the sense, so that the people understood the reading.

And Nehemiah, who was the governor, and Ezra the priest and scribe, and the Levites who taught the people said to all the people, "This day is holy to the LORD your God; do not mourn or weep." For all the people wept when they heard the words of the law. Then Ezra said to them, "Go your way, eat the fat and drink sweet wine and send portions of them to those for whom nothing is prepared, for this day is holy to our LORD; and do not be grieved, for the joy of the LORD is your strength."

READING II *1 Corinthians 12:12–14, 27*

For just as the body is one and has many members, and all the members of the body, though many, are one body, so it is with Christ. For in the one Spirit we were all baptized into one body—Jews or Greeks, slaves or free—and we were all made to drink of one Spirit.

Indeed, the body does not consist of one part but of many.

Now you are the body of Christ and individually parts of it.

[Complete reading: 1 Corinthians 12:12–31]

GOSPEL *Luke 1:1–4; 4:14–21*

Since many have undertaken to set down an orderly account of the events that have been fulfilled among us, just as they were handed on to us by those who from the beginning were eyewitnesses and servants of the word, I too decided, after investigating everything carefully from the very first, to write an orderly account for you, most excellent Theophilus, so that you may know the truth concerning the things about which you have been instructed.

Then Jesus, filled with the power of the Spirit, returned to Galilee, and a report about him spread through all the surrounding country. He began to teach in their synagogues and was praised by everyone.

When Jesus came to Nazareth, where he had been brought up, he went to the synagogue on the sabbath day, as was his custom. He stood up to read, and the scroll of the prophet Isaiah was given to him. He unrolled the scroll and found the place where it was written:

"The Spirit of the Lord is upon me,
    because the Lord has anointed me
      to bring good news to the poor.
The Lord has sent me to proclaim release
      to the captives
    and recovery of sight to the blind,
      to let the oppressed go free,
  to proclaim the year of the Lord's favor."

And Jesus rolled up the scroll, gave it back to the attendant, and sat down. The eyes of all in the synagogue were fixed on him. Then he began to say to them, "Today this scripture has been fulfilled in your hearing."

REFLECTION

The anticipation in the synagogue in Nazareth that day must have been palpable. Here was a hometown boy who had been teaching in the synagogues and about whom people had been talking. Surely at home, in Nazareth, the buzz would have been loudest. They had heard of his great deeds at Capernaum, and here he was, in their synagogue, reading before the entire congregation, promising to deliver a word of great power.

The passage Jesus reads, taken from the prophet Isaiah, speaks of turning the current situation upside down. Those who are poor, who struggle to survive from day to day, will receive good news (you've won the lottery!); prisoners will go free; the blind will see; and those suffering injustice will be vindicated. These are no ordinary events. Many of Jesus' listeners must have expected that someday all this would occur — perhaps when the Romans were ejected from the land, perhaps when the anointed one of God appeared, perhaps at the Day of Judgment. But certainly it was not a present reality. Then Jesus had the audacity to say that the words were fulfilled in him!

Jesus challenges the expected order of things at every step in his ministry. He offers a message of hope and salvation, but not for the faithful, the good citizens or the upstanding members of the community. Jesus spends his time in soup kitchens and in jails, with refugees and victims of ethnic cleansing, on street corners with prostitutes.

We say that we follow him. Are we ready to go where he goes?

■ Reread the words from Isaiah. When do you expect, *really* expect, to see this as a reality? Do you *want* to see that day?

■ Where do you belong in the "body" Paul identifies in 1 Corinthians 12? How do you encounter the "Body of Christ"? How are you using the gifts you have identified for yourself in order to build up the body of Christ?

PRACTICE OF FAITH

SPOKEN WORDS. "Today this scripture has been fulfilled in your hearing." Jesus embodies the call of Isaiah that he proclaims in the synagogue. The word and promise are transformed into being in the person of Jesus.

The Feast of the Conversion of Paul (January 25) is a story of words and promise transformed into being. Paul becomes the embodiment of God speaking in his life.

Thomas Aquinas (January 28) found the convergence of word and promise in celebrating the eucharist. Often this convergence moved him to tears.

For Paul and Thomas, these were moments of spoken word, not fax or e-mail. Invite a friend or family member for a visit — in person. Get together for coffee or a soda, and rely on the spoken word to call your relationship into being.

PRACTICE OF HOPE

HOPES AND FULFILMENT. Don't you dare touch my dreams. I know that one day I will be free. Then I'll plant tomatoes and beans on my front lawn, and I'll bake a wedding cake every week. I'll ring all the doorbells on my block and run away to hide in a tree house. I'll greet every morning with a song, and I'll go to the old woman across the street to tell her what beautiful eyes she has. I'll jump on my bike and ride through the city until I meet a friend whose skin is darker or lighter than mine. We'll open a business together that uses ice cream for currency and pays customers interest on their loans. I'll do all these things when the time comes. Just don't you dare tell me, "Time is now." I might get real nasty.

PRACTICE OF CHARITY

GOOD NEWS FOR THE POOR. In 1970 there were 500,000 more housing units available to low-income households than there were families who needed them. Today there are 4.7 million fewer units than there are families who need them. Housing that is attainable for families is more and more difficult to access. Habitat for Humanity is trying valiantly to address this situation. Houses are rehabilitated or built by volunteers and the new occupants. "Sweat equity" — hours spent working on the house — satisfies much of the down payment cost. Monetary contributions from corporations and individuals enable the building program to continue. Find out where your nearest Habitat for Humanity office is, and offer volunteer hours or financial support. Contact Habitat for Humanity at 121 Habitat Street, Americus, Georgia 31709-3498; 202-628-9171.

WEEKDAY READINGS (Mo) 2 Timothy 1:1 – 8; (Tu) 2 Samuel 6:12 – 19; (We) 7:4 – 17; (Th) 7:18 – 29; (Fr) 11:1 – 17; (Sa) 12:1 – 17

READING I *Jeremiah 1:4–5, 17, 18–19*

Now the word of the LORD came to me saying,

"Before I formed you in the womb I knew you,
and before you were born I consecrated you;
I appointed you a prophet to the nations.

Therefore, gird up your loins; stand up and tell the people everything that I command you. I for my part have made you today a fortified city, an iron pillar, and a bronze wall, against the whole land — against the kings of Judah, its princes, its priests, and the people of the land. They will fight against you; but they shall not prevail against you, for I am with you, says the LORD, to deliver you."

READING II *1 Corinthians 12:31 — 13:13*

Brothers and sisters, strive for the greater gifts. And I will show you a still more excellent way.

If I speak in the tongues of mortals and of angels, but do not have love, I am a noisy gong or a clanging cymbal. And if I have prophetic powers, and understand all mysteries and all knowledge, and if I have all faith, so as to remove mountains, but do not have love, I am nothing. If I give away all my possessions, and if I hand over my body so that I may boast, but do not have love, I gain nothing.

Love is patient; love is kind; love is not envious or boastful or arrogant or rude. It does not insist on its own way; it is not irritable or resentful; it does not rejoice in wrongdoing, but rejoices in the truth. It bears all things, believes all things, hopes all things, endures all things.

Love never ends. But as for prophecies, they will come to an end; as for tongues, they will cease; as for knowledge, it will come to an end. For we know only in part, and we prophesy only in part; but when the complete comes, the partial will come to an end. When I was a child, I spoke like a child, I thought like a child, I reasoned like a child; when I became an adult, I put an end to childish ways. For now we see in a mirror, dimly, but then we will see face to face. Now I know only in part; then I will know fully, even as I have been fully known. And now faith, hope, and love abide, these three; and the greatest of these is love.

GOSPEL *Luke 4:21–30*

Then Jesus began to say to all in the synagogue in Nazareth, "Today this scripture has been fulfilled in your hearing." All spoke well of him and were amazed at the gracious words that came from his mouth. They said, "Is not this Joseph's son?" Jesus said to them, "Doubtless you will quote to me this proverb, 'Doctor, cure yourself!' And you will say, 'Do here also in your hometown the things that we have heard you did at Capernaum.'" And he said, "Truly I tell you, no prophet is accepted in the prophet's hometown. But the truth is, there were many widows in Israel in the time of Elijah, when the heaven was shut up three years and six months, and there was a severe famine over all the land; yet Elijah was sent to none of them except to a widow at Zarephath in Sidon. There were also many lepers in Israel in the time of the prophet Elisha, and none of them was cleansed except Naaman the Syrian."

When they heard this, all in the synagogue were filled with rage. They got up, drove Jesus out of the town, and led him to the brow of the hill on which their town was built, so that they might hurl him off the cliff. But Jesus passed through the midst of them and went on his way.

Monday, February 2, 1998

THE PRESENTATION OF THE LORD

Malachi 3:1–4 *But who can endure the day of his coming?*

Hebrews 2:14–18 *He became like us in every way.*

Luke 2:22–40 *Simeon took the child in his arms.*

The light of Christmas shone feebly at first, rising to shine brightly from a star at Epiphany. Today this light is placed in our very arms. Like old Simeon, we are hand in hand with God.

REFLECTION

The congregation in Nazareth first responded to Jesus' words with admiration. Apparently they did not understand that the upheaval referred to in the words from Isaiah, which Jesus had just read, were to apply to them. Jesus leaves no room for doubt, recounting examples of prophets who had brought "good news to the poor" — not to those in need within Israel but to Gentiles. If the residents of Nazareth had at first thought that they would benefit from the ensuing "year of the Lord's favor," they learn that they were mistaken. Jesus says that his message is directed to those outside Israel. The crowd turns ugly and attempts to kill him, but Jesus, as a man of power, escapes.

This story reflects one of the major themes of the Gospel of Luke: Salvation is granted not only to the recipients of the promises of God from of old but to Gentiles as well. The chosen people of God had always been set apart, commanded to refrain from contact with the impure, the outsiders who did not know the true God. They were to be a "light to the nations" but distinct from those nations. The author of this gospel says that God now extends the promises to the entire world so that "all flesh shall see the salvation of God" (Luke 3:6).

We see here the situation of the Christian church to which the author was writing. The first followers of Jesus were Jewish, members of the chosen people of God. But Christianity had soon come, not without tension, to incorporate Gentiles; the zealous apostle Paul directed his entire mission to those outside the people Israel. In the beautiful poem quoted by Paul in today's second reading, we see his insistence that the ultimate criterion for any action should not be possessions, knowledge or even faith, but rather love.

■ **How often do we want to keep our "good news," our blessings, to ourselves rather than sharing them with the outcast? How would you have reacted had you lived in Nazareth and heard Jesus' teaching?**

■ **Reread, each day this week, some portion of the words from Paul. Allow them to sink into your mind, your heart and your soul.**

PRACTICE OF FAITH

LIGHT OF THE NATIONS. Recognition and response to the light continue to define Jesus as the fulfillment of great promises. How is Jesus recognized as the promise of a light for the nations?

"Lord, let your servant go in peace, your word has been fulfilled. My own eyes have seen the salvation you have prepared in the sight of all peoples, a light to reveal you to the nations."

The feast of the Presentation of the Lord (February 2) comes forty days after Christmas and celebrates Simeon's recognition of the light. The church prays the Canticle of Simeon each night in Night Prayer. The antiphon and the canticle are simple and can be prayed as we gather, at nightfall, with those with whom we "take in our arms and bless God."

PRACTICE OF HOPE

ZAREPHATH AND NAZARETH. Go away, Elijah, hide from the wrath of Ahab and Jezebel and their powers of abomination. Hide out at the torrents of Carith, where my ravens shall feed you morning and evening. Hide out in the land of Sidon and show my bounty to the widow at Zarephath. Her pot of meal shall not be wasted, her cruse of oil not diminished; and her child shall live. As for myself, Elijah, I cannot hide any longer. Nor will I destroy my people that rises up against me, as when you slew the priests of Baal. When they come to cast me down headlong over the hills of Nazareth, I will send no fire to consume them and bear no arms to tear them asunder. I will walk away in the breeze of Horeb until my days are fulfilled.

PRACTICE OF CHARITY

LIVING SAINT. Late in her life, Dorothy Day, founder of the Catholic Worker movement, was invited to speak to the U.S. Catholic Bishops. The bishop who respectfully introduced her said, "I present to you a living saint." Dorothy Day, who often had been at odds with Catholic leadership, especially on issues of war and poverty, replied, "I will not be so easily dismissed." Day had often called for change, and that tends to set people at odds with leadership. Saints, on the other hand, are usually seen as "nice" people who would not disturb the status quo. Jesus is the model for our saints, and he certainly was one who called for change — and suffered for it. Try not to be afraid to speak the truth and work for change, even when it costs.

WEEKDAY READINGS (Mo) Presentation of the Lord, see box; (Tu) 1 Samuel 18:9 — 19:3; (We) 2 Samuel 24:2 – 17; (Th) 1 Kings 2:1 – 12; (Fr) Sirach 47:2 – 11; (Sa) 1 Kings 3:4 – 13

READING I *Isaiah 6:1–8*

In the year that King Uzziah died, I saw the Lord sitting on a throne, high and lofty; and the hem of the Lord's robe filled the temple. Seraphs were in attendance above the Lord; each had six wings: with two they covered their faces, and with two they covered their feet, and with two they flew. And one called to another and said:

"Holy, holy, holy is the LORD of hosts;
the whole earth is full of the glory of the LORD."

The pivots on the thresholds shook at the voices of those who called, and the house filled with smoke. And I said: "Woe is me! I am lost, for I am a man of unclean lips, and I live among a people of unclean lips; yet my eyes have seen the Sovereign, the LORD of hosts!"

Then one of the seraphs flew to me, holding a live coal that had been taken from the altar with a pair of tongs. The seraph touched my mouth with it and said: "Now that this has touched your lips, your guilt has departed and your sin is blotted out." Then I heard the voice of the Lord saying, "Whom shall I send, and who will go for us?" And I said, "Here am I; send me!"

READING II *1 Corinthians 15:1–11*

Now I would remind you, brothers and sisters, of the good news that I proclaimed to you, which you in turn received, in which also you stand, through which also you are being saved, if you hold firmly to the message that I proclaimed to you — unless you have come to believe in vain.

For I handed on to you as of first importance what I in turn had received: that Christ died for our sins in accordance with the scriptures, and that he was buried, and that he was raised on the third day in accordance with the scriptures, and that he appeared to Cephas, then to the twelve. Then he appeared to more than five hundred brothers and sisters at one time, most of whom are still alive, though some have died. Then he appeared to James, then to all the apostles. Last of all, as to one untimely born, Christ appeared also to me. For I am the least of the apostles, unfit to be called an apostle, because I persecuted the church of God. But by the grace of God I am what I am, and God's grace toward me has not been in vain. On the contrary, I worked harder than any of them — though it was not I, but the grace of God that is with me. Whether then it was I or they, so we proclaim and so you have come to believe.

GOSPEL *Luke 5:1–11*

Once while Jesus was standing beside the lake of Gennesaret, and the crowd was pressing in on him to hear the word of God, he saw two boats there at the shore of the lake; those who were fishing had gone out of the boats and were washing their nets. Jesus got into one of the boats, the one belonging to Simon, and asked him to put out a little way from the shore. Then he sat down and taught the crowds from the boat.

When Jesus had finished speaking, he said to Simon, "Put out into the deep water and let down your nets for a catch." Simon answered, "Master, we have worked all night long but have caught nothing. Yet if you say so, I will let down the nets." When they had done this, they caught so many fish that their nets were beginning to break. So they signaled their partners in the other boat to come and help them. And they came and filled both boats, so that they began to sink. But when Simon Peter saw it, he fell down at Jesus' knees, saying, "Go away from me, Lord, for I am a sinful man!" For Simon and all who were with him were amazed at the catch of fish that they had taken; and so also were James and John, sons of Zebedee, who were partners with Simon. Then Jesus said to Simon, "Do not be afraid; from now on you will be catching human beings." When they had brought their boats to shore, they left everything and followed Jesus.

R E F L E C T I O N

Each of today's readings recounts a "call" from God to one sent forth to speak in God's name: the prophet Isaiah, the apostle Paul, and Jesus' disciple Peter. These are important figures in the history of God's dealing with people, yet each one's imperfections are paramount in these accounts. Isaiah laments his uncleanness when confronted with the majesty of God; Paul says he is the least of the apostles, one who had persecuted the nascent church. In the gospel, Peter, in the face of a miraculous catch of fish, recognizes his unworthiness. Jesus does not argue with Peter's claim to be a sinner; he does not assure Peter that he is "good enough" to be a disciple, a student of Jesus. Instead, he comforts Peter as though the decision had already been made, and he announces that Peter "will be catching people" instead of fish.

If God chooses to act through such admittedly impure individuals — even one who had persecuted God's people — then what excuse do we have for refusing to heed God's call? Certainly, we say, *someone* needs to speak up in the face of injustice, *someone* needs to spread the gospel, *someone* needs to minister to the followers of Jesus — but not me! Perhaps we are really afraid, not of being unworthy but of what God's calling will cost us. What will people think? Will I have to give up what I enjoy? How painful will it be? (Isaiah, after all, was purified with a burning coal to the lips!)

Perhaps most striking is the story told of Peter and his fishing partners: "They left everything and followed Jesus." This was no casual Sunday afternoon outing by the lake. These people gave up the sources of their livelihood; they quit their jobs to follow an itinerant preacher.

Speaking for God carries a price. It is demanding. It is uncomfortable. It is our calling, too.

■ **How much are you willing to give up to follow Jesus? Could you quit your job? leave your family? How can human responsibilities be coordinated with the demands of the gospel?**

■ **We are who we are. How are you worthy of the task God sets before you?**

PRACTICE OF

FAITH

MEETING. Many people "meet" with people through a computer by going "online." People go to "chat rooms" to "talk" with others who have similar interests. Contrast an online chat room with Saint Scholastica's impassioned prayer to remain overnight in the physical presence of her brother, Saint Benedict. She prays to "go on until morning, talking about the delights of the spiritual life." She wants to further their annual meeting, in person, to talk of "sacred things."

Plan a flesh-and-blood meeting with someone with whom you can discuss your prayer life and sacred things. Plan to meet somewhere special for powerful conversation. Saints Benedict and Scholastica met at a place between her convent and his monastery. Plan to meet in a place that will be conducive to talk of the spiritual life.

PRACTICE OF

HOPE

THE FISHERMAN. "Depart from me, O Lord, for I am sinful. My spirit is dull and my heart faint. My boats are neglected, and my knots do not hold together. I am a burden to all my companions and a laughingstock to those who know their trade. Depart from me, a sinner!"

"I shall not depart from you, my beloved. I have cast my nets wide, and you are my best catch. See how the net is breaking and the boat begins to sink. You have labored and toiled for many years without hope. Come now to labor and toil with me. I will teach you to walk on the surface of the lake, to cast a net of light into the waters above the abyss. Do not be afraid, for I will walk at your right side."

PRACTICE OF

CHARITY

ORGANIZE. Joe Hill, a famous union organizer, told his friends, "When I die, don't mourn. Organize." That is a credo of social justice. An individual who does good must be commended. But some problems can be solved only by united action. In a society as complex as twentieth-century America, people need to work together to address critical issues and to accomplish systemic change. Once, a factory that made desks for Catholic schools refused to hire African Americans. Parishes banded together and refused to purchase the desks. In response, the factory instituted fair hiring practices. Organizing did it.

Be open to joining with others in your neighborhood or in your workplace in the pursuit of justice.

WEEKDAY READINGS (Mo) 1 Kings 8:1 – 13; (Tu) 8:22 – 30; (We) 10:1 – 10; (Th) 11:4 – 13; (Fr) 11:29 – 32; 12:19; (Sa) 12: 26 – 32; 13:33 – 34

FEBRUARY 15, 1998 Sixth Sunday in Ordinary Time
Sixth Sunday after the Epiphany

READING I *Jeremiah 17:5–10*

Thus says the Lord:
Cursed are those who trust in mere mortals
   and make mere flesh their strength,
      whose hearts turn away from the LORD.
They shall be like a shrub in the desert,
   and shall not see when relief comes.
They shall live in the parched places
      of the wilderness,
   in an uninhabited salt land.

Blessed are those who trust in the LORD,
   whose trust is the LORD.
They shall be like a tree planted by water,
   sending out its roots by the stream.
It shall not fear when heat comes,
   and its leaves shall stay green;
in the year of drought it is not anxious,
   and it does not cease to bear fruit.

The heart is devious above all else;
   it is perverse —
who can understand it?
I the LORD test the mind
   and search the heart,
to give to all according to their ways,
   according to the fruit of their doings.

READING II *1 Corinthians 15:12–20*

Now if Christ is proclaimed as raised from the dead,
how can some of you say there is no resurrection of
the dead? If there is no resurrection of the dead, then
Christ has not been raised; and if Christ has not been
raised, then our proclamation has been in vain and
your faith has been in vain. We are even found to be
misrepresenting God, because we testified of God
that God raised Christ — whom God did not raise if
it is true that the dead are not raised. For if the dead
are not raised, then Christ has not been raised. If
Christ has not been raised, your faith is futile and
you are still in your sins. Then those also who have
died in Christ have perished. If for this life only we
have hoped in Christ, we are of all people most to
be pitied.

But in fact Christ has been raised from the dead,
the first fruits of those who have died.

GOSPEL *Luke 6:17–26*

Jesus came down with the twelve and stood on a
level place, with a great crowd of his disciples and
a great multitude of people from all Judea,
Jerusalem, and the coast of Tyre and Sidon. They
had come to hear him and to be healed of their dis-
eases; and those who were troubled with unclean
spirits were cured. And all in the crowd were trying
to touch him, for power came out from him and
healed all of them.

Then Jesus looked up at his disciples and said:

"Blessed are you who are poor,
   for yours is the dominion of God.
"Blessed are you who are hungry now,
   for you will be filled.
"Blessed are you who weep now,
   for you will laugh.

"Blessed are you when people hate you, and
when they exclude you, revile you, and defame you
on account of the Son-of-Man. Rejoice in that day
and leap for joy, for surely your reward is great in
heaven; for that is what their ancestors did to the
prophets.

"But woe to you who are rich,
   for you have received your consolation.
"Woe to you who are full now,
   for you will be hungry.
"Woe to you who are laughing now,
   for you will mourn and weep.
"Woe to you when all speak well of you, for that is
what their ancestors did to the false prophets."

50

REFLECTION

Lest anyone remain uncertain of the message Jesus preaches, the Gospel of Luke, in today's Sermon on the Plain, seeks once again to make it clear. The message introduced in the Magnificat of Mary (1:46 – 55) and reiterated in the words Jesus read from the prophet Isaiah are here encapsulated in Jesus' preaching. Familiar roles, social standing, wealth, even happiness — all is to be turned upside down. "In that day" — as opposed to the present time — all will be different: The discredited and destitute will have favor, while the comfortable will suffer.

Jesus addresses the homeless, those who stand in bread lines, those whose hearts are broken and those who are ostracized for their faith. He promises a reversal of status to such lowly ones. These are not the poor "in spirit," as in the Sermon on the Mount in Matthew, but those who really do have absolutely nothing; to them is promised "ownership" of a realm beyond human comprehension — the kingdom of God.

The author may have been addressing a contemporary situation, one in which the Gentiles of the community were treated as inferior to the Jews (see also Acts 6) and even excluded from worship. But on Jesus' lips is placed a word of hope: Just as the prophets of old, often reviled and even jailed, had to suffer for their message but were eventually vindicated, so too will Jesus' followers, those poor and in pain, be justified.

At the same time, Jesus warns those who are comfortable, happy, popular and respected. Since they have had the opportunity to enjoy their fill, they will one day know the reality of being without.

Our culture is consumed with "keeping up with the Joneses," with following fashions and trends. The gospel today warns us that a time of profound upheaval is promised. It reminds us that identifying with the poor is not simply generosity but is integral to believing in the gospel.

■ Do you strive to be more like the people you know who have many possessions or more like the ones who have little? How can you simplify your life?

■ Often people who leave behind the trappings of a consumerist society speak of the freedom they find from living in simplicity, living close to the earth. Is this part of Jesus' message?

PRACTICE OF FAITH

WISDOM. The Office of Readings, one of the Hours of the Liturgy of the Hours, invites us this week to read and listen to the Book of Proverbs. The first reading for each day for this Hour is taken from Proverbs.

From the tradition of the church, we read this week from Saint Ephrem, Saint Bernard, Saint Athanasius, Procopius of Gaza, Saint Ambrose and Saint Augustine. All of these readings point us to life in the wisdom of God. The week ends with a reading from *Gaudium et Spes*, the *Pastoral Constitution on the Church in the Modern World*, from Vatican II.

This week, read from Proverbs when you sit down at the table for meals. Consider the call to wisdom and holiness in Proverbs with the call to holiness in marriage and family relationships in the *Pastoral Constitution*.

PRACTICE OF HOPE

BLESSINGS, ONE. Blessed are you when a blooming weed outshines your flowerbed. Blessed are you when a mockingbird comes to sing at your windowsill. Blessed are you when your enemy stretches out his hand for peace. Blessed are you when an old man wishes you well from his deathbed. And woe is you when you shut your ears to the bird's song, for you will grow deaf. But three times blessed are you if you feed the starving singer. Woe is you when you refuse the hand of peace, for your arm will wither. But three times blessed are you if you prepare a feast for the newly won friend. And woe is you when you shrink from the face of death, for your heart will freeze. But three times blessed are you if you cradle a dying man into peaceful sleep.

PRACTICE OF CHARITY

IMAGES OF LIFE. Some images capture an entire chapter in human history: Neil Armstrong stepping on the moon, the glowing faces in the reunion of a family with a returning soldier, the uplifted arms of an athlete in victory, the smoldering embers of an urban riot — and though we aren't inclined to see it this way, Christ on the cross. Create in your own mind three images that would capture chapters of your life. Measure the dominant themes. Do these images elicit gratitude, anger, fear, doubt? Now do the same as if you were an entirely different person — someone who is a national leader, someone who is poor and hungry, someone who is disabled, your favorite saint. Let that image be helpful to your thinking about others this week.

WEEKDAY READINGS (Mo) James 1:1 – 11; (Tu) 1:12 – 18; (We) 1:19 – 27; (Th) 2:1 – 9; (Fr) 2:14 – 26; (Sa) 3:1 – 10

READING I *1 Samuel 26:23–25*

David called aloud to Saul, "The LORD rewards everyone for his righteousness and his faithfulness; for the LORD gave you into my hand today, but I would not raise my hand against the LORD's anointed. As your life was precious today in my sight, so may my life be precious in the sight of the LORD, and may he rescue me from all tribulation."

Then Saul said to David, "Blessed be you, my son David! You will do many things and will succeed in them." So David went his way, and Saul returned to his place.

[Complete reading: 1 Samuel 26:2, 7–9, 12–13, 22–25]

READING II *1 Corinthians 15:35, 42–50*

But someone will ask, "How are the dead raised? With what kind of body do they come?"

What is sown is perishable, what is raised is imperishable. It is sown in dishonor, it is raised in glory. It is sown in weakness, it is raised in power. It is sown a physical body, it is raised a spiritual body. If there is a physical body, there is also a spiritual body. Thus it is written, "The first Adam became a living being"; the last Adam became a life-giving spirit. But it is not the spiritual that is first, but the physical, and then the spiritual. The first human was from the dust of the earth; the second human is from heaven. As was the one made of dust, so are those who are of the dust; and as is the one of heaven, so are those who are of heaven. Just as we have borne the image of the one of dust, we will also bear the image of the one of heaven.

What I am saying, brothers and sisters, is this: flesh and blood cannot inherit the dominion of God, nor does the perishable inherit the imperishable.

[Complete reading: 1 Corinthians 15:35–38, 42–50]

GOSPEL *Luke 6:27–38*

Jesus said:

"But I say to you that listen, Love your enemies, do good to those who hate you, bless those who curse you, pray for those who abuse you. If anyone strikes you on the cheek, offer the other also; and from anyone who takes away your coat do not withhold even your shirt. Give to everyone who begs from you; and if anyone takes away your goods, do not ask for them again. Do to others as you would have them do to you.

"If you love those who love you, what credit is that to you? For even sinners love those who love them. If you do good to those who do good to you, what credit is that to you? For even sinners do the same. If you lend to those from whom you hope to receive, what credit is that to you? Even sinners lend to sinners, to receive as much again. But love your enemies, do good, and lend, expecting nothing in return. Your reward will be great, and you will be children of the Most High, who is kind to the ungrateful and the wicked. Be merciful, just as your Father is merciful.

"Do not judge, and you will not be judged; do not condemn, and you will not be condemned. Forgive, and you will be forgiven; give, and it will be given to you. A good measure, pressed down, shaken together, running over, will be put into your lap; for the measure you give will be the measure you get back."

Wednesday, February 25, 1998

ASH WEDNESDAY

Joel 2:12–18 *Proclaim a fast. Rend your hearts.*

2 Corinthians 5:20 — 6:2 *Now is the time to be reconciled.*

Matthew 6:1–6, 16–18 *Pray, fast and give alms.*

The Spirit urges us into the desert discipline of the Lenten spring. For forty days we will strip away everything that separates us from God, beginning today, as we are marked with a cross of ashes. Death and life in a simple sign!

REFLECTION

How difficult are the words of today's gospel reading! Jesus has just finished telling his listeners of blessings for the marginalized and of directing woes to the well-off. Now he directs his remarks to "you that listen," presumably those who would benefit from the upheaval of the current social and economic situation. But what Jesus asks of these listeners is to go beyond justice, beyond the commandments, beyond right living. Jesus instructs those who are mistreated and reviled by others more powerful than they to pray for their persecutors. To those who are poor and are robbed of what little they have, Jesus says to let go of what remains. These are not general instructions or mere ideals; the commands are in the singular and are directed to each individual in specific circumstances.

Then, as if that isn't difficult enough, Jesus goes on to challenge people engaging in everyday activities to go beyond what is normal, even beyond what is right. It is no "credit" to love one's friends and be generous with them. The word for "credit" (*charis*) also means gift, favor, thanks; it comes into English as "charity." What do you expect to receive for doing these things? asks Jesus. You've already received your reward. It is necessary to go beyond all this.

"Going beyond" is summarized in the final paragraph of the passage. What is asked of us, just as it was of Jesus' earliest listeners, is to be like God — to act in mercy and forgiveness, with generosity and compassion.

But this is not natural, our hearts cry: I am not God! It is often difficult enough to love those who are close to me, to forgive those whom I love. How can I love someone who is my enemy? Enemies are not noted for their kind treatment of their foes; how can I pray for someone who intentionally mistreats me or someone who stands for what I know is wrong?

Jesus does not tell us how to follow these commands. He says simply, "Love."

■ **Think about those who have mistreated you, those whom you dislike, those who have caused you harm. Feel the anger rise within you as you reflect on your dealings with them. Then relax. Let God's spirit flow through you. Forgive. Love.**

PRACTICE OF FAITH

UNITY. The feast of the Chair of Peter, apostle (February 22), reminds us in story and in prayer of the call to what we now have narrowed to "authority." What does it mean to preside over a eucharistic or eucharist-bound community? Whether one is head of a household or a bishop, the presiding chair is filled by one called through a "confession of faith" to gather those at the table into the unity and service of that confession. That confession can be "We believe in God . . ." or "We are family."

The Latin word for a bishop's chair is *cathedra,* from which we get cathedral. The cathedral is the home church of the bishop of each diocese. Make a pilgrimage to your cathedral to visit your bishop's chair or, if possible, the bishop himself.

PRACTICE OF HOPE

PRAYER FOR AN ENEMY. Tonight I will pray for you, my faithful opponent. How committed you are to me! The intimacy of your hatred has outlasted my best friendships. Remember the time of our first courtship? You spat at me when I offered the other cheek, and your persecution of me has been relentless ever since. Year after year, the acid of your sarcasm has spurned me to find my true sources of self-respect. The brutality of your hand has forged my resistance to pain. And your unending obstruction of all my plans has led me to uncover the most hidden recesses of my creativity. Yet, I wish you could love me as I love you. For only when I cling to loving you, unlovable one, am I free to learn your lessons. Rest well, then, my enemy. May the angels protect your sleep.

PRACTICE OF CHARITY

LEND WITHOUT REPAYMENT. Rocky, with his pock-marked face and powerful, tattooed forearms, was a familiar panhandler. Jim saw him outside his office every day. Jim grew more and more irritated that he had to pass this guy every day on his way to lunch. He debated: "I'll ignore him. I'll give him money. I'll tell him to move on. I'll just talk to him." Jim did talk — and found a real person with a mother who, without support, tried her best to raise him, a man with life experiences that included the jungles of Vietnam. Jim grew to like Rocky. Jim took the time to meet a person and grew to "love an enemy." Christlike. There is a Jim — and possibly a Rocky — in all of us. Take a moment to listen. Give that irritating neighbor some time. It can be worth it.

WEEKDAY READINGS (Mo) James 3:13 – 18; (Tu) 4:1 – 10; (We) Ash Wednesday, see box; (Th) Deuteronomy 30:15 – 20; (Fr) Isaiah 58:1 – 9; (Sa) 58:9 – 14

LENT

Wash away my sin.
Cleanse me from my guilt.

You see me for what I am,
a sinner before my birth.

You love those centered in truth;
teach me your hidden wisdom.
Wash me with fresh water,
wash me bright as snow.

Fill me with happy songs,
let the bones you bruised now dance.
Shut your eyes to my sin,
make my guilt disappear.

Save me, bring back my joy,
support me, strengthen my will.
Then will I teach your way
and sinners will turn to you.

Help me, stop my tears,
and I will sing your goodness.
Lord, give me words
and I will shout your praise.

When I offer a Holocaust,
the gift does not please you.
So I offer my shattered spirit;
a changed heart you welcome.

— Psalm 51:7 – 11, 14 – 19

Like a gift we only want to want,
these forty days surround us once more
and you set about washing us, God.
Scrub and scour these stubborn ashes.
Separate what we are
from what we are not
and so bring on the Lenten ordeal:
the prayer by day and night,
the fast that clears our sight,
the alms that set things right.
At the end, when we have lost again,
you alone make dry bones come together
and bruised bones dance
round the cross where sinners live
now and for ever.

— Prayer of the Season

READING I *Deuteronomy 26:1–11*

When you have come into the land that the LORD your God is giving you as an inheritance to possess, and you possess it, and settle in it, you shall take some of the first of all the fruit of the ground, which you harvest from the land that the LORD your God is giving you, and you shall put it in a basket and go to the place that the LORD your God will choose as the place where the name of God dwells. You shall go to the priest who is in office at that time, and say to him, "Today I declare to the LORD your God that I have come into the land that the LORD swore to our ancestors to give us."

When the priest takes the basket from your hand and sets it down before the altar of the LORD your God, you shall make this response before the LORD your God: "A wandering Aramean was my ancestor; he went down into Egypt and lived there as an alien, few in number, and there became a great nation, mighty and populous. When the Egyptians treated us harshly and afflicted us, by imposing hard labor on us, we cried to the LORD, the God of our ancestors; the LORD heard our voice and saw our affliction, our toil, and our oppression. The LORD brought us out of Egypt with a mighty hand and an outstretched arm, with a terrifying display of power, and with signs and wonders; and the LORD brought us into this place and gave us this land, a land flowing with milk and honey. So now I bring the first of the fruit of the ground that you, O LORD, have given me."

You shall set it down before the LORD your God and bow down before the LORD your God. Then you, together with the Levites and the aliens who reside among you, shall celebrate with all the bounty that the LORD your God has given to you and to your house.

READING II *Romans 10:8–13*

"The word is near you, on your lips and in your heart" (that is, the word of faith that we proclaim); because if you confess with your lips that Jesus is Lord and believe in your heart that God raised him from the dead, you will be saved. For one believes with the heart and so is justified, and one confesses with the mouth and so is saved. The scripture says, "No one who believes in the Lord will be put to shame." For there is no distinction between Jew and Greek; the same Lord is Lord of all and is generous to all who ask for help. For, "Everyone who calls on the name of the Lord shall be saved."

GOSPEL *Luke 4:1–13*

Jesus, full of the Holy Spirit, returned from the Jordan and was led by the Spirit in the wilderness, where for forty days he was tempted by the devil. He ate nothing at all during those days, and when they were over, he was famished. The devil said to him, "If you are the Son of God, command this stone to become a loaf of bread." Jesus answered the devil, "It is written, 'One does not live by bread alone.'"

Then the devil led Jesus up and showed him in an instant all the dominions of the world. And the devil said to him, "To you I will give their glory and all this authority; for it has been given over to me, and I give it to anyone I please. If you, then, will worship me, it will all be yours." Jesus answered the devil,

"It is written,
'Worship the Lord your God;
    the Lord alone shall you serve.'"

Then the devil took Jesus to Jerusalem, and placed him on the pinnacle of the temple, saying to him, "If you are the Son of God, throw yourself down from here, for it is written,

'God will command the angels concerning you,
    to protect you,'and
'On their hands they will bear you up,
    so that you will not dash your foot
    against a stone.'"

Jesus answered the devil, "It is said, 'Do not put the Lord your God to the test.'" Having finished every test, the devil departed from Jesus until an opportune time.

REFLECTION

As we begin the long journey through Lent, we read a story about Jesus at the very beginning of his ministry. There is no claim to historicity in this passage; there were no witnesses to record the events. Instead, the story's message pertains to us as we strive to live our lives in faithfulness to God. This Jesus, the one whom we proclaim as Savior, as seated at the right hand of God, indeed as God incarnate — this Jesus was tempted, just as we are. When Jesus enters the desert to pray and fast, he experiences what it means to be human. To be human is to be wonderfully made by God, but human nature is prone to neglect that truth and to strive for something else, to be less than we are, to be less than wonderful.

Jesus, too, in this narrative, was tempted to be less than he was. And his temptations were similar to those that confront us as well. We desire security, the knowledge that our needs will be met. So we purchase "insurance" against the inevitable, finding it too difficult, too foolish, to trust solely in the promises of God. At other times we relish our own authority, thinking of ourselves as powerful and respected, and enjoying every opportunity to wield power over others, whether children, students, coworkers or clients. For some of us, the greatest temptation is to feel a sense of religious superiority, a conviction that God is on our side, at the expense of those who look, think or act differently than we do.

Lent offers us the opportunity to confront our own "devils," to look honestly into our hearts, without recoiling but rather in sorrow and repentance for the attitudes found there that compromise our potential to be truly human, made in the image and likeness of God. Entering the desert time of Lent, when little grows and refreshment is lacking, is not easy; we need guidance. We can take comfort in the knowledge that Jesus too had his desert experiences. We place our trust in one who has been there before.

■ **Is the desert of Lent frightening to you? How can you find comfort and sustenance on this long road?**

■ **It is customary to give something up during Lent. If you choose this practice, concentrate on how it disciplines and strengthens you. But consider also a Lenten discipline involving action, a giving of yourself.**

PRACTICE OF FAITH

FORTY DAYS. Jesus was "in the desert for forty days " (Luke); he "fasted for forty days and forty nights" (Matthew); and he "stayed forty days" (Mark). We enter Lent with several time frames, including "How long until it's over?" for Lent itself and even "How long is it going to be?" for the Easter Vigil. What about days and nights, instead of length, for the time frames? We have forty days and nights to prepare for the Mother of All Nights and the Crowning Glory of All Days.

Honor daylight and morning with rising, morning prayer and a real breakfast. Honor evening with dinner, evening prayer and preparation for sleep. Don't omit the small rituals that signal day into night and night into day.

PRACTICE OF HOPE

THE TEMPTER, ONE. The devil comes in two guises to tempt us. He comes from the sky with billowing garments and flaming eyes, with grandiose gestures and an alluring voice, saying, "I am the master of the universe. There is no power or beauty without me. Come, my child, and I will fill you with my might to make you like God. I will feed you on steroids and poppies and you will grow tall and attractive. You will astound all people with the acuteness of your mind. I will place you in a tower high up in the sky from whence you will command great empires, and the riches of this world will be at your fingertips."

O my soul, arm yourself with Christ's love for the earth when this one draws near you.

PRACTICE OF CHARITY

NO DISTINCTION BETWEEN JEW AND GREEK. On a train in Ireland, I met a traveler from Australia. We talked of the Irish troubles between Catholics and Protestants. The Australian then remarked that the United States simply could not handle racial discord. It occurred to me that an immigrant island in the southern hemisphere had not excelled in its treatment of Aborigines, but we are often blind to our own prejudices. In our United States we have confronted religious prejudice more successfully than many other countries have. There are sad exceptions, but we have learned that Protestants and Catholics can live in mutual respect, and that Muslims, Jews, atheists and New Agers all have rights and insights. Explore efforts in your community that foster respect and tolerance. Participate in an ecumenical Lenten service.

WEEKDAY READINGS (Mo) Leviticus 19:1 – 2, 11 – 18; (Tu) Isaiah 55:10 – 11; (We) Jonah 3:1 – 10; (Th) Esther C:12 – 25; (Fr) Ezekiel 18:21 – 28; (Sa) Deuteronomy 26:16 – 19

MARCH 8, 1998 Second Sunday of Lent

READING I *Genesis 15:1–12, 17–18*

After these things the word of the LORD came to Abram in a vision, "Do not be afraid, Abram, I am your shield; your reward shall be very great." But Abram said, "O Lord GOD, what will you give me, for I continue childless, and the heir of my house is Eliezer of Damascus?" And Abram said, "You have given me no offspring, and so a slave born in my house is to be my heir." But the word of the LORD came to him, "This man shall not be your heir; no one but your very own issue shall be your heir." The LORD brought Abram outside and said, "Look toward heaven and count the stars, if you are able to count them." Then the LORD said to him, "So shall your descendants be." And Abram believed the LORD; and the LORD reckoned it to him as righteousness.

Then the LORD said to Abram, "I am the LORD who brought you from Ur of the Chaldeans, to give you this land to possess." But Abram said, "O Lord GOD, how am I to know that I shall possess it?" The LORD said to him, "Bring me a heifer three years old, a female goat three years old, a ram three years old, a turtledove, and a young pigeon." Abram brought the LORD all these and cut them in two, laying each half over against the other; but he did not cut the birds in two. And when birds of prey came down on the carcasses, Abram drove them away. As the sun was going down, a deep sleep fell upon Abram, and a deep and terrifying darkness descended upon him.

When the sun had gone down and it was dark, a smoking fire pot and a flaming torch passed between these pieces. On that day the LORD made a covenant with Abram, saying, "To your descendants I give this land, from the river of Egypt to the great river, the river Euphrates."

READING II *Philippians 3:17 — 4:1*

Brothers and sisters, join in imitating me, and observe those who live according to the example you have in us. For many live as enemies of the cross of Christ; I have often told you of them, and now I tell you even with tears. Their end is destruction; their god is the belly; and their glory is in their shame; their minds are set on earthly things. But our citizenship is in heaven, and it is from there that we are expecting a Savior, the Lord Jesus Christ. The Lord will transform the body of our humiliation that it may be conformed to the body of his glory, by the power that also enables him to make all things subject to himself.

Therefore, my brothers and sisters, whom I love and long for, my joy and crown, stand firm in the Lord in this way, my beloved.

GOSPEL *Luke 9:28–36*

Now about eight days after these sayings Jesus took with him Peter and John and James, and went up on the mountain to pray. And while he was praying, the appearance of his face changed, and his clothes became dazzling white. Suddenly they saw two men, Moses and Elijah, talking to Jesus. They appeared in glory and were speaking of his departure, which he was about to accomplish at Jerusalem. Now Peter and his companions were weighed down with sleep; but since they had stayed awake, they saw the glory of Jesus and the two men who stood with him. Just as the men were leaving him, Peter said to Jesus, "Master, it is good for us to be here; let us make three dwellings, one for you, one for Moses, and one for Elijah" — not knowing what he said. While he was saying this, a cloud came and overshadowed them; and they were terrified as they entered the cloud. Then from the cloud came a voice that said, "This is my Son, my Chosen; listen to him!" When the voice had spoken, Jesus was found alone. And they kept silent and in those days told no one any of the things they had seen.

REFLECTION

The significance of the transfiguration in the Gospel of Luke cannot be missed. Jesus takes with him Peter, James and John, whom he earlier singled out from among the other disciples, and they climb a mountain to pray. Mountains are traditional sites for experiences of God. Moses met with God on Mount Sinai. Elijah encountered God on the mountain. The Temple in Jerusalem was built at the pinnacle of a mountain. Something about standing high up and being able to see the grandeur of God's creation for miles around makes a mountaintop a perfect setting for meeting with God. And prayer in this gospel always signals a significant event.

In the transfiguration, Jesus meets with two prophets from the past, Moses and Elijah. Moses was, of course, the great lawgiver, but he was also a prophet who spoke for God to the people. Because of their lack of faith, however, Moses was not able to lead the people Israel into the promised land after their exodus from Egypt. He was allowed only to view the promised land from afar. Elijah was a prophet who raised the dead and performed other miracles and was taken alive into heaven; in him was placed an active hope for God's intervention at the end times. Jesus is presented here as sharing in their mission, as being willing to suffer for the sake of others and inaugurating a new era of God's reign. The three glorified figures are said to discuss Jesus' departure (in Greek, *exodos*), his journey to Jerusalem and the decisive events that would take place there.

This passage follows immediately after the confession of Peter that Jesus is the Messiah and Jesus' instructions about his own sufferings and the necessity of his followers to be willing to suffer. Soon after the transfiguration, Jesus leaves Galilee and heads toward Jerusalem. There is no turning back. The glorified one, the chosen one, is on a journey, a journey that will lead to his death.

■ **Have you ever had a mountaintop experience — literal or figurative — in which you encountered the presence of God?**

■ **Jesus is presented here as a Moses figure, as one who journeys through the desert. The road is fraught with perils. What does it mean for his followers to join Jesus in his exodus experience?**

PRACTICE OF FAITH

GOSPEL WRITING. Did the gospel writers struggle with knowing a great ending but not knowing where to begin the story? How to tell the story so as to illuminate fully the glory of the risen Lord?

Reynolds Pricem, in his book *Three Gospels,* has rendered scholarly translations of the gospels of Mark and John along with a gospel of his own. He titles his gospel, "An Honest Account of a Memorable Life." In it, Price attempts an academically and faithfully rendered gospel.

This Lent, read aloud the Gospel of Mark in its entirety. Then have each member of the household write their own gospel. Pre-readers (and writers) can dictate their gospel to a suitable scribe. Take time to listen to the reading aloud of each gospel.

PRACTICE OF HOPE

PRAYER. Why must I go to a mountain to pray? Why not pray in the temple of my heart and leave it at that? I am a creature of the earth. My soul is woven into the soul of the earth, into the mountains, valleys and plains. My heartbeat follows the tides of the ocean, and my thoughts drift with the clouds. The mountain is the prayer of the earth. Slowly, with patience and majesty, it rises above itself to meet the heavens. I climb with effort into air more pure and fragrant. Then, if I am not overcome with sleep or lost in some dark cloud, I might be touched by the dazzling light around me. I might not tell anyone about it. But I can't be sure that the appearance of my countenance will not give it away.

PRACTICE OF CHARITY

DOM HELDER CAMARA. A diminutive, pesky archbishop, Dom Helder Camara, said, "When I pray for the poor, people praise me and call me a Christian. When I help the poor, people call me saintly. When I call for changes in policies that make people poor, people complain and call me a communist." This leader from Recife, Brazil has been both cursed and praised — much like Christ was. He called for economic policies that would not favor the rich and punish the poor. Working to establish processes that free people to attain their own food, clothing and shelter is noble — and can be provocative and dangerous. Speak out. Join with others. You can learn more about feeding the hungry by contacting Bread for the World, 1100 Wayne Avenue, Suite 1000, Silver Spring MD 20910; 301-608-2400.

WEEKDAY READINGS (Mo) Daniel 9:4–10; (Tu) Isaiah 1:10–20; (We) Jeremiah 18:18–20; (Th) 17:5–10; (Fr) Genesis 37:3–28; (Sa) Micah 7:14–20

READING I *Exodus 3:2, 4–7, 8, 11–12*

The angel of the LORD appeared to Moses in a flame of fire out of a bush; Moses looked, and the bush was blazing, yet it was not consumed. When the Lord saw that Moses had turned aside to see, God called to him out of the bush, "Moses, Moses!" And Moses said, "Here I am."

Then God said, "Come no closer! Remove the sandals from your feet, for the place on which you are standing is holy ground." God said further, "I am the God of your father, the God of Abraham, the God of Isaac, and the God of Jacob." And Moses hid his face, for he was afraid to look at God. Then the Lord said, "I have observed the misery of my people who are in Egypt; I have come down to deliver them from the Egyptians."

Moses said to God, "If I come to the Israelites and say to them, 'The God of your ancestors has sent me to you,' and they ask me, 'What is his name?' what shall I say to them?"

God said to Moses, "I AM WHO I AM." He said further, "Thus you shall say to the Israelites, 'I AM has sent me to you.'" God also said to Moses, "Thus you shall say to the Israelites, 'The LORD, the God of your ancestors, the God of Abraham, the God of Isaac, and the God of Jacob, has sent me to you': This is my name forever, and this my title for all generations."

[Complete reading: Exodus 3:1–8, 13–15]

READING II *1 Corinthians 10:1–6, 10–12*

I do not want you to be unaware, brothers and sisters, that our ancestors were all under the cloud, and all passed through the sea, and all were baptized into Moses in the cloud and in the sea, and all ate the same spiritual food, and all drank the same spiritual drink. For they drank from the spiritual rock that followed them, and the rock was Christ. Nevertheless, God was not pleased with most of them, and they were struck down in the wilderness.

Now these things occurred as examples for us, so that we might not desire evil as they did. And do not complain as some of them did, and were destroyed by the destroyer. These things happened to them to serve as an example, and they were written down to instruct us, on whom the ends of the ages have come. So if you think you are standing, watch out that you do not fall.

GOSPEL *Luke 13:1–9*

At that very time there were some present who told Jesus about the Galileans whose blood Pilate had mingled with their sacrifices. Jesus asked them, "Do you think that because these Galileans suffered in this way they were worse sinners than all other Galileans? No, I tell you; but unless you repent, you will all perish as they did. Or those eighteen who were killed when the tower of Siloam fell on them— do you think that they were worse offenders than all the others living in Jerusalem? No, I tell you; but unless you repent, you will all perish just as they did."

Then Jesus told this parable: "A man had a fig tree planted in his vineyard; and he came looking for fruit on it and found none. So he said to the gardener, 'See here! For three years I have come looking for fruit on this fig tree, and still I find none. Cut it down! Why should it be wasting the soil?' The gardener replied, 'Sir, let it alone for one more year, until I dig around it and put manure on it. If it bears fruit next year, well and good; but if not, you can cut it down.'"

Thursday, March 19, 1998

JOSEPH, HUSBAND OF MARY

2 Samuel 7:4–5, 12–14, 16 *I will make David's throne endure.*

Romans 4:13, 16–18, 22 *He is father of us all.*

Matthew 1:16, 18–21, 24 *Joseph, Son of David, fear not!*

Near the beginning of spring, as the earth is about to awaken from its sleep, we tell the story of Joseph. In the Book of Genesis, Joseph is the "dreamer of dreams." In the Gospel of Matthew, Joseph dreams of the coming kingdom. Then he awakens to find himself the father of the king.

R E F L E C T I O N

Today's readings introduce the theme of human suffering and God's response. Part of Moses' encounter with God at the burning bush involves an expression of God's concern for the Hebrew slaves in Egypt. Moses also receives a revelation of God's identity as a god who acts in human life, in the events of history. Paul refers to that decisive Hebrew event, the exodus, and God's favor shown to the Hebrew people. Yet because of their sinfulness, many were "struck down." Paul goes on to indicate that such disasters occurred so that others might learn from the examples given. Suffering is a test, common to all, but God gives the means to endure.

In the gospel reading we encounter the traditional Hebrew understanding of suffering as punishment for sin and Jesus' response to this understanding. Jesus is not unique in rejecting the idea that the righteous are blessed and the wicked punished; several earlier strands of Jewish tradition had found other means of dealing with the issue. But Jesus does not enter into a philosophical debate regarding God's justice, nor does he say *why* people suffer. Instead, he makes a demand: Repent. The word repent signifies not only remorse but also a change of heart and a consequent change of action.

The refusal to repent, to turn around, to change, has disastrous results; those who refuse to repent will perish. Since Jesus has just rejected the idea that calamities befall only the sinful, the message here must be even more profound. The refusal to turn around one's heart and life is to refuse to listen to God, to refuse the invitation to know God. Given the idea of an afterlife, a concept Jesus surely accepted, the absence of God is especially stark. Even the threat of death cannot compare with the emptiness of being forever without God.

But there is hope. Just as the fig tree in the parable is given yet another chance and even greater attention and care, so God's people are given another opportunity. But the time is short; the fig tree does not have an unlimited amount of time to prove its worth.

This is Jesus' response to suffering: Repent. Now.

■ **There are still many people today who believe that pain in life results from wrongdoing and that blessings are rewards for good deeds. Why does this idea persist? What does it say about God?**

PRACTICE OF FAITH

AT TABLE. It seems that fasting and feasting might be in conflict during this week of Lent. This week the church, in its fasting journey toward the Triduum, celebrates the feast of Saint Joseph. In the heart of Lent we remember the faithfulness and humility of Joseph.

The celebration for Joseph on March 19 is called Saint Joseph's Tables. It is a day to call family, friends and especially those who are alone to table. Is this focus on the table and the meal a breaking of the fast? Or is it an honoring of a simple meal, a simple table and simple conversation and the people gathered to it? The abundance and the feast are in the gathering and the building of table, fellowship and memory.

PRACTICE OF HOPE

THE FIG TREE, ONE. As the vinedresser began digging about the fig tree, he saw that its roots were all gnawed. But as much as he searched, he could not find who or what was eating away at the roots. One day the vinedresser's young daughter was walking about in the vineyard. As she came by the fig tree, she heard a startling sound. She stooped down and saw an ugly, earth-colored snake gnawing away at the roots of the tree. "Good afternoon, snake! Why are you eating the roots of my father's tree?"

"I eat roots for hunger. I would prefer choicer foods, but they are not for the likes of me."

"O, dear snake, wait until I bring you a bowl of milk." And from this day on, the daughter went every afternoon to feed the hungry snake under the tree.

PRACTICE OF CHARITY

WORDS. "Sticks and stones may break my bones, but words can never hurt me." Great idea, but check it out. The words we use in public debate make a difference. Witness the words "pro-life" and "pro-choice," or the Pentagon terms "pacification" to describe the taking of a village in Vietnam, "revenue enhancement" for raising taxes, "welfare" for children's support and "mortgage interest deduction" for homeowners. The people in charge of the terms of the debate have power. Followers of Christ will take note of word use and misuse. Read three items in today's paper and check for any special influence that comes through the power of words. Challenge people in discussions when they use words to gain power.

WEEKDAY READINGS (Mo) 2 Kings 5:1 – 15; (Tu) Daniel 3: 25 – 43; (We) Deuteronomy 4:1 – 9; (Th) Joseph, Husband of Mary, see box; (Fr) Hosea 14:2 – 10; (Sa) Hosea 6:1 – 6

READING I *Exodus 17:3–7*

The people thirsted there for water; and the people complained against Moses and said, "Why did you bring us out of Egypt, to kill us and our children and livestock with thirst?"

So Moses cried out to the LORD, "What shall I do with this people? They are almost ready to stone me." The LORD said to Moses, "Go on ahead of the people, and take some of the elders of Israel with you; take in your hand the staff with which you struck the Nile, and go. I will be standing there in front of you on the rock at Horeb. Strike the rock, and water will come out of it, so that the people may drink."

Moses did so, in the sight of the elders of Israel. He called the place Massah and Meribah, because the Israelites quarreled and tested the LORD, saying, "Is the LORD among us or not?"

[Complete reading: Exodus 17:1–7]

READING II *Romans 5:1–8*

Since we are justified by faith, we have peace with God through our Lord Jesus Christ, through whom we have obtained access to this grace in which we stand; and we boast in our hope of sharing the glory of God. And not only that, but we also boast in our sufferings, knowing that suffering produces endurance, and endurance produces character, and character produces hope, and hope does not disappoint us, because God's love has been poured into our hearts through the Holy Spirit that has been given to us. For while we were still weak, at the right time Christ died for the ungodly. Indeed, rarely will anyone die for a righteous person—though perhaps for a good person someone might actually dare to die. But it is proof of God's own love for us in that while we still were sinners Christ died for us.

[Complete reading: Romans 5:1–11]

GOSPEL *John 4:5–15, 19–26, 39*

Jesus came to a Samaritan city called Sychar, near the plot of ground that Jacob had given to his son Joseph.

Jacob's well was there, and Jesus, tired out by his journey, was sitting by the well. It was about noon.

A Samaritan woman came to draw water, and Jesus said to her, "Give me a drink." (His disciples had gone to the city to buy food.) The Samaritan woman said to him, "How is it that you, a Jewish man, ask a drink of me, a woman of Samaria?" (Jewish people do not share things in common with Samaritans.) Jesus answered her, "If you knew the gift of God, and who it is that is saying to you, 'Give me a drink,' you would have asked him, and he would have given you living water." The woman said to him, "Sir, you have no bucket, and the well is deep. Where do you get that living water? Are you greater than our ancestor Jacob, who gave us the well, and with his children and his flocks drank from it?"

Jesus said to her, "Everyone who drinks of this water will be thirsty again, but those who drink of the water that I will give them will never be thirsty. The water that I will give will become in them a spring of water gushing up to eternal life." The woman said to Jesus, "Sir, give me this water, so that I may never be thirsty or have to keep coming here to draw water.

"I see that you are a prophet. Our ancestors worshiped on this mountain, but you say that the place where people must worship is in Jerusalem."

Jesus said to her, "Woman, believe me, the hour is coming when you will worship the Father neither on this mountain nor in Jerusalem. You worship what you do not know; we worship what we know, for salvation is from the Jewish people. But the hour is coming, and is now here, when the true worshipers will worship the Father in spirit and truth, for such worshipers the Father seeks. God is spirit, and those who worship God must worship in spirit and truth." The woman said to him, "I know that Messiah is coming" (who is called Christ). "When he comes, he will proclaim all things to us." Jesus said to her, "Here I am, the one who is speaking to you."

Many Samaritans from that city believed in Jesus because of the woman's testimony.

[Complete reading: John 4:5–42]

REFLECTION

Just as the Israelites in the desert thirsted and demanded refreshment, so we, too, in our Lenten desert, are thirsty. In the story of the woman at the well in the Gospel of John, we read of life-giving water, water that offers lasting relief. Today we pause to anticipate the refreshing baptismal waters of Easter and to prepare ourselves for receiving or renewing our own baptism.

The story of the Samaritan woman is a story of misconstrual and trust, and of inclusion and acceptance. It was absolutely unheard of for a Jewish man to speak with a Samaritan woman! Although the Jews and Samaritans had traditions in common and together revered the well of Jacob, there was unmistakable animosity between the two groups. Jews believed that "salvation is from the Jews," while Samaritans accepted only the Pentateuch, holding fast to the Law of Moses and seeing later accretions, such as worship in Jerusalem, as abominations. Mutual contempt was the norm, and Jews from the region of Galilee would try to avoid traveling through the heart of Samaria on their way to Jerusalem.

Yet here was Jesus, not only stopping to rest but striking up a conversation with one of the "outcasts." And not only a godless Samaritan but a woman! Rabbis avoided speaking even to Jewish women in public. Jesus' simple request — for a drink of water — overturns all the usual expectations and begins to heal the breach between people of different nationalities, of different religions, of different educational levels, of different sexes. Jesus' message is directed not only to his own community but to all who will listen: Age-old barriers are removed.

Here in this richly symbolic text, the water that satisfies, the water eagerly desired by the woman, gives eternal life. The story plays on the term "living" water, understood by the woman to be running water but holding a much deeper meaning for Jesus and the reader. Even after an explanation from Jesus, the woman still misunderstands his meaning, only recognizing her error through Jesus' relationship with her.

We too desire this water. We renounce our past errors and affirm our faith in the one who gives the water of life.

■ **What barriers would Jesus break down in our own society today?**

■ **What do the waters of baptism mean to you?**

PRACTICE OF FAITH

CONFESSION. This week of Lent celebrates two saints, Patrick and Cyril, whose ministries were largely dedicated to instructing catechumens. Patrick and Cyril, each in his own circumstances, instructed and formed people into baptism and life in the church at Easter. Saint Patrick used the three-leafed shamrock to explain the mystery of the Trinity. Saint Cyril has been honored as a Doctor of the Church because of his wise teaching.

As we pray with and support the catechumens in our midst, we can attend to and learn from their formation. Consider sponsoring someone in the catechumenate next Easter. Read *The Confession of Saint Patrick* this week. Share in household prayer the broader story of Saint Patrick's gift to the church.

PRACTICE OF HOPE

THE WELL. I went into the desert to build a garden. I surveyed the expanses of the barren plain until I had found its exact center. There I began to dig for a well. My plan was to build radiating channels to carry the water of the central well all across the parched land. I have been digging for a long time now. Every day I sink deeper into the desert rock. But there is no water — only rocks and dust. I cannot go back. I would perish on the way for lack of food and water. I must work on. But my strength is leaving me. My only hope is that the water itself will seek me and break through the rock before I faint and die. I never knew until this moment how utterly dependent I am on grace.

PRACTICE OF CHARITY

WOMAN AT THE WELL. Marilyn Logan raised seven children and has more than a dozen grandchildren. She's more than seventy years old now, but she still finds ways to help and serve others. She volunteers to read books and newspapers to elderly who are no longer able to read. Marilyn says, "I love it. I get to learn at the same time I'm doing a service for others. And you wouldn't believe how interesting some of the people are. When you've raised seven kids, you just learn to use time well — and find joy in the little things of life." Find out where you can volunteer and be of service to others. Contact a nursing home, senior center or school, or your church.

WEEKDAY READINGS (Mo) 2 Kings 5:1 – 15; (Tu) Daniel 3: 25 – 43; (We) Deuteronomy 4:1 – 9; (Th) Joseph, Husband of Mary, see page 60; (Fr) Hosea 14:2 – 10; (Sa) Hosea 6:1 – 6

READING I *Joshua 5:9–12*

The LORD said to Joshua, "Today I have rolled away from you the disgrace of Egypt." And so that place is called Gilgal to this day. While the Israelites were camped in Gilgal they kept the passover in the evening on the fourteenth day of the month in the plains of Jericho. On the day after the passover, on that very day, they ate the produce of the land, unleavened cakes and parched grain. The manna ceased on the day they ate the produce of the land, and the Israelites no longer had manna; they ate the crops of the land of Canaan that year.

READING II *2 Corinthians 5:17–21*

So if anyone is in Christ, there is a new creation: everything old has passed away; see, everything has become new! All this is from God, who reconciled us through Christ to God, and has given us the ministry of reconciliation; that is, in Christ God was reconciling the world to God's own self, not counting their trespasses against them, and entrusting the message of reconciliation to us. So we are ambassadors for Christ, since God is appealing through us; we entreat you on behalf of Christ, be reconciled to God. For our sake God made Christ to be sin who knew no sin, so that in Christ we might become the righteousness of God.

GOSPEL *Luke 15:1–3, 11–24a*

Now all the tax collectors and sinners were coming near to listen to Jesus. And the Pharisees and the scribes were grumbling and saying, "This fellow welcomes sinners and eats with them."

So Jesus told them this parable: "There was a man who had two sons. The younger of them said to his father, 'Father, give me the share of the property that will belong to me.' So the father divided his property between them. A few days later the younger son gathered all he had and traveled to a distant country, and there he squandered his property in dissolute living. When he had spent everything, a severe famine took place throughout that country, and he began to be in need. So he went and hired himself out to one of the citizens of that country, who sent him to his fields to feed the pigs. He would gladly have filled himself with the pods that the pigs were eating; and no one gave him anything. But when he came to himself he said, 'How many of my father's hired hands have bread enough and to spare, but here I am dying of hunger! I will get up and go to my father, and I will say to him, "Father, I have sinned against heaven and before you; I am no longer worthy to be called your son; treat me like one of your hired hands." ' So he set off and went to his father. But while he was still far off, his father saw him and was filled with compassion; he ran and put his arms around him and kissed him. Then the son said to him, 'Father, I have sinned against heaven and before you; I am no longer worthy to be called your son.' But the father said to his slaves, 'Quickly, bring out a robe—the best one—and put it on him; put a ring on his finger and sandals on his feet. And get the fatted calf and kill it, and let us eat and celebrate; for this son of mine was dead and is alive again; he was lost and is found!'"

[Complete reading: Luke 15:1–3, 11–32]

Wednesday, March 25, 1998

ANNUNCIATION

Isaiah 7:10–14 *A virgin will bear a child.*

Hebrews 10:4–10 *I come to do God's will.*

Luke 1:26–38 *Rejoice, O highly favored daughter!*

Because pregnancy outside of marriage was punishable by death, Mary's "yes" to the angel was an acceptance of death. But in this death, the risen Spirit conquers death. Mary's mortal body conceives the Immortal One. The paschal victory is won.

REFLECTION

The beautiful story of repentance and forgiveness in today's gospel begins on a negative note: The religious leaders of Jesus' day were critical of the company he kept. If Jesus was preaching and teaching something about the reign of God, about how to live rightly, shouldn't he have been associating with them rather than with known sinners, who clearly did not follow God's will?

But Jesus apparently knew what was in their hearts and tells a story in which the sinner captures the attention and sympathy of the audience. To be sure, the younger son begins by acting despicably, demanding and then wasting his share of his father's estate — usually divided only at the father's death. But his misfortune in a foreign land causes a change of heart. Jewish hearers of this parable would know without any doubt that this son had hit rock bottom: He was caring for and even willing to eat the food of that most unclean of animals, the pig.

After treating his father with utter contempt, even as though he were dead, the young son humbles himself and resolves to renounce any familial claims to favor but to accept the role of a servant in his father's house. The reader is drawn to this son, sympathizing with the acknowledgment of his error (brought to the fore, it is true, by hunger) and the humility he displays by swallowing his pride and returning to his father.

Although the anger of the older son, described in 15:24b–32, is justified, his obstinacy and lack of compassion make one wonder if there is still a lost son, one who has not inherited the same love and forgiveness for his brother that was so freely bestowed by the father.

The self-righteous religious leaders to whom this parable is directed cannot help but squirm at the suggestion that God, represented by the father, grants the same favor to sinners as to them. But the father does not rebuke the older son, he merely corrects him: You always have all that is mine; let us share our bounty with this one who has returned.

On another level, the behavior of the father is that asked of us: compassion, forgiveness, generosity.

■ **Do you sometimes feel like the older son, responsible and hardworking yet upset at the unfairness of life?**

■ **Are you more comfortable with the religious leaders you know or with people at rock bottom?**

PRACTICE OF FAITH

ANNUNCIATION. Throughout the season of Lent there are feast days that keep us pointed toward the glorious mystery of each Sunday and the grand Sunday we are yearning toward. The Annunciation of the Lord (March 25) places us in front of the question of recognizing God working in our lives and our response.

The Holy Spirit is the gifted guide in that recognition. If our eyes fail us, the breath of the Spirit will awaken our senses to the arrival and presence of God. The Annunciation is celebrated with wind and fire, the symbols of the Spirit. In the darkness of Lent, we light candles and a warming fire. In Greece, kites are flown on this day. Make a windsock for this day for your front porch, and watch its spirited flight.

PRACTICE OF HOPE

PRODIGAL BROTHERS, ONE. Then the elder son turned away in anger and said to himself, "My father's heart has turned away from me. Let me get rid of my crafty brother." So, at an opportune time, the elder son took his brother into the wilderness and slew him. He scattered his body and buried the head under a tree. To his father he showed his brother's blood-stained shirt and said that a lion had killed and eaten him. The father cried out loudly, and nothing could console him. Day after day, he carried around the blood-stained shirt, and night after night, he drenched it with his tears. As years went by, the elder son saw that he would never take his brother's place in his father's heart. And he began to pity the old man, who was bent low by his grief.

PRACTICE OF CHARITY

NEW CREATION. In a rain forest on the Oregon coast, a dozen people on a weekend retreat prayed in an unfamiliar and ancient manner. Inside a hut made from branches, red-hot rocks threw an oppressive heat. The sweat and silence placed their prayers in the context of North American Indian tradition and ritual. Afterward, the Christian participants admitted that the "sweat lodge" gave them a broader and deeper understanding of the ways in which God speaks to people and touches their lives. Jesus opened eyes and hearts to new ways and invited his followers to live in peace and harmony with nature and all people. Take a moment this week to pray in a new way or place — remembering a friend while riding a bicycle, having a quick thought under your favorite tree. New ways, new prayers, refreshed spirit.

WEEKDAY READINGS (Mo) Isaiah 65:17–21; (Tu) Ezekiel 47:1–12; (We) Annunciation, see box; (Th) Exodus 32:7–14; (Fr) Wisdom 2:1a, 12–22; (Sa) Jeremiah 11:18–20

READING I *1 Samuel 16:1, 4, 6–7, 10–13*

The LORD said to Samuel, "I will send you to Jesse the Bethlehemite, for I have provided for myself a king among his sons." Samuel did what the LORD commanded, and came to Bethlehem.

When Jesse and his sons came, Samuel looked on Eliab and thought, "Surely the LORD's anointed is now before the LORD." But the LORD said to Samuel, "Do not look on his appearance or on the height of his stature, because I have rejected him; for the LORD does not see as mortals see; they look on the outward appearance, but the LORD looks on the heart." Jesse made seven of his sons pass before Samuel, and Samuel said to Jesse, "The LORD has not chosen any of these."

Samuel said to Jesse, "Are all your sons here?" And he said, "There remains yet the youngest, but he is keeping the sheep." And Samuel said to Jesse, "Send and bring him; for we will not sit down until he comes here." Jesse sent and brought him in. Now he was ruddy, and had beautiful eyes, and was handsome. The LORD said, "Rise and anoint him; for this is the one." Then Samuel took the horn of oil, and anointed him in the presence of his brothers; and the spirit of the LORD came mightily upon David from that day forward.

[Complete reading: 1 Samuel 16:1–13]

READING II *Ephesians 5:8–14*

Once you were darkness, but now in the Lord you are light. Live as children of light—for the fruit of the light is found in all that is good and right and true. Try to find out what is pleasing to the Lord. Take no part in the unfruitful works of darkness, but instead expose them. For it is shameful even to mention what such people do secretly; but everything exposed by the light becomes visible, for everything that becomes visible is light.

Therefore it says, "Sleeper, awake! Rise from the dead, and Christ will shine on you."

GOSPEL *John 9:1, 6–17, 34–41*

As Jesus walked along, he saw a man blind from birth. He spat on the ground and made mud with the saliva and spread the mud on the man's eyes, saying to him, "Go, wash in the pool of Siloam" (which means Sent). Then he went and washed and came back able to see.

The neighbors and those who had seen him before as a beggar began to ask, "Is this not the man who used to sit and beg?" Some were saying, "It is he." Others were saying, "No, but it is someone like him." He kept saying, "I am the man." But they kept asking him, "Then how were your eyes opened?" He answered, "The man called Jesus made mud, spread it on my eyes, and said to me, 'Go to Siloam and wash.' Then I went and washed and received my sight." They said to him, "Where is he?" He said, "I do not know."

They brought to the Pharisees the man who had formerly been blind. Now it was a sabbath day when Jesus made the mud and opened his eyes. Then the Pharisees also began to ask him how he had received his sight. He said to them, "He put mud on my eyes. Then I washed, and now I see." Some of the Pharisees said, "This man is not from God, for he does not observe the sabbath." But others said, "How can a man who is a sinner perform such signs?" And they were divided. So they said again to the blind man, "What do you say about him? It was your eyes he opened." He said, "He is a prophet." They answered him, "You were born entirely in sins, and are you trying to teach us?" And they drove him out.

Jesus heard that they had driven him out, and when he found him, he said, "Do you believe in the Son-of-Man?" He answered, "And who is he, sir? Tell me, so that I may believe in him." Jesus said to him, "You have seen him, and he is the one speaking with you." He said, "Lord, I believe." And he worshiped Jesus. Jesus said, "I came into this world for judgment so that those who do not see may see, and those who do see may become blind." Some of the Pharisees near Jesus heard this and said to him, "Surely we are not blind, are we?" Jesus said to them, "If you were blind, you would not have sin. But now that you say, 'We see,' your sin remains."

[Complete reading: John 9:1–41]

REFLECTION

A familiar theme in the Gospel of John is that of the contrast between light and darkness. This gospel as a whole sets out much the same message as that of the passage from Ephesians: Walk as children of the light, and renounce the darkness in which you were once enveloped. But this passage from the Gospel of John, in a story of sight and blindness, turns upside down the ideas of light and darkness.

On a literal level, the story recounts a healing by Jesus. But this healing involves a violation of the sabbath command to rest. The Pharisees, whose role it was to uphold and interpret God's law, object and say that Jesus is a sinner. When the one who was healed declares Jesus to be a prophet, they reject his word, clinging to the traditional deuteronomic understanding of misfortune as a punishment for sinfulness. This occasions an opportunity for Jesus to elicit a faith response from the man who formerly was blind.

But in this gospel, the story goes beyond a simple healing. It is the one who was blind who is really able to see and acknowledge Jesus' heavenly origin. Those who have sight, the religious leaders who supposedly walk in the light of God's favor, are in fact the blind ones. They become consumed with issues of legality in doing God's will and miss the moral demand to assist the less fortunate. The religious leaders refuse to fulfill their role as guides to others, preferring instead to allow those born in "utter sin" to remain in darkness. They have abdicated their responsibility as "enlightened" leaders to share their insight with others; they are instead depicted as stumbling in darkness.

Finally, Jesus says that he is the heavenly judge who reverses the usual categories; nothing is as it appears to be. The blind see, and those who should lead are themselves lost.

■ **Would you rather spend time with the religious leaders you know or with the blind and ignorant? Why?**

■ **Are you ever blind to the activity of God in your life? How can you allow yourself to be healed?**

PRACTICE OF FAITH

VOCABULARY. The journey of the catechumens to baptism invites us all to deepen our identity with the faith.

Many "modern" Catholics lack a Catholic vocabulary. Words that in the past were a common passageway into our shared faith have been lost to some, particularly the young. The catechumenate offers a hopeful model for reclaiming a shared vocabulary with which to open discussion about the faith. In the spirit of the catechumenate, we can review the basics and go over the terms and concepts that are necessary for entering (or reentering) the faith of our church.

Purchase a Catholic catechism or Catholic dictionary for the household.

PRACTICE OF HOPE

THE FIG TREE, TWO. But one day the vinedresser caught his daughter feeding the snake. Filled with fear and anger, he rushed forward, seized the snake by its neck, and cried: "Is it you gnawing at the roots of my master's fig tree? And are you threatening my daughter now? I shall cut off your head with my pruning knife." But the snake opened her mouth and spat venom into the vinedresser's face. The father cried out in pain, for he had lost his eyesight.

In tears, the daughter began to plead with the snake, "O snake, I have shown you nothing but kindness, and now my father is blind. Make him see again, and surely he will let you live under the fig tree."

"I cannot help. But because you were good to me, I will tell you how you may restore your father's eyesight."

PRACTICE OF CHARITY

DARKNESS. Hard shadows were burned into the surfaces of concrete walls in the atomic blast in Hiroshima. So intense was the heat that human bodies disintegrated instantly into ashes — vaporized. A survivor of the inferno was Jesuit priest Father Pedro Arrupe. He later became the worldwide head of the Jesuit Order. Bombs, heat, death — and survival — are dramatic moments in God's world. Most moments are not like that. The dramatic instances teach us to see life more clearly, to notice the gifts around us. Take a moment today to call to mind the two most dramatic events of your life. Thank God for them and for survival. We can be more awake to the human heart when we understand something of the darkness and light of our lives.

WEEKDAY READINGS (Mo) Isaiah 65:17 – 21; (Tu) Ezekiel 47: 1 – 12; (We) Annunciation, see page 64; (Th) Exodus 32:7 – 14; (Fr) Wisdom 2:1, 12 – 22; (Sa) Jeremiah 11:18 – 20

READING I *Isaiah 43:16–21*

Thus says the LORD,
who makes a way in the sea,
a path in the mighty waters,
who brings out chariot and horse,
army and warrior;
they lie down, they cannot rise,
they are extinguished, quenched like a wick:
Do not remember the former things,
or consider the things of old.
I am about to do a new thing;
now it springs forth, do you not perceive it?
I will make a way in the wilderness
and rivers in the desert.
The wild animals will honor me,
the jackals and the ostriches;
for I give water in the wilderness,
rivers in the desert,
to give drink to my chosen people,
the people whom I formed for myself
so that they might declare my praise.

READING II *Philippians 3:8–14*

More than that, I regard everything as loss because of the surpassing value of knowing Christ Jesus my Lord, for whose sake I have suffered the loss of all things, and I regard them as rubbish, in order that I may gain Christ and be found in him, not having a righteousness of my own that comes from the law, but one that comes through faith in Christ, the righteousness from God based on faith. I want to know Christ and the power of his resurrection and the sharing of his sufferings by becoming like him in his death, if somehow I may attain the resurrection from the dead.

Not that I have already obtained this or have already reached the goal but I press on to make it my own, because Christ Jesus has made me his own. Beloved, I do not consider that I have made it my own but this one thing I do: forgetting what lies behind and straining forward to what lies ahead, I press on toward the goal for the prize of the heavenly call of God in Christ Jesus.

GOSPEL *John 8:1–11*

Jesus went to the Mount of Olives. Early in the morning he came again to the temple. All the people came to him and he sat down and began to teach them.

The scribes and the Pharisees brought a woman who had been caught in adultery; and making her stand before the people, they said to Jesus, "Teacher, this woman was caught in the very act of committing adultery. In the law, Moses commanded us to stone such women. Now what do you say?" They said this to test Jesus, so that they might have some charge to bring against him.

Jesus bent down and wrote with his finger on the ground. When the scribes and Pharisees kept on questioning him, Jesus straightened up and said to them, "Let anyone among you who is without sin be the first to throw a stone at her." And once again Jesus bent down and wrote on the ground. When the scribes and Pharisees heard what Jesus had said, they went away, one by one, beginning with the elders; and Jesus was left alone with the woman standing before him.

Jesus straightened up and said to her, "Woman, where are they? Has no one condemned you?" She said, "No one, sir." And Jesus said, "Neither do I condemn you. Go your way, and from now on do not sin again."

REFLECTION

Only in the Gospel of John do we find the story of the woman caught in adultery. This story, which was not in the earliest manuscripts of the gospel, apparently was added during a time of controversies among early Christians over penance: Could such a grievous sin as adultery be forgiven, or was it one of the unforgivable sins that was to have been renounced at baptism? Some clearly saw it as in keeping with the teachings of Jesus to proclaim the possibility of forgiveness for all.

The story itself may in fact go back to the life of Jesus. In Jewish law at the time, the transgression of adultery could be committed only by a woman, apparently as a means of ensuring that a man would have offspring of his own. Jesus himself, as Matthew, Mark and Luke recount, apparently extended the definition of adultery to include husbands who were unfaithful as well.

But in this story, it is a woman who is charged by the Pharisees with adultery. And the question is intended to trap Jesus. Would he deny the validity of the precious law of Moses? Or, if he was such a compassionate and loving person, often critical of religious leaders for their lack of heartfelt concern, could he uphold the law and allow the woman to be put to death?

Jesus does not answer. The woman must have realized that her fate was in the hands of this silent man. When he is further pressed, his response — let the one who is without sin cast a stone — penetrates their hearts. The oldest and wisest of the crowd initiate the exodus; of course no one can deny the reality of sinfulness. But they had not thought that they themselves would be charged; they were concerned with upholding the Mosaic law.

Jesus never does address the question of the validity of the law. He shows compassion for the woman, who stands alone before him. But he also tells her not to sin again. Forgiveness for past wrongs allows for the strength to renounce wrongdoing. Compassion and righteousness are not opposed to one another but are intimately entwined.

■ **What do you think was Jesus' response to the law of Moses? Did he intend to uphold it or to abrogate it?**

■ **How do you respond when you are confronted with the clear wrongdoing of others? Are you able to forgive and yet demand right behavior? How?**

PRACTICE OF FAITH

PEACE AND QUIET. In the gospel, Jesus goes off to the Mount of Olives before returning to the temple area, where he brings reconciliation and peace to the woman caught in adultery. Jesus goes off for the night in solitude and prayer. Saint Francis of Paola (March 29) spent a good part of his life dedicated to prayer and solitude as a hermit. Out of this solitude emerged peacemaking between countries. The wisdom of Saint Francis helped engineer peace between France, Great Britain and Spain.

Health magazines have joined with the church in an appreciation of the benefits of quiet and solitude. They add the health benefits to the spiritual benefits the church has known for ages. Set aside a time daily to spend in solitude. Find a quiet time and place to "hear" the wisdom of silence.

PRACTICE OF HOPE

THE TEMPTER, TWO. Again, he comes to us from the depths of the earth, hissing into our ears: "I am the master of the earth. I have dominion over every rock on which you walk. With me there is law and security for ever and ever. Come, miserable humans, forsake the gods above. Throw yourselves onto the earth, creep into its dust, take on the life of the sediment, and bring others along with you. Hate them, judge them, rape them, cast stones at them, put them in prisons and death camps. Crush them to the ground and grind them up until all is motionless, silent, equal and secure. Then will the earth be your kingdom."

O my soul, arm yourself with Christ's love for humankind when this one draws near you.

PRACTICE OF CHARITY

WRITING AND READING. Are you utterly intrigued by Jesus writing on the ground? What could he have been writing — not once, but twice? It's the only instance in the scriptures that notes Jesus writing. He taught by word and example, especially by telling stories — parables. In Rock Island, Illinois, some years ago, a literacy campaign was announced by passing out flyers door to door. A written message to announce literacy training — once the humor of it passed, several neighbors did learn to read and write. Whole worlds of information and stories, flights of imagination and learning opened up for them. Contact your neighborhood school to volunteer to tutor students, or assist at your local adult literacy training center.

WEEKDAY READINGS (Mo) Daniel 13:41 – 62; (Tu) Numbers 21:4 – 9; (We) Daniel 3:14 – 20, 91 – 95; (Th) Genesis 17:3 – 9; (Fr) Jeremiah 20:10 – 13; (Sa) Ezekiel 37:21 – 28

READING I *Ezekiel 37:12–14*

"Thus says the Lord GOD: I am going to open your graves, and bring you up from your graves, O my people; and I will bring you back to the land of Israel. And you shall know that I am the LORD, when I open your graves, and bring you up from your graves, O my people. I will put my spirit within you, and you shall live, and I will place you on your own soil; then you shall know that I, the LORD, have spoken and will act," says the LORD.

[Complete reading: Ezekiel 37:1–14]

READING II *Romans 8:6–11*

To set the mind on the flesh is death, but to set the mind on the Spirit is life and peace. For this reason the mind that is set on the flesh is hostile to God; it does not submit to God's law—indeed it cannot, and those who are in the flesh cannot please God.

But you are not in the flesh; you are in the Spirit, since the Spirit of God dwells in you. Anyone who does not have the Spirit of Christ does not belong to Christ. But if Christ is in you, though the body is dead because of sin, the Spirit is life because of righteousness. If the Spirit of the one who raised Jesus from the dead dwells in you, the one who raised Christ from the dead will give life to your mortal bodies also through this Spirit dwelling in you.

GOSPEL *John 11:3–7, 17, 20–27, 33–45*

The sisters sent a message to Jesus, "Lord, he whom you love is ill." But when Jesus heard it, he said, "This illness does not lead to death; rather it is for God's glory, so that the Son of God may be glorified through it." Accordingly, though Jesus loved Martha and her sister and Lazarus, after having heard that Lazarus was ill, he stayed two days longer in the place where he was.

Then after this he said to the disciples, "Let us go to Judea again." When Jesus arrived, he found that Lazarus had already been in the tomb four days.

When Martha heard that Jesus was coming, she went and met him, while Mary stayed at home. Martha said to Jesus, "Lord, if you had been here, my brother would not have died. But even now I know that whatever you ask from God, God will give you." Jesus said to her, "Your brother will rise again." Martha said to him, "I know that he will rise again in the resurrection on the last day." Jesus said to her, "I am the resurrection and the life. Those who believe in me, even though they die, will live, and everyone who lives and believes in me will never die. Do you believe this?" She said to him, "Yes, Lord, I believe that you are the Messiah, the Son of God, the one coming into the world."

Jesus was greatly disturbed in spirit and deeply moved. He said, "Where have you laid him?" They said to him, "Lord, come and see." Jesus began to weep. So the Judeans said, "See how he loved him!" But some of them said, "Could not the one who opened the eyes of the blind man have kept this man from dying?"

Then Jesus, again greatly disturbed, came to the tomb. It was a cave, and a stone was lying against it. Jesus said, "Take away the stone." Martha, the sister of the dead man, said to him, "Lord, already there is a stench because he has been dead four days." Jesus said to her, "Did I not tell you that if you believed, you would see the glory of God?"

So they took away the stone. And Jesus looked upward and said, "Father, I thank you for having heard me. I knew that you always hear me, but I have said this for the sake of the crowd standing here, so that they may believe that you sent me." When Jesus had said this, he cried with a loud voice, "Lazarus, come out!" The dead man came out, his hands and feet bound with strips of cloth, and his face wrapped in a cloth. Jesus said to them, "Unbind him, and let him go."

Many of the Judeans therefore, who had come with Mary and had seen what Jesus did, believed in him.

[Complete reading: John 11:1–45]

REFLECTION

Death is very near; it dominates all of today's readings. But death, though central, is not the only reality present here. The promise of life is also expressed. Just as in Ezekiel God promises new life to Israel during the Babylonian exile, and just as Paul speaks of the offer of life to those dead in sin, so also the gospel passage illustrates that death does not have the final word. The story of the raising of Lazarus anticipates Jesus' own death and resurrection. In the Gospel of John, the event that reveals Jesus' purpose and message is his death, in which he is raised up to glory. Death is paradoxical; it provides the opportunity to be exalted. It is also the supreme way of living the command that Jesus discusses at some length at the Last Supper: Love.

All of these themes are captured in miniature in the story of Lazarus. Here Jesus' compassion and love are foremost; he grieves the loss of his friend. Here too, Jesus reveals his purpose and identity to Martha, who faithfully trusts in the promise of a future resurrection of the dead. The Gospel of John makes clear, however, that all hope of life, of resurrection, resides properly in the person of Jesus; he not only restores life, he is the source of life.

The dramatic account of the raising of Lazarus and the affirmation of Jesus as the "Messiah, the Son of God" who gives life to all is set against the backdrop of Jesus' movement toward his own death. Immediately after the account in today's gospel is the story of the plot of the Sanhedrin against Jesus. Not only do the religious leaders find it necessary to put a stop to Jesus' many signs, but in order not to upset the Romans, who held Judea with a tight fist, the high priest Caiaphas is presented as prophesying Jesus' death for the sake of all.

After the happy event of today's gospel and Martha's profession of faith, the mood begins to darken. The plot thickens. Death is near.

■ **How do you think it feels to know that death is near? What do you think Jesus must have been thinking and feeling?**

■ **It is difficult to miss the significance of raising someone from the dead. What "signs" of God's activity (perhaps more subtle than this) have you witnessed?**

PRACTICE OF FAITH

APPROACH. We approach Passion (Palm) Sunday with Jesus and his friends. There is much movement in relationships and the truth in the raising of Lazarus. As each person approaches Jesus with already established relationships, they are invited by Jesus into the more mysterious relationship that will include his death.

We move toward the beginning of Holy Week by approaching Jesus and Lazarus. We are preparing to approach the cross and the tomb. Pray with and for the catechumens in their intense preparation for Holy Saturday's Vigil of Easter. Look ahead to each day of Holy Week and plan your celebration or observance. Include home, parish and diocesan prayer and worship in your movement through the days of Holy Week.

PRACTICE OF HOPE

PRODIGAL BROTHERS, TWO. One day, the elder son spoke to his father, saying, "What does your heart desire, that I may get it for you?"

And the father answered: "O my son, if I only had a bone from your brother's body, this would end my suffering."

The elder son stood up and led his father into the wilderness, to the place where he had slain his brother. He dug up the skull from under the tree and said: "Behold the head the lion spared. I buried it in silence to spare you."

But lo, at the touch of his father's hand the skull began to speak: "Dear father, it was not the lion but my jealous brother who killed me and scattered my bones in the wilderness."

PRACTICE OF CHARITY

LIVING IN THE SPIRIT. A wise woman once said, "All human beings owe it to themselves to walk on the beach alone at least once a year." No social justice can occur without quiet reflection, without the lonely search for real solutions. Poverty, for example, is usually not the result of irresponsibility or personal failure. Much more often it is caused by societal forces that all but overwhelm a person or family. Quiet reflection in a park, an airport chapel or the back yard, or a walk on the beach, can actually become the beginning force in a Christian's journey to address these issues. International leaders Nelson Mandela, Anwar Sadat and Vaclav Havel all spent time alone in reflection. In solitude we can do as Jesus did, touch the troubled places in our spirit, our deepest emotions.

WEEKDAY READINGS (Mo) Daniel 13:41 – 62; (Tu) Numbers 21:4 – 9; (We) Daniel 3:14 – 20, 91 – 95; (Th) Genesis 17:3 – 9; (Fr) Jeremiah 20:10 – 13; (Sa) Ezekiel 37:21 – 28

READING I *Isaiah 50:4–7*

The Lord GOD has given me
    the tongue of a teacher,
that I may know how to sustain
    the weary with a word.
Morning by morning the Lord GOD wakens—
    wakens my ear
    to listen as those who are taught.
The Lord GOD has opened my ear,
    and I was not rebellious,
    I did not turn backward.
I gave my back to those who struck me,
    and my cheeks to those who pulled out the beard;
I did not hide my face
    from insult and spitting.
The Lord GOD helps me;
    therefore I have not been disgraced;
therefore I have set my face like flint,
    and I know that I shall not be put to shame.

READING II *Philippians 2:6–11*

Although being in the form of God, Jesus did not regard equality with God as something to be exploited, but relinquished it all, taking the form of a slave, being born in human likeness. And being found in human form, he humbled himself and became obedient to the point of death—even death on a cross.

Therefore God also highly exalted him and gave him the name that is above every name, so that at the name of Jesus every knee should bend, in heaven and on earth and under the earth, and every tongue should confess that Jesus Christ is Lord, to the glory of God, the Father.

GOSPEL *Luke 22:14 — 23:25, 32–56*

When the hour came, Jesus took his place at the table, and the apostles with him. He said to them, "I have eagerly desired to eat this Passover with you before I suffer; for I tell you, I will not eat it until it is fulfilled in the dominion of God." Then Jesus took a cup, and after giving thanks he said, "Take this and divide it among yourselves; for I tell you that from now on I will not drink of the fruit of the vine until the dominion of God comes." Then he took a loaf of bread, and when he had given thanks, he broke it and gave it to them, saying, "This is my body, which is given for you. Do this in remembrance of me." And Jesus did the same with the cup after supper, saying, "This cup that is poured out for you is the new covenant in my blood. But see, the one who betrays me is with me, and his hand is on the table. For the Son-of-Man is going as it has been determined, but woe to that one by whom he is betrayed!" Then they began to ask one another which one of them it could be who would do this.

A dispute also arose among them as to which one of them was to be regarded as the greatest. But Jesus said to them, "The rulers of the Gentiles are domineering; and those in authority over them are called benefactors. But not so with you; rather the greatest among you must become like the youngest, and the leader like one who serves. For who is greater, the one who is at the table or the one who serves? Is it not the one at the table? But I am among you as one who serves.

"You are those who have stood by me in my trials; and I confer on you, just as my Father has conferred on me, a dominion, so that you may eat and drink at my table in my dominion, and you will sit on thrones judging the twelve tribes of Israel.

"Simon, Simon, listen! Satan has demanded to sift all of you like wheat, but I have prayed for you that your own faith may not fail; and you, when once you have turned back, strengthen the community." And Simon Peter said to Jesus, "Lord, I am ready to go with you to prison and to death!" Jesus said, "I tell you, Peter, the cock will not crow this day, until you have denied three times that you know me." Jesus said to them, "When I sent you out without a purse, bag, or sandals, did you lack anything?" They said, "No, not a thing." He said to them, "But now, the one who has a purse must take it, and likewise a bag. And the one who has no sword must sell a cloak to buy one. For I tell you, this scripture must be fulfilled in me, 'And he was counted among the lawless'; and indeed what is written about me is being fulfilled." They said, "Lord, look, here are two swords." He replied, "It is enough."

Jesus came out and went, as was his custom, to the Mount of Olives; and the disciples followed him. When he reached the place, he said to them, "Pray that you may not come into the time of trial." Then he withdrew from them about a stone's throw, knelt down, and prayed, "Father, if you are willing, remove this cup from me; yet, not my will but yours be done." Then an angel from heaven appeared to Jesus and gave him strength. In his anguish Jesus prayed more earnestly, and his sweat became like great drops of blood falling down on the ground. When he got up from prayer, he came to the disciples and found them sleeping because of grief, and he said to them, "Why are you sleeping? Get up and pray that you may not come into the time of trial."

While Jesus was still speaking, suddenly a crowd came, and the one called Judas, one of the twelve, was leading them. Judas approached Jesus to kiss him; but Jesus said to him, "Judas, is it with a kiss that you are betraying the Son-of-Man?" When those who were around him saw what was coming, they asked, "Lord, should we strike with the sword?" Then one of them struck the slave of the high priest and cut off his right ear. But Jesus said, "No more of this!" And Jesus touched the slave's ear and healed him. Then Jesus said to the chief priests, the officers of the temple police, and the elders who had come for him, "Have you come out with swords and clubs as if I were a bandit? When I was with you day after day in the temple, you did not lay hands on me. But this is your hour, and the power of darkness!"

Then they seized Jesus and led him away, bringing him into the high priest's house. But Peter was following at a distance. When they had kindled a fire in the middle of the courtyard and sat down together, Peter sat among them. Then a servant, seeing Peter in the firelight, stared at him and said, "This man also was with him." But he denied it, saying, "Woman, I do not know him." A little later someone else, on seeing Peter, said, "You also are one of them." But Peter said, "Man, I am not!" Then

about an hour later still another kept insisting, "Surely this man also was with Jesus; for he is a Galilean." But Peter said, "Man, I do not know what you are talking about!" At that moment, while he was still speaking, the cock crowed. The Lord turned and looked at Peter. Then Peter remembered the word of the Lord, who had said to him, "Before the cock crows today, you will deny me three times." And he went out and wept bitterly.

Now the men who were holding Jesus began to mock him and beat him; they also blindfolded him and kept asking him, "Prophesy! Who is it that struck you?" They kept heaping many other insults on him.

When day came, the assembly of the elders of the people, both chief priests and scribes, gathered together, and they brought Jesus to their council. They said, "If you are the Messiah, tell us." Jesus replied, "If I tell you, you will not believe; and if I question you, you will not answer. But from now on the Son-of-Man will be seated at the right hand of the power of God." All of them asked, "Are you, then, the Son of God?" Jesus said to them, "You say that I am." Then they said, "What further testimony do we need? We have heard it ourselves from his own lips!"

Then the assembly rose as a body and brought Jesus before Pilate. They began to accuse Jesus, saying, "We found this man perverting our nation, forbidding us to pay taxes to the emperor, and saying that he himself is the Messiah, a king." Then Pilate asked Jesus, "Are you the king of the Jews?" Jesus answered, "You say so." Then Pilate said to the chief priests and the crowds, "I find no basis for an accusation against this man." But they were insistent and said, "He stirs up the people by teaching throughout all Judea, from Galilee where he began even to this place."

When Pilate heard this, he asked whether the man was a Galilean. And when he learned that he was under Herod's jurisdiction, Pilate sent Jesus off to Herod, who was himself in Jerusalem at that time. When Herod saw Jesus, he was very glad, for he had been wanting to see him for a long time, because he had heard about Jesus and was hoping to see him perform some sign. Herod questioned him at some length, but Jesus gave him no answer. The chief priests and the scribes stood by, vehemently accusing him. Even Herod with his soldiers treated Jesus with contempt and mocked him; then he put an elegant robe on him, and sent him back to Pilate. That same day Herod and Pilate became friends with each other; before this they had been enemies.

Pilate then called together the chief priests, the leaders, and the people, and said to them, "You brought me this man as one who was perverting the people; and here I have examined him in your presence and have not found this man guilty of any of your charges against him. Neither has Herod, for he sent him back to us. Indeed, he has done nothing to deserve death. I will therefore have him flogged and release him."

Then they all shouted out together, "Away with this fellow! Release Barabbas for us!" (This was a man who had been put in prison for an insurrection that had taken place in the city, and for murder.) Pilate, wanting to release Jesus, addressed them again; but they kept shouting, "Crucify, crucify him!" A third time Pilate said to them, "Why, what evil has he done? I have found in him no ground for the sentence of death; I will therefore have him flogged and then release him." But they kept urgently demanding with loud shouts that Jesus should be crucified; and their voices prevailed. So Pilate gave his verdict that their demand should be granted. He released the man they asked for, the one who had been put in prison for insurrection and murder, and he handed Jesus over as they wished.

Two others also, who were criminals, were led away to be put to death with Jesus. When they came to the place that is called The Skull, they crucified Jesus there with the criminals, one on his right and one on his left. Then Jesus said, "Father, forgive them; for they do not know what they are doing." And they cast lots to divide his clothing. And the people stood by, watching; but the leaders scoffed at him, saying, "He saved others; let him save himself if he is the Messiah of God, the chosen one!" The soldiers also mocked him, coming up and offering him sour wine, and saying, "If you are the King of the Jews, save yourself!" There was also an inscription over him, "This is the King of the Jews."

One of the criminals who were hanged there kept deriding Jesus and saying, "Are you not the Messiah? Save yourself and us!" But the other rebuked him, saying, "Do you not fear God, since you are under the same sentence of condemnation? And we indeed have been condemned justly, for we are getting what we deserve for our deeds, but this man has done nothing wrong." Then he said, "Jesus, remember me when you come into your kingdom." He replied, "Truly I tell you, today you will be with me in Paradise."

It was now about noon, and darkness came over the whole land until three in the afternoon, while the sun's light failed; and the curtain of the temple was torn in two. Then Jesus, crying with a loud voice, said, "Father, into your hands I commend my spirit." Having said this, he breathed his last. When the centurion saw what had taken place, he praised God and said, "Certainly this man was innocent." And when all the crowds who had gathered there for this spectacle saw what had taken place, they returned home, beating their breasts. But all his acquaintances, including the women who had followed him from Galilee, stood at a distance, watching these things.

Now there was a good and righteous man named Joseph, who, though a member of the council, had not agreed to their plan and action. He came from the Jewish town of Arimathea, and he was waiting expectantly for the dominion of God. This man went to Pilate and asked for the body of Jesus. Then he took it down, wrapped it in a linen cloth, and laid it in a rock-hewn tomb where no one had ever been laid. It was the day of Preparation, and the sabbath was beginning. The women who had come with Jesus from Galilee followed, and they saw the tomb and how his body was laid. Then they returned, and prepared spices and ointments.

[Complete reading: Luke 22:14 — 23:56]

REFLECTION

The hour has come, the darkest hour, the time of entering the depths of despair, the hour of death.

We first encounter Jesus in the midst of friends, at a holiday celebration. But by the time of his death, he is surrounded by those who revile him. Gradually those closest to him turn away. First his betrayer is seen to be one of his own; the greatest danger sometimes lies not with enemies or strangers but with those most trusted. The other disciples are all absent after the arrest of Jesus. Only Peter loiters nearby, offering him the occasion to save his own hide by denying that he ever knew Jesus. In the end, the one who had attracted crowds of admirers eager to listen to his words finds himself standing alone, in the midst of a crowd eager to see him die. Yet even in this dark hour, the theme of compassion, of concern for the lowly, which is so prevalent in this gospel, comes to the fore.

Once again, all expectations are turned upside down. To the disciples who missed the significance of the events at hand and spent their last meal with Jesus arguing about which of them was the greatest, Jesus presents himself, their teacher, as a servant. Although his friends deny him, a common criminal acknowledges him and speaks the truth about him. A godless Gentile, one of the soldiers charged with his execution, recognizes his innocence. Those worthy of trust are not friends, religious leaders or government officials but the lowly, even the guilty. Things are not always as they appear.

We leave this narrative tired, spent. The forces of hatred, ignorance and death have prevailed. But this cannot be the final word. It is a typically Lukan theme of reversal, a message so often difficult to hear, which now gives us hope. Death does not have the last laugh. There is yet more to come.

■ **When someone dies, the bereaved may feel abandoned by God, by the one who died and by friends. If you know someone who is grieving, say a simple and sincere "I'm so sorry," and then listen. Use the name of the deceased person. Join in the mourning.**

PRACTICE OF FAITH

WALK WITH ME. "If you're going to talk to me, fellow, you'll have to walk." These are the words of Wendell Berry's character Old Jack Beechum. This quote is carried down through generations of the community as the old listen to the young.

If we are going to talk with Jesus this week, we are going to have to walk. We need to walk with Jesus through this week. Much of our ritual this week is the holy remembrance of walking the walk of Jesus to the cross and finally out of the tomb. Our prayer is the talk of the walk.

Pray the Stations of the Cross this week in a setting where you can walk them as you talk them. An outdoor setting of the Stations would be ideal.

PRACTICE OF HOPE

PRODIGAL BROTHERS, THREE. Upon these words, the elder son turned ashen. With a loud cry, he seized his dagger and plunged it into his own heart. Dying, he fell into the arms of his father and said: "Father, forgive me! I have failed in your love. It is I who killed the son you loved!"

But the old man rested his faltering hand on his son's bloodied brow and said to him: "My son, your crime was born of hatred, but it was your love for me that brought us to this place and this hour, for you took pity on my grief. I do forgive you. Moreover, when you close your eyes, I too will lay down my head, for I am weary. And truly, I say unto you, this night you will be with me and your brother in paradise."

PRACTICE OF CHARITY

EMPTYING ONESELF. In the movie *Dead Man Walking*, Sister Helen Prejean, played by Susan Sarandon, urges the death row inmate, played by Sean Penn, to empty himself, to humble himself, as he faces the lethal injection. Finally, strapped to the cross-like gurney, he does. Before he could face himself and God, he had to confront his crime of rape and murder and consider the families of the victims. Our crimes may not be so horrendous, but we are still called to own our faults and make peace with our victims. Twelve-step recovery programs like Alcoholics Anonymous require this. Great insights about the process of honestly and healthily accepting our faults, of emptying ourselves, can be gained by watching *Dead Man Walking*. Better yet, read Sister Prejean's book, and consider questions about the death penalty itself.

WEEKDAY READINGS (Mo) Isaiah 42:1 – 7; (Tu) 49:1 – 6; (We) Isaiah 50:4 – 9

PASCHAL TRIDUUM

Holy is God! Holy and Strong!
Holy, immortal One, have mercy on us!

All you sheltered by the Most High,
who live in Almighty God's shadow,
say to the Lord, "My refuge, my fortress,
my God in whom I trust!"

God will free you from the hunters' snares,
will save you from deadly plague,
will cover you like a nesting bird.
God's wings will shelter you.

No nighttime terror shall you fear,
no arrows shot by day,
no plague that prowls the dark,
no wasting scourge at noon.

You have only to open your eyes
to see how the wicked are repaid.
You have the Lord as refuge,
have made the Most High your stronghold.

No evil shall ever touch you,
no harm come near your home.
God instructs angels
to guard you wherever you go.

"I deliver all who cling to me,
raise the ones who know my name,
answer those who call me,
stand with those in trouble.
These I rescue and honor,
satisfy with long life,
and show my power to save."

—Psalm 91: 1 – 6, 8 – 11, 14 – 16

Holy God,
praise be yours for this tree of Paradise,
this tree that made Noah's saving Ark,
this tree whose branches embraced Jesus
and so shade and shelter us all.
Here may all the weary rest
these holy days,
hungry and thirsty for your word,
eating and drinking only your word
until, in the darkness between
Saturday and Sunday,
Heaven and earth shall here be wed.
Then drowning waters shall be
waters of life
and the Savior's blood a banquet.
Holy God, praise be yours.

— Prayer of the Triduum

THE THREE DAYS

Holy Thursday brings the end to the Forty Days of Lent, which began on Ash Wednesday. The Forty Days make up the season of anticipation of the great Three Days. Composed of prayer, almsgiving, fasting and the preparation of the catechumens for baptism, the season of Lent is brought to a close and the Three Days begin as we approach the liturgy of Holy Thursday evening. As those to be initiated into the church have prepared themselves for their entrance into the fullness of life, so have we been awakening in our bodies, minds and hearts our own entrances into the life of Christ, experienced in the life of the church.

The Three Days, this Easter *Triduum* (Latin for "three days"), is the center, the core, of the entire year for Christians. These days mark the mystery around which our entire lives are played out. Adults in the community are invited to plan ahead so that the whole time from Thursday night until Easter Sunday is free of social engagements, free of entertainment and free of meals except for the simplest nourishment. We measure these days — indeed, our very salvation in the life of God — in step with the catechumens themselves; our own rebirths are revitalized as we participate in their initiation rites and as we have supported them along the way.

We are asked to fast on Good Friday and to continue fasting, if possible, all through Holy Saturday as strictly as we can so that we come to the Easter Vigil hungry and full of excitement, parched and longing to feel the sacred water of the font on our crusty skin. Good Friday and Holy Saturday are days of paring down distractions so that we may be free for prayer and anticipation, for reflection, preparation and silence. The church is getting ready for the Great Night of the Easter Vigil.

As one who has been initiated into the church, as one whose life has been wedded to this community gathered at the table, you should anticipate the Triduum with concentration and vigor. With you, the whole church knows that our presence for the liturgies of the Triduum is not just an invitation. All are needed. We "pull out all the stops" for these days. As human persons, wedded to all humanity by the joys and travails of life and grafted onto the body of the church by the sanctifying waters of baptism, we lead the new members into new life in this community of faith.

To this end, it is important that the Three Days be seen not as three liturgies distinct from one another but as one movement. These days have been connected intimately and liturgically from the early days of the Christian church. As a member of this community, you should be personally committed to preparing for and anticipating the Triduum and its culmination in the Vigil of the Great Night, Holy Saturday.

The church proclaims the direction of the Triduum by the opening antiphon of Holy Thursday, which comes from Paul's Letter to the Galatians (6:14). With this verse the church sets a spiritual environment into which we as committed Christians enter the Triduum:

> We should glory in the cross of our Lord Jesus Christ, for he is our salvation, our life and resurrection; through him we are saved and made free.

HOLY THURSDAY

On Thursday evening we enter into this Triduum together. Whether presider, baker, lector, preacher, wine maker, greeter, altar server, minister of the eucharist, decorator or person in a remote corner in the last pew of the church, we begin, as always, by hearkening to the word of God. These are the scriptures for the liturgy of Holy Thursday:

Exodus 12:1 – 8, 11 – 14
Ancient instructions for the meal of the Passover

1 Corinthians 11:23 – 26
Eat the bread and drink the cup until the return of the Lord

John 13:1 – 15
Jesus washes the feet of the disciples

After the readings, we, like Jesus, do something strange: We wash feet. Jesus gave us this image of what the church is supposed to look like, feel like, act like. Our position — whether as washer or washed, servant or served — is a difficult one for us to take. Yet we learn from the discomfort, from the awkwardness.

Then we celebrate the eucharist. Because it is connected to the other liturgies of the Triduum on Good Friday and Holy Saturday night, the evening liturgy of Holy Thursday has no ending. Whether we stay to pray awhile or leave, we are now in the quiet, peace and glory of the Triduum.

GOOD FRIDAY

We gather quietly in community on Friday and again listen to the word of God:

Isaiah 52:13 — 53:12
The servant of the Lord was crushed for our sins

Hebrews 4:14 – 16; 5:7 – 9
The Son of God learned obedience through his suffering

John 18:1 — 19:42
The passion of Jesus Christ

After the homily, we pray at length for all the world's needs — for the church; for the Pope, the clergy and all the baptized; for those preparing for initiation; for the unity of Christians; for Jews; for non-Christians; for atheists; for all in public office; and for those in special need.

Then there is another once-a-year event: The holy cross is held up in our midst and we come forward one by one to do reverence with a kiss, a bow or a genuflection. This communal reverence of an instrument of torture recalls the painful price, in the past and today, of salvation, the way in which our redemption is wrought, the stripes and humiliation of Jesus Christ that bring direction and life back to a humanity that is lost and dead. During the veneration of the cross, we sing not only of the sorrow but of the glory of the cross by which we have been saved.

Again, we bring to mind the words of Paul: "The cross of Jesus Christ . . . our salvation, our life and resurrection; through him we are saved and made free."

We continue in fasting and prayer and vigil, in rest and quiet, through Saturday. This Saturday for us is God's rest at the end of creation. It is Christ's repose in the tomb. It is Christ's visit with the dead.

EASTER VIGIL

Hungry now, pared down to basics, lightheaded from vigilance and full of excitement, we committed members of the church, the already baptized, gather in darkness and light a new fire. From this blaze we light a great candle that will make this night bright for us and will burn throughout the Easter season.

We hearken again to the word of God with some of the most powerful narratives and proclamations of our tradition:

Genesis 1:1 — 2:2 *Creation of the world*

Genesis 22:1 – 18 *The sacrifice of Isaac*

Exodus 14:15 — 15:1 *The Red Sea*

Isaiah 54:5 – 14 *You will not be afraid*

Isaiah 55:1 – 11 *Come, come to the water*

Baruch 3:9 – 15, 32 — 4:4 *The shining light*

Ezekiel 36:16 – 28 *The Lord says: I will sprinkle water*

Romans 6:3 – 11 *United with him in death*

Luke 24:1 – 12 *Jesus has been raised up*

After the readings, we pray to all our saints to stand with us as we go to the font and bless the waters. The chosen of all times and all places attend to what is about to take place. The catechumens renounce evil, profess the faith of the church and are baptized and anointed.

All of us renew our baptism. For us these are the moments when death and life meet, when we reject evil and give our promises to God. All of this is in the communion of the church. So together we go to the table and celebrate the Easter eucharist.

EASTERTIME

Christ is risen! Christ is truly risen!

Give thanks, the Lord is good,
God's love is for ever!
Now let Israel say,
"God's love is for ever!"

I was pushed to falling,
but the Lord gave me help.
My strength, my song is the Lord,
who has become my savior.

I shall not die but live
to tell the Lord's great deeds.
The Lord punished me severely,
but did not let me die.

The stone the builders rejected
has become the cornerstone.
This is the work of the Lord,
how wonderful in our eyes.

This is the day the Lord made,
let us rejoice and be glad.
Lord, give us the victory!
Lord, grant us success!

Blest is the one who comes,
who comes in the name of the Lord.
We bless you from the Lord's house.
The Lord God is our light:
adorn the altar with branches.

— *Psalm 118:1 – 2, 13 – 14, 17 – 18, 22 – 27*

The heavens rumble alleluias,
earth dances to the tune
and the wail of the graves
itself becomes song.
All are singing with you, savior God,
at this wedding feast
for you have turned the world around,
inside out and upside down.
Now the homeless are at home
and the martyred embrace their assassins
and the rulers and bosses wonder
whose world this is after all.
After all, let us stand and sing
with the heavens and earth and the graves
and so proclaim that we live now only
in Christ who is Lord for ever and ever.

— *Prayer of the Season*

READING I *Acts 10:34–43*

Peter began to speak to the people: "I truly understand that God shows no partiality, but in every nation anyone who is God-fearing and does what is right is acceptable to God.

"You know the message God sent to the people of Israel, preaching peace by Jesus Christ — who is Lord of all. That message spread throughout Judea, beginning in Galilee after the baptism that John announced: how God anointed Jesus of Nazareth with the Holy Spirit and with power; how Jesus went about doing good and healing all who were oppressed by the devil, for God was with him. We are witnesses to all that he did both in Judea and in Jerusalem. They put him to death by hanging him on a tree; but God raised him on the third day and allowed him to appear, not to all the people but to us who were chosen by God as witnesses, and who ate and drank with him after he rose from the dead.

"Jesus commanded us to preach to the people and to testify that he is the one ordained by God as judge of the living and the dead. All the prophets testify about him that everyone who believes in him receives forgiveness of sins through his name."

READING II *Colossians 3:1–4*

So if you have been raised with Christ, seek the things that are above, where Christ is, seated at the right hand of God. Set your minds on things that are above, not on things that are on earth, for you have died, and your life is hidden with Christ in God. When Christ who is your life is revealed, then you also will be revealed with him in glory.

GOSPEL *Luke 24:1–12*

But on the first day of the week, at early dawn, the women came to the tomb, taking the spices that they had prepared. They found the stone rolled away from the tomb, but when they went in, they did not find the body. While they were perplexed about this, suddenly two men in dazzling clothes stood beside them. The women were terrified and bowed their faces to the ground, but the men said to them, "Why do you look for the living among the dead? He is not here, but has risen. Remember how he told you, while he was still in Galilee, that the Son-of-Man must be handed over to sinners, and be crucified, and on the third day rise again."

Then the women remembered his words, and returning from the tomb, they told all this to the eleven and to all the rest. Now it was Mary Magdalene, Joanna, Mary the mother of James, and the other women with them who told this to the apostles. But these words seemed to the apostles an idle tale, and they did not believe them. But Peter got up and ran to the tomb; stooping and looking in, he saw the linen cloths by themselves; then he went home, amazed at what had happened.

REFLECTION

The darkness lifts; the dawn arrives. The events of the passion of Jesus, in which we have immersed ourselves in these recent days, have given way to an awe-inspiring event. Rejoice!

Never in any of the canonical gospels is an attempt made to describe the resurrection of Jesus. Instead, silent witness is provided by the empty tomb, and the appearances of Jesus, who is somehow transformed and not immediately recognizable, provide further evidence for the claim that death has been conquered, victory wrenched from its greedy hand.

All the gospels agree that it was women, approaching the tomb to perform the ritual of anointing the body of the deceased, who were the first recipients of the wondrous news that Jesus was alive. In the Gospel of Luke, these women are clearly presented as having been among the close followers of Jesus; they are reminded of a message he had given regarding his death. The "two men in dazzling clothes" recall the glorified figures at the transfiguration, during which Jesus discussed his journey toward death. But here they are figures who correct the mistaken impression of the women that "the living one" would be found within a tomb.

Unfortunately, women were not trusted as legal witnesses, and the (male) apostles did not believe them; only after confirming their claims for himself did Peter allow himself to be amazed.

We too are asked to be filled with awe, for the narrative itself involves the reader. The women leave the tomb and give their message to the eleven and to "all the rest." We have been witnesses of the events that have occurred. We too are among "the rest." We are given the message that Jesus is alive, and we are asked to believe. But how can it be that something as sure as death, something we know will come to us all, has been overcome? How can it be that God could give the promise of life to those who, like Jesus' followers, run away at the first sign of adversity? We do not understand, and yet we believe. It is our responsibility to question, to seek to understand, and, at the same time, to trust in the goodness of God.

■ **Why do you suppose that the resurrection of Jesus is not described in any of the gospels and that the gospels differ in their discussions of the empty tomb and the appearances of Jesus?**

PRACTICE OF FAITH

AMAZEMENT. We are often amazed by advances in technology. We look with wonder at what a new machine or instrument can do for us. "I did all of this at home on my computer" has become the punctuation on much of our work. In the face of technology, can resurrection dazzle us? Can an encounter with the empty tomb leave us "full of amazement"?

Can we celebrate resurrection by putting away technology, occasionally, in order to be open to the moments of encounter in our lives? The memories of these encounters will live in story, not video. Put away the video camera and watch, with naked eye, amazement in children today. Keep these kinds of memories in story form. Carry this kind of technology-free amazement into the season-long proclamation of "Alleluia" that begins today.

PRACTICE OF HOPE

THE FIG TREE, THREE. "Go to the valley of the snakes in the middle of the desert. There you will find the salve that can heal your father's eyes."

The girl journeyed for many days until she reached the valley of the snakes. It was the most fearsome place she had ever seen. Horrible reptiles hissed and snatched at her from every side. But she walked on to the middle of the valley where a large, gold-patterned snake spoke to her: "I know your errand, little girl. Because you have stepped among my adders without fear, I will give you the salve you desire." And when she returned, she put the ointment on her father's eyes, and he saw. And when the master came to his vineyard, the fig tree was heavy with fruit, and a beautiful emerald serpent lay basking on its branches.

PRACTICE OF CHARITY

WOMEN AT THE TOMB. "Welfare is like a traffic accident. It can happen to anybody, but it especially happens to women." Johnnie Tillman said that in 1972. Women on welfare must sometimes feel like the women at the tomb. They tell their stories and find, in gospel terms, their stories treated as "an idle tale, nonsense." After all, 47 percent of American citizens receive benefits from the government. The benefits for businesses, homeowners and others are called subsidies, compensation, grants, incentives, aid, tax deductions and social security. Two thirds of the recipients of "welfare" are children. Learn more about this by contacting the Children's Defense Fund, 25 E Street NW, Washington, DC 20001; 202-628-8787.

WEEKDAY READINGS (Mo) Acts 2:14, 22 – 32; (Tu) 2:36 – 41; (We) 3:1 – 10; (Th) 3:11 – 26; (Fr) 4:1 – 12; (Sa) 4:13 – 21

READING I *Acts 5:12–16*

Many signs and wonders were done among the people through the apostles. And the believers were all together in Solomon's Portico. None of the rest dared to join them, but the people held them in high esteem. Yet more than ever believers were added to the Lord, great numbers of both men and women, so that they even carried out the sick into the streets, and laid them on cots and mats, in order that Peter's shadow might fall on some of them as he came by. A great number of people would also gather from the towns around Jerusalem, bringing the sick and those tormented by unclean spirits, and they were all cured.

READING II *Revelation 1:4–11, 12–13, 17–19*

John to the seven churches that are in Asia: Grace to you and peace from the one who is and who was and who is to come, and from the seven spirits who are before God's throne, and from Jesus Christ, the faithful witness, the firstborn of the dead, and the ruler of the rulers of the earth. To the one who loves us and freed us from our sins by his blood, and made us to be a dominion, priests serving his God and Father, to Jesus Christ be glory and dominion forever and ever. Amen.

Look! He is coming with the clouds; every eye will see him, even those who pierced him; and on his account all the tribes of the earth will wail. So it is to be. Amen.

"I am the Alpha and the Omega," says the Lord God, who is and who was and who is to come, the Almighty.

I, John, your brother who share with you in Jesus the persecution and the kingdom and the patient endurance, was on the island called Patmos because of the word of God and the testimony of Jesus. I was in the spirit on the Lord's day, and I heard behind me a loud voice like a trumpet saying, "Write in a book what you see and send it to the seven churches." Then I turned to see whose voice it was that spoke to me, and on turning I saw seven golden lampstands, and in the midst of the lampstands I saw one like the Son-of-Man, clothed with a long robe and with a golden sash across his chest. When I saw him, I fell at his feet as though dead. But he placed his right hand on me, saying, "Do not be afraid; I am the first and the last, and the living one. I was dead, and see, I am alive forever and ever; and I have the keys of Death and of Hades. Now write what you have seen, what is, and what is to take place after this."

GOSPEL *John 20:19–31*

When it was evening on that day, the first day of the week, and the doors of the house where the disciples had met were locked for fear of the Judeans, Jesus came and stood among them and said, "Peace be with you." After he said this, he showed them his hands and his side. Then the disciples rejoiced when they saw the Lord. Jesus said to them again, "Peace be with you. As the Father has sent me, so I send you." When he had said this, he breathed on them and said to them, "Receive the Holy Spirit. If you forgive the sins of any, they are forgiven them; if you retain the sins of any, they are retained."

But Thomas (who was called the Twin), one of the twelve, was not with them when Jesus came. So the other disciples told him, "We have seen the Lord." But he said to them, "Unless I see the mark of the nails in his hands, and put my finger in the mark of the nails and my hand in his side, I will not believe."

A week later his disciples were again in the house, and Thomas was with them. Although the doors were shut, Jesus came and stood among them and said, "Peace be with you." Then he said to Thomas, "Put your finger here and see my hands. Reach out your hand and put it in my side. Do not doubt but believe." Thomas said to Jesus, "My Lord and my God!" Jesus said to him, "Have you believed because you have seen me? Blessed are those who have not seen and yet have come to believe."

Now Jesus did many other signs in the presence of his disciples, which are not written in this book. But these are written so that you may come to believe that Jesus is the Messiah, the Son of God, and that through believing you may have life in his name.

REFLECTION

Following the initial joy of Easter come the difficult tasks of assessing the significance of what has happened and being willing to proclaim those wondrous events to others. Today's gospel passage recounts two appearances of Jesus to his followers after his resurrection. Although he is recognizable and his friends respond, with joy to his presence, he is not the same; he is able to enter the room despite its locked doors. Jesus is alive, but he has been transformed.

It is interesting that the disciples are holed up in fear despite the report they had received from Mary that she had seen and talked with the Lord. Although the story of "doubting Thomas" implies that only he had difficulty believing that Jesus was really alive, the narrative actually presents all of the disciples as cowering in fear and doubt. Only with the gift of the Holy Spirit, breathed into them by Jesus, do they have the courage to go forth, sent by Jesus. The Spirit of God, the wind or breath of God, was that which moved over the formless waters in Genesis. It was that which gave life to the first humans in the creation story. That same breath of life inspired the prophets and inspired Jesus in his ministry. Here, Jesus too, exalted with God, breathes the life-giving breath of God into his followers.

Thomas was not present to receive the inspiration (literally "breathing into") from Jesus. His doubting, though, is not that of one who obstinately refuses to acknowledge the truth before him. Instead, Thomas is one who asks for evidence, who does not want to be swayed by mere gossip. He is like so many of us who do not wish to fall for the latest fads or miracle cures but instead test each claim in order to assess its validity. Thomas is an empiricist. Not only is he like us, he stands in the story as one of us. None of us has known Jesus as he walked on earth, nor have any of us heard him preach. The story of Thomas provides an occasion for the evangelist to say that those who did not directly know Jesus can also believe in and proclaim him. Indeed, Thomas's confession is one of the strongest statements of Jesus' divinity in the New Testament: "Blessed are those who have not seen and yet believe."

■ **Do you generally consider yourself one who trusts easily, or are you more of a doubting Thomas? Are you happy with this?**

PRACTICE OF FAITH

ALLELUIA. The brackets are off the Alleluia now. The Liturgy of the Hours for the Lent and Easter seasons are presented together in one volume sharing many psalms, readings and prayers, the difference sometimes being only the bracketed "Alleluia" to be omitted during Lent but proclaimed joyfully during Easter.

Release "Alleluia" into all of your household prayer. Sing it as acclamation and response, and proclaim it as punctuation of every prayer. Now is the time to begin or reclaim singing in household prayer if it has been lost or uncomfortable. There are many easy, sung settings for Alleluia. Give one a try at table.

PRACTICE OF HOPE

THE EYE OF THE HEART. And Jesus said to Thomas, "Put your finger here and see my hands; and place your hand in my side."

And Thomas replied, "I once knew a man who brought light into my life — or so I thought. We shared meals together, and we wandered all across the land speaking to people about love and hope and faith. But they brought him before the judge, they nailed him to the cross, and they pierced his side. He is dead now. His body is rotting in an unknown place. I cannot believe my eyes and hands. I do not know who you are."

Jesus said to him, "Thomas, remember! When first we met, I whispered into your ear these words, inaudible to any other: 'He whom you love is here. Come and follow me.'"

Then Thomas cried, "My Lord and my God!"

PRACTICE OF CHARITY

SIGNS AND WONDERS. They carried the sick out into the streets on cots and mats. They were all cured. AIDS victims must long for such miracles today. In some countries in Africa, nearly half the population is afflicted with the disease. The apostle Peter's shadow won't do today, so AIDS research and education must advance. The great tennis star Arthur Ashe died of the disease. Before his death, he lobbied in Washington, wrote a wonderful autobiography, *Amazing Grace,* and called for understanding for victims. There are as yet no miracle cures, but science has made significant advances. Read Ashe's book. He was writing it within a few weeks of his death. The tenderness and peace to which he witnesses, particularly in his love for his wife and daughter, are admirable. It is grace-filled reading.

WEEKDAY READINGS (Mo) Acts 4:23 – 31; (Tu) 4:32 – 37; (We) 5:17 – 26; (Th) 5:27 – 33; (Fr) 5:34 – 42; (Sa) 1 Peter 5:5 – 14

READING I *Acts 5:27–32, 40–41*

When the temple police had brought the apostles, they had them stand before the council. The high priest questioned them, saying, "We gave you strict orders not to teach in this name, yet here you have filled Jerusalem with your teaching and you are determined to bring this man's blood on us." But Peter and the apostles answered, "We must obey God rather than any human authority. The God of our ancestors raised up Jesus, whom you had killed by hanging him on a tree. God exalted this Jesus to be Leader and Savior at God's right hand, to give repentance to Israel and forgiveness of sins. And we are witnesses to these things, and so is the Holy Spirit who has been given to those who obey God."

Then the council ordered the apostles not to speak in the name of Jesus, and let them go. As they left the council, they rejoiced that they were considered worthy to suffer dishonor for the sake of the name.

READING II *Revelation 5:11–14*

Then I looked, and I heard the voice of many angels surrounding the throne and the living creatures and the elders; they numbered myriads of myriads and thousands of thousands, singing with full voice, "Worthy is the Lamb that was slaughtered to receive power and wealth and wisdom and might and honor and glory and blessing!" Then I heard every creature in heaven and on earth and under the earth and in the sea, and all that is in them, singing, "To the one seated on the throne and to the Lamb be blessing and honor and glory and might forever and ever!" And the four living creatures said, "Amen!" And the elders fell down and worshiped.

GOSPEL *John 21:1–14*

Jesus showed himself again to the disciples by the Sea of Tiberias; and he showed himself in this way. Gathered there together were Simon Peter, Thomas called the Twin, Nathanael of Cana in Galilee, the sons of Zebedee, and two others of his disciples. Simon Peter said to them, "I am going fishing." They said to him, "We will go with you." They went out and got into the boat, but that night they caught nothing.

Just after daybreak, Jesus stood on the beach; but the disciples did not know that it was Jesus. Jesus said to them, "Children, you have no fish, have you?" They answered him, "No." He said to them, "Cast the net to the right side of the boat, and you will find some." So they cast it, and now they were not able to haul it in because there were so many fish. That disciple whom Jesus loved said to Peter, "It is the Lord!" When Simon Peter heard that it was the Lord, he put on some clothes, for he was naked, and jumped into the sea. But the other disciples came in the boat, dragging the net full of fish, for they were not far from the land, only about a hundred yards off.

When they had gone ashore, they saw a charcoal fire there, with fish on it, and bread. Jesus said to them, "Bring some of the fish that you have just caught." So Simon Peter went aboard and hauled the net ashore, full of large fish, a hundred fifty-three of them; and though there were so many, the net was not torn. Jesus said to them, "Come and have breakfast." Now none of the disciples dared to ask him, "Who are you?" because they knew it was the Lord. Jesus came and took the bread and gave it to them, and did the same with the fish. This was now the third time that Jesus appeared to the disciples after he was raised from the dead.

[Complete reading: John 21:1–19]

REFLECTION

Meals figure prominently in the New Testament. During his ministry, Jesus shared meals with his friends and was often chastised for eating with sinners. Meals provided a means for Jesus to display his powers as well as provide sustenance for his hearers.

The Christian community depicted in the Acts of the Apostles and in the letters of Paul gathers to share meals in remembrance of Jesus. Perhaps the most memorable meal is that of the Last Supper, the final gathering of Jesus and his followers prior to his death. So it is fitting that the risen Jesus should share in a meal, an experience of communion with others. Jesus is different now — he is hard to recognize — and yet he is the same, breaking bread with his friends.

Although we are told that this is the third appearance of the risen Jesus to the disciples, it has all the markings of an initial appearance. The disciples do not seem to realize that Jesus is risen; they have returned to their jobs in Galilee. This tale recalls that of a miraculous catch of fish early in Jesus' ministry and may reflect a common tradition. Both stories are "call narratives" in which Jesus commissions Peter to "catch people" or "feed my sheep."

In the verses that follow the meal scene (vv. 15 – 19), Jesus asks Peter if he loves him. The threefold query, which offends Peter by its repetition, recalls and reverses Peter's threefold denial of Jesus prior to the crucifixion. Peter's denial had led to heartfelt remorse and sincere repentance. By asking him if he loves him, Jesus extends to Peter his acceptance and forgiveness. Peter is thus worthy to be given authority and responsibility; the commissioning story surely reflects the role Peter came to take in the nascent Christian community.

Meals, during which we share in communion with others, provide a wonderful opportunity for extending forgiveness. Let us set aside our differences and truly forgive before breaking bread with others, whether in our homes or at the eucharist — that great celebration of our forgiveness in Christ and the Christian meal par excellence.

■ **Read verses 15 – 19 of John 21. How would you have felt had you been Peter?**

■ **Reread the passage from Acts. Would you be able to rejoice if you had to suffer for the name of Jesus?**

PRACTICE OF FAITH

AN EXTRAORDINARY LIFE. Two women I have placed in front of my twelve-year-old daughter as models of seeking and living in truth are Saint Catherine of Siena (April 29) and Jo March. In a cinematic version of Louisa May Alcott's *Little Women*, the willful Jo is challenged by her mother not to expect an ordinary life in possession of her extraordinary gifts.

Catherine of Siena was called out of solitude by God to share her extraordinary gifts with a greater audience. Catherine, like Jo, possessed an intensity in seeking the truth and bringing people to that truth. Both women brought their own truths to the world through writing.

This week, write an overdue letter to someone who needs encouragement or a note from a friend.

PRACTICE OF HOPE

COME AND HAVE BREAKFAST. Recently, I made a dramatic change in my life. Don't worry — I didn't convert to a fundamentalist sect or sign myself up for some weight-loss visualization class. *I pulled the plug on my TV!* I got rid of that unsocial, manipulative, brain-eating, life-draining bug-eye in my living room. Don't give me all that "radical" and "back to the stone age" stuff. Life without the predominant paradigm is terrific! I read the papers to keep in touch with humanity at large. And I'm finally getting back in touch with the kind of humanity that walks about in flesh and blood, the kind you can touch and talk to, go fishing with and share meals with on the beach, the kind that will ask and answer great questions like, "Who are you?"

PRACTICE OF CHARITY

WORK TOGETHER. SPEAK OUT. Saul Alinsky, the controversial pioneer in community organizing, taught organizers always to work with people's strengths. "Speak in terms they can understand." Some years ago he suggested, for example, that Catholic bishops should be addressed not in terms of theology but in terms of fundraising. We can assume the suggestion was made tongue-in-cheek, but Alinsky's dictum is solid. To work together, people must understand each other and share insights, hopes and feelings. They need not always agree, but they can understand. The apostles recognized this when they were ordered to be silent. The Spirit in them impelled them to speak out, to work together. Keep this in mind at the next parents meeting, family reunion or management meeting you attend.

READING I *Acts 13:14, 43–52*

Paul and Barnabas went on from Perga and came to Antioch in Pisidia. And on the sabbath day they went into the synagogue and sat down.

When the meeting of the synagogue broke up, many Jews and devout converts to Judaism followed Paul and Barnabas, who spoke to them and urged them to continue in the grace of God.

The next sabbath almost the whole city gathered to hear the word of the Lord. But when the Jewish officials saw the crowds, they were filled with jealousy; and blaspheming, they contradicted what was spoken by Paul. Then both Paul and Barnabas spoke out boldly, saying, "It was necessary that the word of God should be spoken first to you. Since you reject it and judge yourselves to be unworthy of eternal life, we are now turning to the Gentiles. For so the Lord has commanded us, saying,

'I have set you to be a light for the Gentiles,
so that you may bring salvation to the ends of the earth.'"

When the Gentiles heard this, they were glad and praised the word of the Lord; and as many as had been destined for eternal life became believers. Thus the word of the Lord spread throughout the region. But the officials incited the devout women of high standing and the leading men of the city, and stirred up persecution against Paul and Barnabas, and drove them out of their region. So they shook the dust off their feet in protest against them, and went to Iconium. And the disciples were filled with joy and with the Holy Spirit.

READING II *Revelation 7:9–17*

After this I looked, and there was a great multitude that no one could count, from every nation, from all tribes and peoples and languages, standing before the throne and before the Lamb, robed in white, with palm branches in their hands. They cried out in a loud voice, saying, "Salvation belongs to our God who is seated on the throne, and to the Lamb!"

And all the angels stood around the throne and around the elders and the four living creatures, and they fell on their faces before the throne and worshiped God, singing, "Amen! Blessing and glory and wisdom and thanksgiving and honor and power and might be to our God forever and ever! Amen."

Then one of the elders addressed me, saying, "Who are these, robed in white, and where have they come from?" I said to him, "Sir, you are the one that knows." Then he said to me, "These are they who have come out of the great ordeal; they have washed their robes and made them white in the blood of the Lamb. For this reason they are before the throne of God, and worship God day and night within the temple, and the one who is seated on the throne will shelter them. They will hunger no more, and thirst no more; the sun will not strike them, nor any scorching heat; for the Lamb at the center of the throne will be their shepherd, and will guide them to springs of the water of life, and God will wipe away every tear from their eyes."

GOSPEL *John 10:22–30*

At that time the festival of the Dedication took place in Jerusalem. It was winter, and Jesus was walking in the temple, in the portico of Solomon. So the Judeans gathered around him and said to him, "How long will you keep us in suspense? If you are the Messiah, tell us plainly." Jesus answered, "I have told you, and you do not believe. The works that I do in my Father's name testify to me; but you do not believe, because you do not belong to my sheep. My sheep hear my voice. I know them, and they follow me. I give them eternal life, and they will never perish. No one will snatch them out of my hand. What my Father has given me is greater than all else, and no one can snatch it out of the Father's hand. The Father and I are one."

R E F L E C T I O N

In this Easter season, we have been hearing accounts of the earliest Christians, as told in the Acts of the Apostles, and of the visions of John, recounted in Revelation, which express the hope of Christians for future vindication despite persecution and suffering in the present.

All of today's readings stress inclusion in a community. The passage from Acts claims that the gospel was first declared to and attractive to the Jewish people. Jesus had observed the Jewish rituals and feasts (today's gospel takes place during Hanukkah), had preached to the people of Israel and was followed by Jewish disciples. But, says the author of Acts, many of the intended recipients of Jesus' message refused to allow the inclusion of outsiders—Gentiles—and instead rejected the gospel. Thus Christianity very quickly became primarily a Gentile movement.

The vision of John in today's second reading shows a huge multitude, from every nation, of followers of "the Lamb." The gospel is available to all; it offers forgiveness and renewed purity. But it also entails "great tribulation." Those who are faithful despite opposition — and the vision is of those who have died for their beliefs — are included in the heavenly assembly; they are followers of the Lamb, who is their shepherd.

The Gospel of John often depicts Jesus as the Lamb of God; indeed Jesus is presented as a sacrificial lamb of the Passover celebration. In this gospel only, Jesus is crucified just as the paschal lambs were being slaughtered. Just as the lambs recall the life-giving blood sprinkled on the doorposts to save the lives of the Hebrews before their exodus from Egypt, so also Jesus' blood is shed in order to give life. But in today's gospel, Jesus is the shepherd, the one who calls his flock together, guides them and gives them life. The image of sheep and shepherd is used to emphasize the care Jesus offers his followers and the importance of their remaining united in community. Jesus is able to offer unity and life because of his oneness with God.

■ **How important is your faith community to you? How do you demonstrate your inclusion in it? How do you as a community welcome others to join your flock?**

PRACTICE OF FAITH

COME AND SEE. Philip and James, apostles (May 3), are remembered as followers. Philip's invitation to Nathanael to "come and see" Jesus portrays the openness of his own response. Jesus, through Philip, is the invitation to life. We are invited to look in our own lives for our response to invitation. We are given the opportunity to consider our own willingness to trust and believe. We are also challenged in this story to share the good things we find. We can examine our tendency to keep a good thing for ourselves for fear of losing it by sharing it. The joy of finding Jesus begs to be passed on in openness and trust.

Invite someone to "come and see" the life of Jesus in your small faith community, your family, your friendships or your prayer group.

PRACTICE OF HOPE

RECOGNITION. From all eternity have I known you, my beloved. We have roamed together on countless journeys among the stars and planets, across the deep seas and mountain ranges. We have done and undone so many deeds, so many dreams. We have hunted the saber-toothed tiger, we have cared for the fire of the tribe, we have built a pyramid for Pharaoh, we have conquered the city of Troy. And just as often have we parted, in peace or in pain, with love, with hatred or with indifference. We have waged war on each other; we have fled from each other into the desert. Perhaps we even have killed each other. When we meet again, we've changed beyond recognition. And yet I hear your voice in a million. And yet you cannot resist my call. And our journey begins anew.

PRACTICE OF CHARITY

WIPE TEARS FROM THEIR EYES. Mother Teresa's followers pick up dying men and women from the streets, move them to hospices and minister to them so that they may at least die with dignity. This astonishing work continues the miracle of the gospels. Jesus and the Spirit cured the sick, and now followers of that same Jesus, filled with that same Spirit, give witness to the sacred character of each human person. I met Mother Teresa once several years ago and was startled by how small and frail she appeared. But she was not small in spirit. She was a towering, loving giant. Her work with the poor continues throughout the world. Her healing mission can be supported by contributing financially or volunteering. Contact: Gift of Love, 1596 Fulton Street, San Francisco CA 94117; 415-563-9446.

WEEKDAY READINGS (Mo) Acts 11:1 – 18; (Tu) 11:19 – 26; (We) 12:24 — 13:5; (Th) 13:13 – 25; (Fr) 13:26 – 33; (Sa) 13:44 – 52

READING I *Acts 14:21–27*

Paul and Barnabas returned to Lystra, then on to Iconium and Antioch. There they strengthened the souls of the disciples and encouraged them to continue in the faith, saying, "It is through many persecutions that we must enter the kingdom of God." And after they had appointed elders for them in each church, with prayer and fasting they entrusted them to the Lord in whom they had come to believe.

Then they passed through Pisidia and came to Pamphylia. When they had spoken the word in Perga, they went down to Attalia. From there they sailed back to Antioch, where they had been commended to the grace of God for the work that they had completed. When they arrived, they called the church together and related all that God had done with them, and how he had opened a door of faith for the Gentiles.

READING II *Revelation 21:1–6*

I saw a new heaven and a new earth; for the first heaven and the first earth had passed away, and the sea was no more. And I saw the holy city, the new Jerusalem, coming down out of heaven from God, prepared as a bride adorned for her husband. And I heard a loud voice from the throne saying, "See, the home of God is among mortals. God will dwell with them as their God; they will be God's people, and that very God will be with them, and will wipe every tear from their eyes. Death will be no more; mourning and crying and pain will be no more, for the first things have passed away."

And the one who was seated on the throne said, "See, I am making all things new," and also said, "Write this, for these words are trustworthy and true." Then the one seated on the throne said to me, "It is done! I am the Alpha and the Omega, the beginning and the end. To the thirsty I will give water as a gift from the spring of the water of life."

GOSPEL *John 13:31–35*

When Judas had gone out, Jesus said, "Now the Son-of-Man has been glorified, and God has been glorified in him. If God has been glorified in him, God will also glorify him in God's own self and will glorify him at once. Little children, I am with you only a little longer. You will look for me; and as I said to the Judeans so now I say to you, 'Where I am going, you cannot come.' I give you a new commandment, that you love one another. Just as I have loved you, you also should love one another. By this everyone will know that you are my disciples, if you have love for one another."

Thursday, May 21, 1998

THE ASCENSION OF THE LORD

Acts 1:1–11 *Why stand staring at the skies?*

Ephesians 1:17–23 *The fullness of Christ has filled the universe.*

Luke 24:46–53 *You are witnesses of all this.*

On this fortieth day of Easter, we are told to stop gazing at the clouds and to start spreading the good news. The resurrection of Christ didn't end with the Lord Jesus. All creation is ascending into glory. All the universe is becoming divine.

Note: In the dioceses of Alaska, California, Hawaii, Idaho, Montana, Nevada, Oregon, Utah and Washington, the Ascension of the Lord is transferred to Sunday, May 24.

REFLECTION

The vision that comes to John in Revelation includes the sight of a new Jerusalem adorned in splendor. It is even more glorious than the earthly Jerusalem, on which the rabbis claimed were bestowed nine of the ten measures of beauty given to the world. The new Jerusalem here is a metaphor for the people of God, for it is with human beings, not in a distant heaven, that God dwells. That "they shall be God's people" recalls the covenant written on the heart in Jeremiah; all things are new, yet we have heard this before. The new Jerusalem is a transformation of the old, a return to the promises of old, renewed and expanded in light of the passion, death and resurrection of Jesus. There is a return to a primordial Paradise in which crying, mourning and pain are no more. What was intended from the beginning for God's holy people is fulfilled in Christ.

Today's gospel reading, taken from the long discourses that characterize Jesus' final meal in this gospel, speaks also of something new, a new commandment. Jesus commands his listeners to love one another. But this is *not* a new commandment. The law of Moses included, as integral to its fulfillment, the command to love: "Love your neighbor as yourself. I am the Lord" (Leviticus 19:18). Part of the Jewish tradition was the notion that the less fortunate were to be taken care of, not as charity cases, not grudgingly or out of pity, but as a responsibility by those blessed with plenty. Loving one's neighbor is one of the things the chosen people do in order to be holy, even as God is holy. What can this mean then, this "new" command to love?

Perhaps the revelation to John can put us on a path to understanding Jesus' words. Just as the new Jerusalem represents a return to a paradisaical state, so also the command to love is a restoration of the earlier commandment. But there is more. Jesus specifies how the commandment is to be lived: "even as I have loved you." The commandment to love one another involves loving as Jesus has, that is, loving even to death.

■ **Read Jeremiah 31:31 – 34. How is this similar to, and how is it different from, the message of Jesus in the gospel reading?**

■ **For whom or for what would you be willing to give your life?**

PRACTICE OF FAITH

ANCHORITE. Spiritual direction and counseling as a fixed role in parish life was common in the time and place of Julian of Norwich (May 13). From her place of solitude in Norwich, England, Julian prayed, read and offered guidance. One can easily envy the locals to whom Julian of Norwich was just the parish anchorite. She was placed in their midst to give spiritual guidance. In the anchorite, a person and place were dedicated to prayer and spiritual growth.

Find a place and a person to whom you can go for prayer and spiritual guidance. Naming the person and the conversation can give it proper direction. Identify an anchorite in your life. Don't overlook the potential anchorites as close as the house next door to you, the room down the hall or the next pew over.

PRACTICE OF HOPE

A PLACE OF LOVE. I once went to a place where people had love for one another. It was a most unusual experience, and it made me cry as soon as I entered it. For you see, I had not been used to so much love. A crust of ice had trapped my soul for many years. Now the unaccustomed warmth began to melt the ice around my heart, and I started hurting like you hurt when you thaw a frozen limb. It was torture, but I began to feel alive in the pain. I returned to the place again and again, until every inch of the frozen crust around my heart had melted away. When finally I moved away from this place, I didn't have to say good-bye. I took the place with me. It had entered my heart.

PRACTICE OF CHARITY

NEW HEAVEN AND NEW EARTH. In the last century, the British Parliament debated publicly and then decided explicitly to supply opium to China as a balance of trade measure for tea, silk and porcelain, all things the empire coveted. The readings today suggest quite different standards for Christian nations: wipe away every tear, pray and fast, a new heaven and a new earth. Last century's leaders in England were elected. So are our local and national leaders. Officials we elect carry their values into office. Take the time this week to learn the name of your city council representative and your state representative, and find out how to contact them. Call each of them and discuss an issue, or ask them what they consider to be of current importance. These people represent you. China did not need opium. We all need a new earth.

WEEKDAY READINGS (Mo) Acts 14:5 – 18; (Tu) 14:19 – 28; (We) 15:1 – 6; (Th) 1:15 – 26; (Fr) 15:22 – 31; (Sa) 16:1 – 10

READING I *Acts 15:22–29*

The apostles and the elders, with the consent of the whole church, decided to choose men from among their members and to send them to Antioch with Paul and Barnabas. They sent Judas called Barsabbas, and Silas, leaders within the community, with the following letter: "The apostles and the elders, to the believers of Gentile origin in Antioch and Syria and Cilicia, greetings. Since we have heard that certain persons who have gone out from us, though with no instructions from us, have said things to disturb you and have unsettled your minds, we have decided unanimously to choose representatives and send them to you, along with our beloved Barnabas and Paul, who have risked their lives for the sake of our Lord Jesus Christ.

"We have therefore sent Judas and Silas, who themselves will tell you the same things by word of mouth. For it has seemed good to the Holy Spirit and to us to impose on you no further burden than these essentials: that you abstain from what has been sacrificed to idols, and from blood and from what is strangled and from fornication. If you keep yourselves from these, you will do well. Farewell."
[Complete reading: Acts 15:1–2, 22–29]

READING II *Revelation 21:10, 22 — 22:5*

And in the spirit the angel carried me away to a great, high mountain and showed me the holy city Jerusalem coming down out of heaven from God. I saw no temple in the city, for its temple is the Lord God the Almighty and the Lamb. And the city has no need of sun or moon to shine on it, for the glory of God is its light, and its lamp is the Lamb. The nations will walk by its light, and the rulers of the earth will bring their glory into it. Its gates will never be shut by day — and there will be no night there. People will bring into it the glory and the honor of the nations. But nothing unclean will enter it, nor anyone who practices abomination or falsehood, but only those who are written in the Lamb's book of life.

Then the angel showed me the river of the water of life, bright as crystal, flowing from the throne of God and of the Lamb through the middle of the street of the city. On either side of the river is the tree of life with its twelve kinds of fruit, producing its fruit each month; and the leaves of the tree are for the healing of the nations. Nothing accursed will be found there any more. But the throne of God and of the Lamb will be in it, and the servants of God will do homage; they will see God's face, and on their foreheads shall be God's name. And there will be no more night; they need no light of lamp or sun, for the Lord God will be their light, and they will reign forever and ever.
[Complete reading: Revelation 21:10–14, 22 — 22:5]

GOSPEL *John 14:23–29*

Jesus said, "Those who love me will keep my word, and my Father will love them, and we will come to them and make our home with them. Whoever does not love me does not keep my words; and the word that you hear is not mine, but is from the Father who sent me.

"I have said these things to you while I am still with you. But the Advocate, the Holy Spirit, whom the Father will send in my name, will teach you everything, and remind you of all that I have said to you. Peace I leave with you; my peace I give to you. I do not give to you as the world gives. Do not let your hearts be troubled, and do not let them be afraid. You heard me say to you, 'I am going away, and I am coming to you.' If you loved me, you would rejoice that I am going to the Father, because the Father is greater than I. And now I have told you this before it occurs, so that when it does occur, you may believe."

REFLECTION

The Spirit is a spirit of power who carries the visionary John to the top of a high mountain, a spirit who directs the earliest Christians on how to respond to the question of including Gentiles among the followers of Jesus (and the resultant question regarding the necessity of those Gentiles to keep the law of Moses), a spirit whom Jesus promises to send to his beloved friends. The gospel does not speak of a new experience or of a new revelation the disciples of Jesus will have upon receiving the Spirit; rather, the Spirit helps the disciples to remember what they already know. The Spirit educates, literally "draws out" from them what God already has placed there.

Faith, we know, is a gift; it is not something that can be earned. It can, however, be rejected. It is the activity of the Spirit, the gentle blowing of this divine counselor, who recalls that gift of faith, activates it and brings it to life. The Spirit blows away the cobwebs of the mind and heart to allow one to heed the words of Jesus, to prepare a place for Jesus and the Father to dwell.

Finally, Jesus gives a gift and a command: Peace. It is not the peace known to the world; it is not simply the cessation of war or a time of prosperity. It is instead something that lives within each individual; it is heartfelt. It is this peace that should allow Jesus' listeners (who include the hearers of the gospel) to love him, to let him go. His disciples must allow him to go forth to his death, to be with his Father. We, who have no direct contact with the one whom we revere, are yet asked to believe. We let go of our desires for control, for certainty, so that the Spirit can be present, filling hearts with peace and joy, while we know that Jesus is in his rightful place, one with God.

■ **What is your experience of the Spirit? How do you think of the Spirit and know that the Spirit is active?**

■ **Mystics sometimes speak of having "desert" experiences during which God seems absent. Have you ever known this desert? Are you able, in the midst of such an experience, to recall the teachings of Jesus, to know peace in your heart? What sustains you at such times?**

PRACTICE OF FAITH

PREACHING. The proclamation of the risen Lord during this and the very first Easter season sums up the point of preaching: Simply put, it is the proclamation of the resurrection of our Lord through the lived experience in time and history of the preacher.

Saint Bernadine of Siena (May 20) was a traveling preacher. He preached and proclaimed the risen Lord through his life. He traveled on foot to bring the spoken Word to many people.

Take time on Sundays to bring the spoken word to one another in your household. Turn off the electronic word for a time and gather at table to allow each person the chance to respond to the question, "What did you hear today?" Even a few words from each person will form a verbal collage of each particular Sunday.

PRACTICE OF HOPE

GIFTS. Not as the world gives do I give unto you. Not as the king gives, who seeks your submission by displaying his power to build and destroy you. Not as the prince gives, who presses you into service through gifts you cannot return. Not as the general gives, who ponders the strength of your armor before choosing a gift to appease or allure you. Not as the merchant gives, who inquires of your coffers and calibrates his gift to the size of his profit. No, not as these give do I give unto you, but as the mother gives, whose love flows freely through the milk of her breast, whose body shields her children from the falling rock and whose blood will feed them when famine is in the land.

PRACTICE OF CHARITY

COMFORT THE AFFLICTED. Jazz music has it roots in the soul music of the slave fields of the South. Louie Armstrong, John Coltrane and Dizzy Gillespie played music of anguish as well as music of joy. Today's scripture readings tell of dissension and disturbed, unsettled minds — and of peace and no distress. The message of Jesus both comforts the afflicted and afflicts the comfortable. Slaves suffered terribly, as all oppressed people do. But sometimes people who suffer also find a deeper joy, a peace, when the spirit makes a home in them. Refugees fleeing danger are the "slaves" in today's world. Little music can be made by them. Amnesty International fosters contact and intervention on their behalf. You can participate by contacting Amnesty International, USA, 322 Eighth Avenue, New York NY 10001; 212-807-8400.

WEEKDAY READINGS (Mo) Acts 16:11 – 15; (Tu) 16:22 – 34; (We) 17:15 — 18:1; (Th) Ascension, see page 90; (Fr) Acts 18:9 – 18; (Sa) 18:23 – 28

MAY 24, 1998 Seventh Sunday of Easter

READING I *Acts 7:55–60*

Standing before the high priest and the council, Stephen, filled with the Holy Spirit, gazed into heaven and saw the glory of God and Jesus standing at the right hand of God. "Look," he said, "I see the heavens opened and the Son of Man standing at the right hand of God!" But they covered their ears, and with a loud shout all rushed together against him. Then they dragged him out of the city and began to stone him; and the witnesses laid their coats at the feet of a young man named Saul. While they were stoning Stephen, he prayed, "Lord Jesus, receive my spirit." Then he knelt down and cried out in a loud voice, "Lord, do not hold this sin against them." When he had said this, he died.

READING II *Revelation 22:12–14, 16–17, 20–21*

"See, I am coming soon; my reward is with me, to repay according to everyone's work. I am the Alpha and the Omega, the first and the last, the beginning and the end."

Blessed are those who wash their robes, so that they will have the right to the tree of life and may enter the city by the gates. "It is I, Jesus, who sent my angel to you with this testimony for the churches. I am the root and the descendant of David, the bright morning star." The Spirit and the bride say, "Come." And let everyone who hears say, "Come." And let everyone who is thirsty come. Let anyone who wishes take the water of life as a gift.

The one who testifies to these things says, "Surely I am coming soon." Amen. Come, Lord Jesus! The grace of the Lord Jesus be with all the saints. Amen.

GOSPEL *John 17:20–26*

Jesus prayed: "I ask not only on behalf of these, but also on behalf of those who will believe in me through their word, that they may all be one. As you, Father, are in me and I am in you, may they also be in us, so that the world may believe that you have sent me. The glory that you have given me I have given them, so that they may be one, as we are one, I in them and you in me, that they may become completely one, so that the world may know that you have sent me and have loved them even as you have loved me. Father, I desire that those also, whom you have given me, may be with me where I am, to see my glory, which you have given me because you loved me before the foundation of the world.

"Righteous Father, the world does not know you, but I know you; and these know that you have sent me. I made your name known to them, and I will make it known, so that the love with which you have loved me may be in them, and I in them."

REFLECTION

Jesus' poignant prayer for unity demands that we examine our own families, communities and friendship groups. Jesus' prayer is for future believers, those outside the intimate community he has created. In his prayer, Jesus proclaims that the unity of all those who believe in him reflects the unity of the Godhead, the oneness of him with his Father. He shares with his followers the glory God has bestowed on him so that their unity may be complete. Such unity shows the love believers have for one another and is a demonstration to the world of the truth of the gospel. And the proclamation of the gospel is precisely that the way to know God most fully is to know Jesus, who, through his death on the cross, is revealed to all as supreme Love.

Throughout this gospel, Jesus is the revealer, and it is by being "lifted up" on the cross that he reveals his message. Paradoxically, Jesus is "lifted up" in glory in this gospel precisely by being raised to his death on the cross. What he reveals is the same thing he has been asking of his followers—love. Today's gospel makes it clear that this love is not simply the reflection of one's inner feelings but displays itself in action. The high christology of this gospel—the claim that Jesus is one with God, that he is divine—is expressed principally through action, through living the command to love.

■ **Examine each of the communities, whether large or small, to which you belong. Is there real unity in these communities, or is there sometimes bickering and divisiveness? Is there a diversity of people, which makes oneness both more challenging and more rewarding? How is conflict handled? Would others look at your community and say that they see the love of God revealed?**

■ **If God is complex, is love, what does that say about love in our lives? Can a community as a whole express love, or is that possible only for an individual? What do you do if a few people seem to want to separate themselves from others in the community?**

■ **Read 1 Corinthians 12. How can Paul's words help to clarify, in concrete terms, the demands of today's gospel reading?**

PRACTICE OF FAITH

NOVICE. The person who is new to something and just learning and beginning is the novice. During these Easter weeks, we are hearing of and from many novices in the life of the resurrection. They are beginning and learning in the novitiate of witnessing, baptizing, preaching, worshiping and communing.

On May 25 we celebrate Saint Mary Magdalene de Pazzi, a mistress of novices and teacher of young nuns in her convent. This is a day to remember first teachers and our "novice masters or mistresses" with a letter or note, if possible. There are also the first grade teachers, the preschool teachers and the junior high principals who guide our children with great care in many beginnings and firsts. Take time to thank them.

PRACTICE OF HOPE

CROSSING OVER. I look at you across a deep canyon with no bridge between our two mountainsides. How can I reach you? I stretch out my arm, but it is too short—much too short. How can I reach you? I call across the abyss in the hope that one day the echo will carry back a new melody. One different note would tell me you're answering my call. I could respond by changing more notes, and a rhythm here and there, and before long there would be a beautiful conversation between us. Our wordless tunes would waft back and forth, weaving ropes in the air, making knots, stretching out across the chasm. At last, a bridge of song might appear swinging in the air between us, and the most daring of us could make a dash to cross over.

PRACTICE OF CHARITY

ALL MAY BE ONE. Thomas Merton, a Catholic monk and best-selling author, suggested that Buddhist, Hindu and Christian monks would probably meet in faith if each lived true to the depths of their own tradition. Perhaps this is implied when Jesus says he is the beginning and the end, the first and the last. So often in our world today, conflicts, rather than solutions, are the result of religious differences. Factions are often identified by religion: Protestant and Catholic in Ireland, Jew and "Arab" in the Middle East, Muslim and Christian in Bosnia. Paul was a party to religious, factional hatred and persecution. Stephen was stoned at his feet. Christ prays that the world may know God. Find out today about the Muslim faith. Read some of the Koran.

WEEKDAY READINGS (Mo) Acts 19:1 – 8; (Tu) 20:17 – 27; (We) 20:28 – 38; (Th) 22:30; 23:6 – 11; (Fr) 25:13 – 21; (Sa) 28: 16 – 20, 30 – 31

READING I *Acts 2:1–11*

When the day of Pentecost had come, they were all together in one place. And suddenly from heaven there came a sound like the rush of a violent wind, and it filled the entire house where they were sitting. Divided tongues, as of fire, appeared among them, and a tongue rested on each of them. All of them were filled with the Holy Spirit and began to speak in other languages, as the Spirit gave them ability.

Now there were devout Jews from every nation under heaven living in Jerusalem. And at this sound the crowd gathered and was bewildered, because each one heard them speaking in the native language of each. Amazed and astonished, they asked, "Are not all these who are speaking Galileans? And how is it that we hear, each of us, in our own native language? Parthians, Medes, Elamites, and residents of Mesopotamia, Judea and Cappadocia, Pontus and Asia, Phrygia and Pamphylia, Egypt and the parts of Libya belonging to Cyrene, and visitors from Rome, both Jewish-born and proselytes, Cretans and Arabs — in our own languages we hear them speaking about God's deeds of power."

READING II *1 Corinthians 12:3–7, 12–13*

No one can say "Jesus is Lord" except by the Holy Spirit.

Now there are varieties of gifts, but the same Spirit; and there are varieties of services, but the same Lord; and there are varieties of activities, but it is the same God who activates all of them in everyone. To each is given the manifestation of the Spirit for the common good.

For just as the body is one and has many members, and all the members of the body, though many, are one body, so it is with Christ. For in the one Spirit we were all baptized into one body — Jews or Greeks, slaves or free — and we were all made to drink of one Spirit.

GOSPEL *John 20:19–23*

When it was evening on that day, the first day of the week, and the doors of the house where the disciples had met were locked for fear of the Judeans, Jesus came and stood among them and said, "Peace be with you." After he said this, he showed them his hands and his side. Then the disciples rejoiced when they saw the Lord. Jesus said to them again, "Peace be with you. As the Father has sent me, so I send you." When he had said this, he breathed on them and said to them, "Receive the Holy Spirit. If you forgive the sins of any, they are forgiven them; if you retain the sins of any, they are retained."

**Saturday night through Sunday dawn,
May 30 – 31**

PENTECOST VIGIL

Genesis 11:1–19 *At Babel the Lord confused their speech.*

or

Exodus 19:3–8,16–20 *Fire and wind descended on Sinai.*

or

Ezekiel 37:1–14 *O spirit, breathe on the dead!*

or

Joel 3:1–5 *On the Day of the Lord I will impart my own spirit.*

Romans 8:22–27 *We have the Spirit as first fruits.*

John 7:37–39 *Let the thirsty come to drink of living waters.*

We end Eastertime the way we began it, with a nighttime vigil, poring over the scriptures. We keep watch on Mount Sinai, where we meet God face to face and receive the life-giving Spirit. Our paschal journey, begun so long ago in ashes, is finished in fire.

R E F L E C T I O N

There are several accounts of Jesus' promise to his disciples that he would send to them a helper, a comforter, a spirit of God who would remain with them during his absence. In this short gospel passage, which comes just after the exchange between Jesus and Mary Magdalene outside the tomb, Jesus himself mentions both the Father and the Holy Spirit. Although a formalized trinitarian speculation took several centuries to develop, the high Johannine christology so intimately united the Father and the Son that they can be said to be one. Because of this christology, the early Christian community very quickly came to realize that Jesus was exalted with God and was even, as is clear from the fourth gospel, divine, having been with God from eternity.

Again Jesus tells his disciples to keep his commandments; this is a demonstration of their love for him. But to assist them, he will send the Spirit of Truth, who will dwell within them and give them peace. The Acts of the Apostles recounts, in creative language, the bestowal of the Spirit. The tongues of fire and the rushing wind grab the attention of both the characters and the audience. But the most spectacular event was the ability of the followers of Jesus to speak to people from many nations and be understood. Here we encounter a reversal of the story of Babel, in which the diversity of languages was described as a way of dividing people so that they would not get too powerful. In the Pentecost story, diverse languages serve to draw people together, to create greater understanding. It is an experience of the power of God active in human life.

It is this Spirit which enables the Christians to call out, "Abba!" Through the activity of the Spirit is one able to use this intimate, familial address for God. And so it is by the Spirit that Christians are adopted as children of God, heirs to the promises of God.

■ **Paul's claim in Romans that Christians are adopted children of God closes with a sobering note. Being children of God, heirs with Christ, involves suffering, just as Christ suffered. Glorification follows pain. The joyous events of Pentecost are not isolated from the passion. How do you understand the idea of being glorified with Christ? And how does suffering fit into that?**

PRACTICE OF FAITH

IDENTITY. Unity in identity and identity in unity. We celebrate now as at the first Pentecost the new life in the church in the form of the new members who wish to identify and unify with us.

Saint Justin (June 1) and Saint Boniface (June 5) show us some of the specific issues in celebrating our unity in identity. Both these saints were concerned with preserving the truths of Christian worship. We can approach Trinity Sunday next week fortified by the example of Justin and Boniface regarding the importance of passing on practices and rituals that are responsible to the truth.

As households we can treasure the rituals that allow us to deepen our unity and identity. Keep family prayer "things" together in a book or place of prayer. Hand on the forms of family prayer in record and in practice.

PRACTICE OF HOPE

FEAR TO BREATHE. I live behind locked doors with all my fears for company. They are sitting around my table, twelve of them, their hollow eyes flickering underneath dark hoods. There are the fear of life and the fear of death across the table. There is the fear of self, facing the fear of the other. There is the fear of change and, opposite, the fear of boredom. The fear of yesterday glances anxiously at the fear of tomorrow. The fear of hurting is staring gloomily at the fear of being hurt. And the fear of loving makes grimaces at the fear of being loved. The chair across from me is empty. O Lord, enter my house through the locked door, and breathe on me and my tablemates. Then, perhaps, I'll be able to change them into disciples, one by one.

PRACTICE OF CHARITY

SEE GOD. Jason, a cocaine addict, said, "I had to show up for my recovery to happen. The real me had to be there. Otherwise I'd go through life handcuffed to a stranger—that's what happens. The stranger is the real you." All of us struggle to be authentic. Christ says, "Whoever sees me, sees God." Can that be true of Jason, of me? When the Pentecost spirit enables us to be fully ourselves, it is true. Seeing and hearing Jason makes God's love visible, audible, more authentic. Members of Alcoholics and Narcotics Anonymous understand the necessity of God's help. Memorial Day is a time for us to remember that the spirit of God resides in everyone and brings authenticity to soldier, addict, coworker, enemy, friend. Visit a grave this week to remember God's spirit.

WEEKDAY READINGS (Mo) 2 Peter 1:2 – 7; (Tu) 3:12 – 18; (We) 2 Timothy 1:1 – 12; (Th) 2:8 – 15; (Fr) 3:10 – 17; (Sa) 4:1 – 8

SUMMER ORDINARY TIME

You crown the year with riches.
All you touch is fertile.

Praise is yours, God in Zion.
Now is the moment
to keep our vow.

You soak the furrows
and level the ridges.
With softening rain
you bless the land with growth.

You crown the year with riches.
All you touch comes alive:
untilled lands yield crops,
hills are dressed in joy,

flocks clothe the pastures,
valleys wrap themselves in grain.
They all shout for joy
and break into song.

—Psalm 65: 2, 11 – 14

God who called each day's creation good,
all we have for our food
and shelter and clothing
are the crust and air, the light and water
   of this planet.
Give us care like yours for this earth:
to share its bounty
with generations to come
and with all alike in this generation,
to savor its beauty and respect its power,
to heal what greed and war and foolishness
have done to your earth and to us.
Bring us finally to give thanks,
always and everywhere.

— Prayer of the Season

JUNE 7, 1998
Trinity Sunday
First Sunday after Pentecost

READING I *Proverbs 8:1–4, 22–31*

Does not Wisdom call,
  and does not Understanding raise her voice?
On the heights, beside the way,
  at the crossroads she takes her stand;
beside the gates in front of the town,
  at the entrance of the portals she cries out:
"To you, O people, I call,
  and my cry is to all that live.

"The LORD created me at the beginning of creation,
  the first of the LORD's acts of long ago.
Ages ago I was set up,
  at the first, before the beginning of the earth.
When there were no depths I was brought forth,
  when there were no springs abounding
    with water.
Before the mountains had been shaped,
  before the hills, I was brought forth —
when the LORD had not yet made earth and fields,
  or the world's first bits of soil.
I was there when the LORD established the heavens,
  and drew a circle on the face of the deep,
and made firm the skies above,
  and established the fountains of the deep,
and assigned to the sea its limit,
  so that the waters might not transgress the
    LORD's command,
when the foundations of the earth were marked out,
  then I was beside the LORD, like a master worker;
and I was daily the LORD's delight,
  rejoicing before the LORD always,
rejoicing in the LORD's inhabited world
  and delighting in the human race."

READING II *Romans 5:1–5*

Therefore, since we are justified by faith, we have peace with God through our Lord Jesus Christ, through whom we have obtained access to this grace in which we stand; and we boast in our hope of sharing the glory of God. And not only that, but we also boast in our sufferings, knowing that suffering produces endurance, and endurance produces character, and character produces hope, and hope does not disappoint us, because God's love has been poured into our hearts through the Holy Spirit that has been given to us.

GOSPEL *John 16:12–15*

"I still have many things to say to you, but you cannot bear them now. When the Spirit of truth comes, you will be guided into all the truth; for the Spirit will not speak out of the Spirit's own authority, but will speak whatever the Spirit hears, and will declare to you the things that are to come. The Spirit will glorify me, taking what is mine and declaring it to you. All that the Father has is mine. For this reason I said that the Spirit will take what is mine and declare it to you."

REFLECTION

Christian trinitarian speculation arose from the complexity of beliefs that characterized the faith of the Jews at the turn of the era. The concept of Jesus as one with God, as divine, is based in part on the understanding of Wisdom in the Hebrew tradition. Even in early Wisdom literature, such as Proverbs, Wisdom is personified and given an exalted role. (See, for example, Proverbs 1:20–33.) Through her was created the world with all its diversity. Wisdom is not simply something that the wise have obtained; she is active with God, cocreator with God.

In the New Testament, Jesus takes this role of God's activity in the world. He is, according to the prologue to the Gospel of John, the very communication of God to the world. He is God's reason, God's inner workings, and the expression of that reason in understandable form. The Greek *logos* (reason, word) conveys the richness of this line of thinking. (See John 1:1–18.)

Today's gospel seems to indicate that humans cannot comprehend the greatness of that communication of God all at once. Although the fourth gospel indicates that Jesus is the bearer of all truth, is in fact the essence of Truth, his listeners cannot comprehend that truth in its fullness. And so Jesus promises the Spirit of Truth, who will continue the revelation of his message. And what Jesus has to give is that which the Father gives; for all that belongs to the Father is his.

Here, in embryonic form, is the idea of a trinity of persons who share in the same truth, who reveal different aspects of the Godhead. How there can be a relationship of Father, Son, and Spirit while maintaining monotheism is a complex question that took Christians many years to resolve, and the question must be reexamined in every age and place. But the threefold formula was present from the beginning. It was used in prayer and at liturgy, and especially at baptism. And as Christians pray, so also we believe.

■ **Look up "trinity" in a religious encyclopedia or resolve to learn more about the trinitarian debates of the fourth century. The material is not easy to understand; persevere in your attempts to learn more about your faith.**

■ **What is truth, and how can it be affirmed? What criteria do you use in determining what is truthful and what is false?**

PRACTICE OF FAITH

GLORY TO THE FATHER. The celebration of Trinity Sunday begins with Evening Prayer I and Psalm 113, which begins with the following verses:

Praise, O servants of the Lord;
  praise the name of the Lord,
Blessed be the name of the Lord
  from this time on and forevermore.
From the rising of the sun to its setting
  the name of the Lord is to be praised.

Many of us dismiss these persistent calls to prayer and witness as meant for others whose lifestyles are more suited to it than our own. We overlook the simple, ample prayer of praise to the Trinity and the name of the Lord in "Glory to the Father and to the Son and to the Holy Spirit, as it was in the beginning, is now and will be forever. Amen." It can be prayed alone or with psalms and canticles.

PRACTICE OF HOPE

THE THREEFOLD VESSEL. O Spirit divine, teach me according to my strength. For even now, I cannot bear much. My head is filled with vapors and numbed by a swelling of numbers and words. My heart is lost in a sea of passions, and my courage is inconstant like the clouds. The grip of my hand is weak, and my fingers tremble at the touch of a flower. How can I bear the flame of your wisdom in my scattered mind? How can I keep the spark of your love in the embers of my soul? How can I carry the blaze of your will through the sloughs of my inaction? O Spirit divine, threefold power of God, form your vessel so that whatever wells up in it from the fiery ocean of your being may be gathered and not spilled.

PRACTICE OF CHARITY

SPIRIT OF TRUTH. The President of the United States delivered a major address on low-income housing at a luncheon meeting in a resort hotel. The waiter and bus boy who served him had ridden two hours by bus over mountain passes to get to work that day because they could not afford to live nearby. The Archdiocese of Denver took note of this and marshaled resources to develop more than 150 units of safe, affordable housing. Jesus' call to bring the Spirit of God to life is answered. The current need for low-income housing in our country is 4.7 million units. Find out what the people of Denver did. Contact the Archdiocesan Housing Committee, 1580 Logan St., Suite 700, Denver CO 80203; 303-830-0215.

WEEKDAY READINGS (Mo) 1 Kings 17:1–6; (Tu) 17:7–16; (We) 18:20–39; (Th) Acts 11:21–26, 13:1–3; (Fr) 1 Kings 19:9a–16; (Sa) 19:19–21

READING I *Genesis 14:18–20*

When Abram heard that his nephew, Lot, had been taken captive, he led forth his trained men, and routed the abductors. After Abram's return King Melchizedek of Salem brought out bread and wine; he was priest of God Most High. He blessed Abram and said,

> "Blessed be Abram by God Most High,
> maker of heaven and earth;
> and blessed be God Most High,
> who has delivered your enemies
> into your hand!"

And Abram gave him one tenth of everything.

READING II *1 Corinthians 11:23–26*

For I received from the Lord what I also handed on to you, that the Lord Jesus on the night when he was betrayed took a loaf of bread, and when he had given thanks, he broke it and said, "This is my body that is for you. Do this in remembrance of me." In the same way he took the cup also, after supper, saying, "This cup is the new covenant in my blood. Do this, as often as you drink it, in remembrance of me." For as often as you eat this bread and drink the cup, you proclaim the Lord's death until he comes.

GOSPEL *Luke 9:11–17*

Jesus spoke to the crowds about the kingdom of God, and healed those who needed to be cured. The day was drawing to a close, and the twelve came to him and said, "Send the crowd away, so that they may go into the surrounding villages and countryside, to lodge and get provisions; for we are here in a deserted place." But Jesus said to them, "You give them something to eat." They said, "We have no more than five loaves and two fish—unless we are to go and buy food for all these people." For there were about five thousand men. And Jesus said to his disciples, "Make the people sit down in groups of about fifty each." They did so and made them all sit down. And taking the five loaves and the two fish, he looked up to heaven, and blessed and broke them, and gave them to the disciples to set before the crowd. And all ate and were filled. What was left over was gathered up, twelve baskets of broken pieces.

REFLECTION

The story of the loaves and fishes was especially beloved by early Christians. It is a story of welcome, of sharing, and of nourishment provided by Jesus; it is a story of being drawn together in community. When the crowds press upon Jesus and the time grows late, his intimate companions urge him to send people away so that they may be comfortable for the night. Although the twelve express concern for the well-being of the people, they surely also have their own well-being in mind. In this gospel, "the Twelve" signifies a renewed Israel, and only these twelve are called "apostles" by this author. They have been specially chosen. So they suggest crowd control to deal with the pressing mob of common folk.

Imagine the shock and disbelief on the faces of these twelve when Jesus tells them to feed the large crowd with their meager supplies. They did not have enough food for themselves, and he wanted them to share what little they had with thousands of people? Jesus counters their exclusion and lack of hospitality. He instructs them not simply to give "charity" after they have cared for their own needs but to give despite their need.

Just how there came to be enough food is not the point of the story. (Did Jesus, it is debated, increase the amount himself, or did he inspire generosity among the people?) Rather, the message is that in sharing what we have, we find our abundance. Hospitality requires a broad, inclusive understanding of community. A real community, a real family, is not one which closes its doors in order to be together but one which opens the doors and invites others to join in.

This is eucharist. In giving thanks for what is given, we also offer to share what we have. It is what Jesus did, as we see in the words of Paul, who gives us the earliest surviving account of the eucharistic words of Jesus. To take part in the meal that remembers and makes real again what Jesus offered requires being willing to share it with others. And what Jesus offered was not only nourishment but his very life.

■ **Pope Paul VI said, "Give not from your excess but from your want." Why do you think this distinction is important? Think of some creative ways to make this a reality.**

■ **Recall a time when you were especially touched by someone's generosity toward you.**

PRACTICE OF FAITH

THIS FEAST. "How holy this feast in which Christ is our food." This antiphon from Evening Prayer reminds us that Jesus makes simple bread a feast. The life gift of the feast is also in the gathering around the bread. The feasting continues in the living together in Christ.

The food is a reason for gathering, but it is not the only reason. We gather around the feast of the Body and Blood of Christ because we need the food but also because we need to gather. We need to hold the food and the gathering itself as partners in the continued life of Christ.

When we share food at home and at church, we need to call all members to the table as well as to the food. We need to invite all members to the sustenance of meal, the sharing of food and presence.

PRACTICE OF HOPE

LOAVES. "Billions and billions served!" I pass by one of these signs almost every day. Thinking of this gospel, I say to myself: "They crossed the five thousand mark a long time ago." Or have they? Try to bake a loaf of bread from scratch. Get your wheat and rye grains from the farmer's market. Grind them coarsely with a hand mill. Set up your sourdough in the basement. Mix the flour in a large bowl. Knead the dough until it is consistent and smooth. Then be still. Let the dough rise. Then knead some more. Form the loaves and shove them into the preheated oven. When your house fills with the most heavenly smell on earth, you discover it: There is no such thing as fast food — not for five thousand, not for billions. So look up to heaven, bless the loaves and share freely.

PRACTICE OF CHARITY

CHRISTMAS IN JUNE. Several parishioners were irate that the parish rectory was being converted into a seventeen-bed Catholic Worker shelter for homeless folks. Josie riled other angry voices when she declared, "It's a shame. Those dirty people in that beautiful house." Julia, on the other hand, silenced the entire meeting when she said simply, "I think it's good. Jesus said, 'Feed the hungry.'" The body and blood of Jesus refers not just to ritual in worship. It means feeding the hungry and giving drink to the thirsty, housing to the homeless and clothing to families in crisis. Volunteer an hour this week at a shelter. Or better yet, make Christmas in June by giving a nicely wrapped gift to someone in a shelter.

WEEKDAY READINGS (Mo) 1 Kings 21:1 – 16; (Tu) 21:17 – 29; (We) 2 Kings 2:1 – 14; (Th) Sirach 48:1 – 14; (Fr) Ezekiel 34:11 – 16; (Sa) 2 Chronicles 24:17 – 25

JUNE 14, 1998
**Roman Catholic: See pages 102–103
Other churches: Second Sunday after Pentecost**

READING I *1 Kings 21:1–4, 7–10, 15–17, 19*

Naboth the Jezreelite had a vineyard in Jezreel, beside the palace of King Ahab of Samaria. And Ahab said to Naboth, "Give me your vineyard, so that I may have it for a vegetable garden, because it is near my house; I will give you a better vineyard for it; or, if it seems good to you, I will give you its value in money." But Naboth said to Ahab, "The LORD forbid that I should give you my ancestral inheritance."

Ahab went home resentful and sullen because of what Naboth the Jezreelite had said to him. His wife Jezebel said to him, "Do you now govern Israel? Get up, eat some food, and be cheerful; I will give you the vineyard of Naboth the Jezreelite."

So Jezebel wrote letters in Ahab's name and sealed them with his seal; she sent the letters to the elders and the nobles who lived with Naboth in his city. She wrote in the letters, "Proclaim a fast, and seat Naboth at the head of the assembly; seat two scoundrels opposite him, and have them bring a charge against him, saying, 'You have cursed God and the king.' Then take him out, and stone him to death."

As soon as Jezebel heard that Naboth had been stoned and was dead, Jezebel said to Ahab, "Go, take possession of the vineyard of Naboth the Jezreelite, which he refused to give you for money; for Naboth is not alive, but dead." As soon as Ahab heard that Naboth was dead, Ahab set out to go down to the vineyard of Naboth the Jezreelite, to take possession of it.

Then the word of the LORD came to Elijah the Tishbite, saying: Go down to meet King Ahab of Israel, who rules in Samaria. You shall say to him, "Thus says the LORD: In the place where dogs licked up the blood of Naboth, dogs will also lick up your blood."
[Complete reading: 1 Kings 21:1–21]

READING II *Galatians 2:15–16, 19–20*

We ourselves are Jews by birth and not Gentile sinners; yet we know that a person is justified not by the works of the law but through faith in Jesus Christ. And we have come to believe in Christ Jesus, so that we might be justified by faith in Christ, and not by doing the works of the law, because no one will be justified by the works of the law.

My brothers and sisters, through the law I died to the law, so that I might live to God. I have been crucified with Christ; and it is no longer I who live, but it is Christ who lives in me. And the life I now live in the flesh I live by faith in the Son of God, who loved me and gave himself for me.
[Complete reading: Galatians 2:15–21]

GOSPEL *Luke 7:36–39, 44–50*

One of the Pharisees asked Jesus to eat with him, and Jesus went into the Pharisee's house and took his place at the table. And a woman in the city, who was a sinner, having learned that he was eating in the Pharisee's house, brought an alabaster jar of ointment. She stood behind Jesus at his feet, weeping, and began to bathe his feet with her tears and to dry them with her hair. Then she continued kissing his feet and anointing them with the ointment. Now when the Pharisee who had invited Jesus saw it, he said to himself, "If this man were a prophet, he would have known who and what kind of woman this is who is touching him — that she is a sinner."

Turning toward the woman, Jesus said to Simon, "Do you see this woman? I entered your house; you gave me no water for my feet, but she has bathed my feet with her tears and dried them with her hair. You gave me no kiss, but from the time I came in she has not stopped kissing my feet. You did not anoint my head with oil, but she has anointed my feet with ointment. Therefore, I tell you, her sins, which were many, have been forgiven; hence she has shown great love. But the one to whom little is forgiven, loves little." Then Jesus said to the woman, "Your sins are forgiven." But those who were at the table with him began to say among themselves, "Who is this who even forgives sins?" And Jesus said to the woman, "Your faith has saved you; go in peace."
[Complete reading: Luke 7:36 — 8:3]

104

R E F L E C T I O N

Forgiveness freely given is the theme of today's New Testament readings. Paul's theme of justification by faith addresses the question of how to be set right with God — forgiven — without benefit of the means God had earlier provided in the Jewish law. The theme of compassion in the Gospel of Luke comes to the fore in this account of the woman who anoints Jesus' feet with oil and dries them with her hair.

The story of the woman who anoints Jesus' feet appears in each of the gospels, but in the other three, Jesus comments on the continuing presence of the poor in response to concern regarding waste of expensive nard. The ointment is connected with Jesus' burial, and the scene leads into the plot of Judas to betray him.

In this gospel, however, the question posed to Jesus is not that of waste but of the sinfulness of the woman. Jesus is able to teach his host something about generosity, both the generosity of the woman and that of God, who forgives sins great and small.

What upsets Jesus' listeners is not the idea of the woman's extravagance nor Jesus' rebuke of a religious leader; it is his claim to forgive sins. The gospel presents Jesus as sharing the power and authority of God. But the theme of Jesus' death appears here as well, despite the relatively early location of this pericope in the gospel narrative. Jesus' hearers knew that the sins of all Israel were ritually deposited on a scapegoat on the Day of Atonement. For Jesus to claim to forgive sins presents him as the scapegoat, the one who suffers for the transgressions of many. Although not explicitly mentioned, his salvific death is in the background of this account; Jesus has the authority to forgive the woman's sins, because through him all sins are forgiven.

■ **If you were the lesser debtor in this story, what would be your response upon hearing that you and the other borrower both had your debts completely canceled? How do you respond to the idea of forgiveness rather than retribution for criminals?**

■ **How do you show your gratitude for the forgiveness you have received?**

PRACTICE OF FAITH

FORGIVEN. Today's gospel is full of rich images. We can enter the story through sight, smell, touch or hearing. We hear Jesus say, "Your faith has saved you; go in peace." The woman in the story shows her penitence in movement and contriteness in actions.

The words "I'm sorry" are important to say or learn to say. At the same time, we may live with people who prefer to show their regret in conscious, caring gestures. The adolescent who finds the words difficult will quietly set the dinner table rather than apologize. For full reconciliation, the words and the gesture are important, but the gesture is the bridge in the journey to that fullness. Let us "listen" to the gestures that can begin reconciliation. And for those who find words easy, there is the challenge of contrite action.

PRACTICE OF HOPE

HIRED, FIRED. They hired me right off the street to embarrass him, told me, "Bust him at the party at this Pharisee's place." Throw myself at him, and do the "Hey, remember me?" act. Some good money waiting for me, too. And I kind of liked the idea: Show those propped-up, holier-than-thou folks a thing or two. It was gonna be a scream. Well, they didn't tell me it was gonna be *him*. He looked at me and saw right through me. And I lost it, started crying and groveling at his feet, and yelling at myself, "I'm bad," and he saying to me inside my head, "You're good." He even told the Pharisee's bouncer to leave me alone. What am I to do now? I'm on fire. I can't go back, can I?

PRACTICE OF CHARITY

VAGRANCY LAWS. Seattle has a law that forbids sitting down on the sidewalk. Dallas forbids sleeping in public. Santa Ana, California, allows sleeping on the sidewalk, but the person can't be covered. Ever wonder why these laws are passed? Dallas passed their law a few months before the World Cup was coming to town. The city found $150,000 for free rent for three months for homeless individuals. The three months ended just after the World Cup ended. Jesus, David, Nathan and Paul in today's scriptures all say that laws are not the source of the true spirit of God. True love and forgiveness come from a deeper place in the heart. The National Law Center on Homelessness and Poverty is an excellent source on how laws can help people. Contact them at 918 F Street, Suite 412, Washington, DC 20004; 202-638-2535.

WEEKDAY READINGS (Mo) 1 Kings 21:1 – 16; (Tu) 21:17 – 29; (We) 2 Kings 2:1 – 14; (Th) Sirach 48:1 – 14; (Fr) Ezekiel 34:11 – 16; (Sa) 2 Chronicles 24:17 – 25

READING I *Zechariah 12:10–11*

The Lord says this: "I will pour out a spirit of compassion and supplication on the house of David and the inhabitants of Jerusalem, so that, when they look on the one whom they have pierced, they shall mourn for him, as one mourns for an only child, and weep bitterly over him, as one weeps over a firstborn. On that day the mourning in Jerusalem will be as great as the mourning for Hadad-rimmon in the plain of Megiddo."

READING II *Galatians 3:23–29*

Now before faith came, we were imprisoned and guarded under the law until faith would be revealed. Therefore the law was our disciplinarian until Christ came, so that we might be justified by faith. But now that faith has come, we are no longer subject to a disciplinarian, for in Christ Jesus you are all children of God through faith. As many of you as were baptized into Christ have clothed yourselves with Christ. There is no longer Jew or Greek, there is no longer slave or free, there is no longer male and female; for all of you are one in Christ Jesus. And if you belong to Christ, then you are Abraham's offspring, heirs according to the promise.

GOSPEL *Luke 9:18–22*

One day when Jesus was praying alone, with only the disciples near him, he asked them, "Who do the crowds say that I am?" They answered, "John the Baptist; but others, Elijah; and still others, that one of the ancient prophets has arisen." Jesus said to them, "But who do you say that I am?" Peter answered, "The Messiah of God." Jesus sternly ordered and commanded the disciples not to tell anyone, saying, "The Son of Man must undergo great suffering, and be rejected by the elders, chief priests, and scribes, and be killed, and on the third day be raised."

Wednesday, June 24, 1998

THE BIRTH OF JOHN THE BAPTIST

VIGIL

Jeremiah 1:4–10 *Before I formed you in the womb, I knew you.*

1 Peter 1:8–12 *Rejoice with inexpressible joy.*

Luke 1:5–17 *Many will rejoice at John's birth.*

DAY

Isaiah 49:1–6 *From my mother's womb I am given my name.*

Acts 13:22–26 *John's message is for all children of Abraham.*

Luke 1:57–66, 80 *What will the child be?*

John said that he must decrease if Christ is to increase. At this time of the year, the daytime begins to decrease. It is the midsummer nativity. John is born to be the best man of the Bridegroom, the lamp of the Light and the voice of the Word. Rejoice in John's birth!

REFLECTION

Today's reading from the Gospel of Luke falls between the accounts of the feeding of the five thousand and the transfiguration. It is a turning point in the narrative. Only after the confession of Peter is Jesus revealed in his glory, but his final glorification occurs only after his death, toward which the rest of the gospel relentlessly advances.

The feeding of the five thousand taught the twelve about inclusiveness and generosity. Here Jesus takes his disciples apart from the crowd. A distinction must be made between the popular perception of his mission and the understanding of his intimate followers. While "the people" recognize his prophetic role, Peter acknowledges him as the anointed one of God. The title Messiah, or Christ, is a rich one, recalling the anointing of kings and the promises made to the royal line of David, as well as the expectation of a future savior and judge who would rule with justice, establish the dominion of Israel and inaugurate the final days.

But Jesus has something else to add to the title: He identifies it with the Son of Humanity in Daniel 7, the one to whom was given an everlasting dominion; but Jesus claims that this heavenly figure must suffer and die, and then be raised. Surely here is the faith of the early church, believing Jesus had risen, placed on the lips of Jesus. But Jesus himself may indeed have recognized the necessity and inevitability of suffering for the message he preached.

Most significant, though, is not any insight regarding Jesus' own fate but the claim that his followers must be willing to suffer, to deny themselves, to turn everything upside down for him. The Gospel of Luke, so comforting in its emphasis on compassion, here makes a harsh demand. There is no room for comfort here. There is no explanation for the paradox presented, only the demand. To save one's life, one must be willing to lose it.

■ **Have you ever experienced letting go of something — a desire, a person, a possession — only to find that, when you truly relinquished your hold on it, it became yours? How does such an experience change you?**

PRACTICE OF FAITH

GROWING IN STORY. The church celebrates the witness of Thomas More on June 22. In a sense, Thomas More is a very adult saint. His story might seem too complex and dark for children. We worry that all they will take from the story is a beheading. For my eight-year-old son, Thomas, having a patron who was beheaded is a matter of some pride and fascination. How do Thomas More and other adult witnesses fit into a child's growing faith? It does not fit as much as it grows. The story grows as the child grows in the hearing of it. Each year of growth and experience allows my son to hear more of who Thomas More was.

Celebrate your child's saint day each year by honoring the child, the saint and the story.

PRACTICE OF HOPE

THE CHRIST OF GOD. "Who do you say I am?" You are the earth that presses against my feet. You are the vault that rises above my head. You are the singing sand of the dune. You are the wide-wombed ocean that rises to meet its lover. You are the laughter of the roadside flower in midsummer. You are the dance of the snowflake in winter's dark. You are the vast expectation of a newborn's gaze. You are the silent plea of the abandoned child. You are the innocence of a girl's first kiss. You are the blessing of an old woman's hand. You are the solitary lamp flickering in the night of despair. You are the stake in the desert dividing abyss from abyss. You are the Christ of God. You are the power that swells the space where people meet in love.

PRACTICE OF CHARITY

NEITHER MALE NOR FEMALE. When I saw the pope in Chicago in 1979, it was thrilling: Five hundred thousand people at Mass in Grant Park in Chicago. That evening I received four phone calls from friends. Each was a woman, each a deep and devout Catholic. Each mentioned how the excitement of the Pope's visit captured the country. And each expressed sadness that women were not yet fully recognized in the church. None of the four was bitter or angry, just sad, disheartened. Years later, in 1993 in Denver, during the Pope's visit there, I was attending a prayer vigil for women's ordination. The Pope's helicopter, as it landed nearby, in a strangely coincidental moment, drowned out the prayers. Saint Paul says there is no male or female. Pray as the church struggles on this issue.

WEEKDAY READINGS (Mo) 2 Kings 17:5 – 18; (Tu) 19:9 – 36; (We) Birth of John the Baptist, see box; (Th) 2 Kings 24:8 – 17; (Fr) 25:1 – 12; (Sa) Lamentations 2:2 – 19

READING I *1 Kings 19:15–16, 19–21*

Then the LORD said to Elijah, "Go, return on your way to the wilderness of Damascus; when you arrive, you shall anoint Hazael as king over Aram. Also you shall anoint Jehu son of Nimshi as king over Israel; and you shall anoint Elisha son of Shaphat of Abel-meholah as prophet in your place."

So Elijah set out from there, and found Elisha son of Shaphat, who was plowing. There were twelve yoke of oxen ahead of him, and he was with the twelfth. Elijah passed by him and threw his mantle over Elisha. He left the oxen, ran after Elijah, and said, "Let me kiss my father and my mother, and then I will follow you." Then Elijah said to him, "Go back again; for what have I done to you?" Elisha returned from following Elijah, took the yoke of oxen, and slaughtered them; using the equipment from the oxen, he boiled their flesh, and gave it to the people, and they ate. Then Elisha set out and followed Elijah, and became his servant.

READING II *Galatians 5:1, 13–18*

For freedom Christ has set us free. Stand firm, therefore, and do not submit again to a yoke of slavery.

For you were called to freedom, brothers and sisters; only do not use your freedom as an opportunity for self-indulgence, but through love become slaves to one another. For the whole law is summed up in a single commandment, "You shall love your neighbor as yourself." If, however, you bite and devour one another, take care that you are not consumed by one another.

Live by the Spirit, I say, and do not gratify the desires of the flesh. For what the flesh desires is opposed to the Spirit, and what the Spirit desires is opposed to the flesh; for these are opposed to each other, to prevent you from doing what you want. But if you are led by the Spirit, you are not subject to the law.

[Complete reading: Galatians 5:1, 13–25]

GOSPEL *Luke 9:51–62*

When the days drew near for Jesus to be taken up, he set his face to go to Jerusalem. And he sent messengers ahead of him. On their way they entered a village of the Samaritans to make ready for him; but the people did not receive him, because his face was set toward Jerusalem. When his disciples James and John saw it, they said, "Lord, do you want us to command fire to come down from heaven and consume them?" But Jesus turned and rebuked them. Then they went on to another village.

As they were going along the road, someone said to Jesus, "I will follow you wherever you go." And Jesus said to him, "Foxes have holes, and birds of the air have nests; but the Son-of-Man has nowhere to lay his head." To another Jesus said, "Follow me." But he said, "Lord, first let me go and bury my father." But Jesus replied, "Let the dead bury their own dead; but as for you, go and proclaim the dominion of God." Another said, "I will follow you, Lord; but let me first say farewell to those at my home." Jesus replied, "No one who puts a hand to the plow and looks back is fit for the dominion of God."

Monday, June 29

PETER AND PAUL, APOSTLES

VIGIL

Acts 3:1–10 *Peter cried, "Look at us!"*

Galatians 1:11–20 *God chose to reveal Christ to me.*

John 21:15–19 *Simon Peter, so you love me!*

DAY

Acts 12:1–11 *The chains dropped from Peter's wrists.*

2 Timothy 4:6–8, 17–18 *I have kept the faith.*

Matthew 16:13–19 *I entrust to you the keys of the kingdom.*

This season is the beginning of the grain harvest. So today we keep a festival in honor of the two apostles who began the harvest of God's reign. They preached from Jerusalem to Rome, keeping the Easter commandment to bring the good news to the ends of the earth.

REFLECTION

Jesus is on his final journey. Although his path may twist and turn, his "way" leads straight to his destination — the holy city of Jerusalem and his death. We too are on a journey with Jesus, for this travel account in the Gospel of Luke is concerned with discipleship. The author uses the journey motif to teach something about the road that Christians must walk. It is similar to the road Jesus trod, involving misunderstanding and rejection and requiring a great deal of stamina. It is demanding to follow Jesus, but the demands made of him were ultimate.

First Jesus encounters misunderstanding of his purpose from the Samaritans, who reject him because he is heading toward Jerusalem. For Jesus' followers too, Jerusalem, which represents his death as a political criminal, is an obstacle. To follow Jesus is to follow a criminal.

Jesus is misunderstood also by his disciples, who can appeal to traditions about earlier prophets, notably Elijah, for their desire to see the Samaritan village destroyed. This common desire, to see enemies vanquished, is not the way of Jesus, who continues on his journey.

The final section of the gospel passage is troubling. To one who expresses the willingness to follow him, Jesus describes his itinerant ministry, his homelessness. In the next instance, one who intends to fulfill both a legal and a personal obligation to bury a parent is instructed to proclaim God's reign instead. Finally, the desire to bid farewell to family members before following Jesus is met with an agricultural image: One cannot plow a field or accomplish the task ahead by looking back.

To be a disciple of Jesus requires total commitment. It involves homelessness, not belonging anywhere. It must supersede all other obligations. The leisurely attitude of Elijah in accepting a disciple is gone. The stakes are too high now, the time too short. This journey is final, its consequences ultimate.

■ **The earliest Christians expected Jesus to return in glory and to bring the present world to an end. Given our perspective 2000 years later, how do you understand the demands to leave everything behind? Is it ever possible to reconcile these demands with personal and professional obligations?**

PRACTICE OF FAITH

MISSIONARY. Saint Paul shares a feast day with Saint Peter on June 29. Paul, the missionary, took the witness of his faith experience "on the road." Peter traveled mainly out of himself and his limitations.

Household prayer, like the companionship that Paul enjoyed with his friends and the apostolic community in Peter's life, can be a safe haven for faith. Paul and Peter learned that what is learned and gained in the safe havens begs to be shared with the world.

The safe haven of household prayer can go out to the world by being the inspiration for greater involvement in the larger faith community. It can help us to see private prayer as a path to communal prayer instead of an alternative to it.

PRACTICE OF HOPE

REBUKE. "Burn, burn, all you houses of infamy. Be consumed, all you places of shame. The King of Truth is approaching, and you have closed your doors on him. Therefore will he send down napalm from heaven and reduce your memory to smoke and ashes forever." And you, O Master, censured them only once? Did you not foresee that the temptation was too great and the smell of burning flesh all too alluring? Where was your reprimand when they dragged heretics to the stake? Where was your rebuke when they slaughtered pagans like cattle? Where was your anger when they waged war on each other for your name's sake? They have built foxholes in your name, they bury their dead in your name, and they expect harvest every season. Let me follow you, Lord, on to another village.

PRACTICE OF CHARITY

NOWHERE TO LAY HIS HEAD. As she finished her commute each day to her Manhattan office, Karen Olson saw the woman huddled on the sidewalk. One day she bought a sandwich to give the woman. She grasped Karen's hand — she wanted to meet. Twenty minutes later Karen went into work a changed person. She founded the Interfaith Hospitality Network (IHN). Uniting eight to thirteen religious congregations — Jewish, Protestant, Catholic — plus day centers and social service agencies, IHN provides shelter and support for homeless families. One host congregation furnishes safe overnight lodging and nutritious meals for three to five families. Love your neighbor as yourself. Inquire about your church's participation. Contact the National Interfaith Hospitality Network, 120 Morris Avenue, Summit NJ 07901; 908-273-1100.

WEEKDAY READINGS (Mo) Peter and Paul, see box; (Tu) Amos 3:1 – 8; 4:11 – 12; (We) 5:14 – 24; (Th) 7:10 – 17; (Fr) Ephesians 2:19 – 22; (Sa) Amos 9:11 – 15

JULY 5, 1998
Fourteenth Sunday in Ordinary Time
Fifth Sunday after Pentecost

READING I *Isaiah 66:10–14*

Rejoice with Jerusalem, and be glad for the city,
　all you who love her;
rejoice with Jerusalem in joy,
　all you who mourn over her —
that you may nurse and be satisfied
　from her consoling breast;
that you may drink deeply with delight
　from her glorious bosom.
For thus says the LORD:
I will extend prosperity to Jerusalem like a river,
　and the wealth of the nations
　　like an overflowing stream;
and you shall nurse and be carried on her arm,
　and dandled on her knees.
As a mother comforts her child,
　so I will comfort you;
　you shall be comforted in Jerusalem.
You shall see, and your heart shall rejoice;
　your bodies shall flourish like the grass;
and it shall be known that my hand is with
　　my servants,
　and my indignation is against my enemies.

READING II *Galatians 6:14–18*

May I never boast of anything except the cross of
our Lord Jesus Christ, by which the world has been
crucified to me, and I to the world. For neither cir-
cumcision nor uncircumcision is anything; but a
new creation is everything! As for those who will
follow this rule — peace be upon them, and mercy,
and upon the Israel of God.

From now on, let no one make trouble for me; for
I carry the marks of Jesus branded on my body.

May the grace of our Lord Jesus Christ be with
your spirit, brothers and sisters. Amen.
[Complete reading: Galatians 6:1 – 18]

GOSPEL *Luke 10:1–11, 16–20*

After this the Lord appointed seventy others and
sent them on ahead of him in pairs to every town
and place where he himself intended to go. Jesus
said to them, "The harvest is plentiful, but the laborers are few; therefore ask the Lord of the harvest to
send out laborers for the harvesting. Go on your
way. See, I am sending you out like lambs into the
midst of wolves. Carry no purse, no bag, no sandals;
and greet no one on the road. Whatever house you
enter, first say, 'Peace to this house!' And if anyone is
there who shares in peace, your peace will rest on
that person; but if not, it will return to you. Remain
in the same house, eating and drinking whatever
they provide, for the laborer deserves to be paid. Do
not move about from house to house. Whenever you
enter a town and its people welcome you, eat what
is set before you; cure the sick who are there, and
say to them, 'The dominion of God has come near to
you.' But whenever you enter a town and they do
not welcome you, go out into its streets and say,
'Even the dust of your town that clings to our feet,
we wipe off in protest against you. Yet know this:
the dominion of God has come near.'"

"Whoever listens to you listens to me, and whoever rejects you rejects me, and whoever rejects me
rejects the one who sent me."

The seventy returned with joy, saying, "Lord, in
your name even the demons submit to us!" Jesus
said to them, "I watched Satan fall from heaven like
a flash of lightning. See, I have given you authority
to tread on snakes and scorpions, and over all the
power of the enemy; and nothing will hurt you.
Nevertheless, do not rejoice at this, that the spirits
submit to you, but rejoice that your names are written in heaven."

R E F L E C T I O N

The sending of the seventy recalls an earlier sending of the twelve (9:1–11) to go forth to homes and villages, sharing the good news and healing. It also repeats themes from last Sunday: These "laborers" are to go forth in poverty, unburdened even by apparently necessary possessions; and they are not to condemn those who reject their message but are to move on.

The commission of the seventy, as an advance guard preceding Jesus on his journey, is odd; their mission is not clear. This story appears, rather, to be an account of the earliest Christian missionary movement, in which itinerant preachers would travel from place to place depending upon the hospitality of their hosts. The message that "the dominion of God has come near" is much the same as the message of Jesus; how welcome such a proclamation would be depends on the status of the hearer. And these missionaries will meet with opposition, just as Jesus did; they are "lambs in the midst of wolves." To proclaim the overturning of conventional categories, as this gospel consistently does, results in both eager acceptance and strong rejection. There is no possibility of a lukewarm response; the gospel requires all or nothing.

These missionaries, these apostles (literally, "those who are sent"), return triumphant and joyful, amazed at their success and the power active in them. Jesus' response is to claim the decisive defeat of evil, recalling the traditional belief that Satan once dwelled in heaven with God but had fallen. As signs of the victory over evil, the disciples have spectacular powers, demonstrating the awesome power of God. They are to rejoice, though not in the power of God active in them or even in the success of their message: Joy comes from the promise of life that has been given to them.

■ Reread the first and second readings. How do they complement this gospel selection?

■ In what activities and beliefs do you find the most profound joy?

■ How is Jesus' agricultural imagery of harvest and laborers useful in looking at today's society? In what ways do you take on the tasks of one of the needed laborers? Do you ever feel like a lamb amid wolves?

PRACTICE OF FAITH

VISITORS. Saint Benedict's definition of hospitality as treating every visitor like Christ has become a guidepost for monastic communities.

Busy households with many people coming and going can benefit from the reminder of Benedict's rule. We can take the example of some monasteries and post a written reminder over the front door: "Every visitor is treated like Christ."

We can extend ourselves to make visitors comfortable enough to come to our table and join us in our prayer. Often just a quick explanation helps a visitor know what's coming and how they can participate. The leader of prayer can make an effort to include guests without putting them on the spot.

PRACTICE OF HOPE

DEMONS. Don't you wish you had a visitor like one of those apostle types? They bless your house, take care of your chronic fatigue syndrome, are content with leftover take-out food and chat placidly about the nearness of the Kingdom. Beats a visit from your in-laws, right? Wrong! These guys drive out demons. They see through every cubic inch of you. They, following the example of Jesus, are likely to turn your life upside down by taking away some of your favorite little poltergeists. They're no consumers, they're visionaries — and they may turn out to be socialists. And then what? But what if the Christ-messengers really do turn fear into hope? What would my house look like if all the demons moved?

PRACTICE OF CHARITY

LAMBS AMONG WOLVES. The leader at the table clicked two loose bullets in his hand. The room was stifling, the attitude nasty. He challenged each person who stood to speak about the rally for fair housing: "Are you going to burn this town with us?" I knew Jim could not answer "yes" when his turn came. With integrity he said, "Am I going to burn? How can you ask me that? Where were you when I was talking to the man? Where were you when we worked day and night? I'll be here tomorrow and next week and next year." He sat down, values intact, point made. Even the demons are subject to fullness of spirit. Fair housing laws are supported by the report *No Room for the Inn*, available from the National Law Center on Homelessness and Poverty, 918 F St. NW, #412, Washington, DC 20004-1406; 202-638-2535.

WEEKDAY READINGS (Mo) Hosea 2:16 – 22; (Tu) 8:4 – 13; (We) 10:1 – 12; (Th) 11:1 – 9; (Fr) 14:2 – 10; (Sa) Isaiah 6:1 – 8

READING I *Deuteronomy 30:9 – 14*

The LORD your God will make you abundantly prosperous in all your undertakings, in the fruit of your body, in the fruit of your livestock, and in the fruit of your soil. For the LORD will again take delight in prospering you, delighting in you as in your ancestors, when you obey the LORD your God by observing the commandments and decrees of the LORD that are written in this book of the law, because you turn to the LORD your God with all your heart and with all your soul.

Surely, this commandment that I am commanding you today is not too hard for you, nor is it too far away. It is not in heaven, that you should say, "Who will go up to heaven for us, and get it for us so that we may hear it and observe it?" Neither is it beyond the sea, that you should say, "Who will cross to the other side of the sea for us, and get it for us so that we may hear it and observe it?" No, the word is very near to you; it is in your mouth and in your heart for you to observe.

READING II *Colossians 1:15 – 20*

Christ is the image of the invisible God, the firstborn of all creation; for in Christ all things in heaven and on earth were created, things visible and invisible, whether thrones or dominions or rulers or powers — all things have been created through him and for him. Christ himself is before all things, and in him all things hold together. Christ is the head of the body, the church; Christ is the beginning, the firstborn from the dead, so that he might come to have first place in everything. For in Christ all the fullness of God was pleased to dwell, and through Christ God was pleased to reconcile to himself all things, whether on earth or in heaven, by making peace through the blood of his cross.

[Complete reading: Colossians 1:1 – 20]

GOSPEL *Luke 10:25 – 37*

Just then a lawyer stood up to test Jesus. "Teacher," he said, "what must I do to inherit eternal life?" Jesus said to him, "What is written in the law? What do you read there?" He answered, "You shall love the Lord your God with all your heart, and with all your soul, and with all your strength, and with all your mind; and your neighbor as yourself." And Jesus said to him, "You have given the right answer; do this, and you will live."

But wanting to justify himself, the lawyer asked Jesus, "And who is my neighbor?" Jesus replied, "A man was going down from Jerusalem to Jericho, and fell into the hands of robbers, who stripped him, beat him, and went away, leaving him half dead. Now by chance a priest was going down that road; and when he saw him, he passed by on the other side. So likewise a Levite, when he came to the place and saw him, passed by on the other side. But a Samaritan while traveling came near him; and when the Samaritan saw him, he was moved with pity. He went to him and bandaged his wounds, having poured oil and wine on them. Then he put him on his own animal, brought him to an inn, and took care of him. The next day the Samaritan took out two denarii, gave them to the innkeeper, and said, 'Take care of him; and when I come back, I will repay you whatever more you spend.'

"Which of these three, do you think, was a neighbor to the man who fell into the hands of the robbers?" The lawyer said, "The one who showed him mercy." Jesus said to him, "Go and do likewise."

R E F L E C T I O N

The moving story of the Good Samaritan is unparalleled in the gospels; it appears only in Luke. Jesus tells the parable in response to a question from a lawyer, one educated in the Jewish law, regarding eternal life. Both the lawyer and Jesus agree that the core of the Jewish legal tradition is found in the commands to love God and to love neighbor.

But the lawyer continues to press Jesus: "Who is my neighbor?" Does the law require extending care for another, as profound as one's care for oneself, beyond the family unit, beyond the household, beyond the "neighborhood" or community? Jesus does not answer him directly; he does not directly address the question of the neighbor's identity. Rather, he tells a story of what it is to love, to act neighborly.

The injured man may not have evoked a great deal of sympathy from Jesus' hearers. Most likely he was a trader, probably dishonest himself. But certainly the audience would have felt horror at the idea of a man lying naked in the ditch and near death. The religious leaders in the story, who knew the commands of the law as did the lawyer, were repulsed and passed by. We are not told why. Were they afraid the man might die, and thus they would become impure by touching a corpse? Were they afraid that the robbers might still have been lying in wait, or that it was a setup, and they would be attacked themselves? Did they think the man must have gotten what he deserved? Or did they simply not want to get involved?

The appearance of a Samaritan, one of the traditional enemies of the Jewish people despite their common ancestry and customs, is surprising. An outsider demonstrates how to live rightly by having compassion, by recognizing the man in the ditch as someone worthy of love. The lawyer's question about having a neighbor is answered by action. *Being* a neighbor is what matters.

■ **In a study that used this parable with seminarians, the issue of time was the most significant factor in the generosity of the seminarians toward an injured person. Have we become too busy to care for those in need?**

■ **I recall seeing a city shopowner kicking a man, probably drunk, lying in front of the door to his shop. I was horrified but did not intervene. Why is it so hard to "get involved"?**

PRACTICE OF FAITH

NEIGHBORS AND NEARNESS. Today's gospel challenges us to see our neighbor as anyone we pass by, anyone in need whom we come by. Deuteronomy puts God's presence even closer: "The word is very near to you; it is in your mouth and in your heart."

Our fear of nearness to neighbor must then share our insides with the word of God. The word is near in the elderly neighbor who needs help with the yard, in the single parent who needs rides for the children and in those who cannot get to church without a ride. We can overcome our fear of nearness by helping a neighbor with the fears of loneliness and isolation. The word is near and our fear is diminished when we speak the words "How can I help?"

PRACTICE OF HOPE

ACTING UP. Imagine yourself in a play featuring the parable of the Good Samaritan. One actor has the part of the victim. You get to play all the other parts. First, you are the robber. You almost beat the brains out of your man, but you don't care: You got his money! So dump him on the roadside! Take your exit quickly, and change into a priest's robe.

You reappear, full of church-going and law-abiding self-righteousness. "What is that bloody mess on the roadside? Whoever this is probably deserved his fate. Better not get involved." You exit and come back as the Samaritan.

Your heart opens at the sight of a human being in distress, and all you can do is help. What happened? By assuming all three roles you have given immeasurable hope to the priest and the robber — in you.

PRACTICE OF CHARITY

WHO IS MY NEIGHBOR? The TV cameras quickly surrounded the man when he shouted, "We don't want these people in our neighborhood." He was on the evening news. Two voices not given the spotlight had said, "We welcome the group home. We know it will be well run by the Mental Health Center because they have one near our brother's house. The disabled people have enriched the entire neighborhood." Too often, rational, caring neighbors are ignored. Some people say, "I believe in the work you do, but this just isn't the right place."

The Samaritan took care of his neighbor. Christ commended him for it. Be a Good Samaritan and speak out against the fear which leads to the homelessness of others.

WEEKDAY READINGS (Mo) Isaiah 1:10 – 17; (Tu) 7:1 – 9; (We) 10:5 – 16; (Th) 26:7 – 19; (Fr) 38:1 – 22; (Sa) Micah 2:1 – 5

READING I *Genesis 18:1–10*

The LORD appeared to Abraham by the oaks of Mamre, as he sat at the entrance of his tent in the heat of the day. Abraham looked up and saw three men standing near him. When he saw them, he ran from the tent entrance to meet them, and bowed down to the ground. He said, "My lord, if I find favor with you, do not pass by your servant. Let a little water be brought, and wash your feet, and rest yourselves under the tree. Let me bring a little bread, that you may refresh yourselves, and after that you may pass on — since you have come to your servant." So they said, "Do as you have said." And Abraham hastened into the tent to Sarah, and said, "Make ready quickly three measures of choice flour, knead it, and make cakes." Abraham ran to the herd, and took a calf, tender and good, and gave it to the servant, who hastened to prepare it. Then he took curds and milk and the calf that he had prepared, and set it before them; and he stood by them under the tree while they ate.

They said to him, "Where is your wife Sarah?" And he said, "There, in the tent." Then one said, "I will surely return to you in due season, and your wife Sarah shall have a son."

READING II *Colossians 1:21–28*

You who were once estranged and hostile in mind, doing evil deeds, Christ has now reconciled in his fleshly body through death, so as to present you holy and blameless and irreproachable before God — provided that you continue securely established and steadfast in the faith, without shifting from the hope promised by the gospel that you heard, which has been proclaimed to every creature under heaven. I, Paul, became a servant of this gospel.

I am now rejoicing in my sufferings for your sake, and in my flesh I am completing what is lacking in Christ's afflictions for the sake of his body, that is, the church. I became its servant according to God's commission that was given to me for you, to make the word of God fully known, the mystery that has been hidden throughout the ages and generations but has now been revealed to the saints. To them God chose to make known how great among the Gentiles are the riches of the glory of this mystery, which is Christ in you, the hope of glory. It is Christ whom we proclaim, warning everyone and teaching everyone in all wisdom, so that we may present everyone mature in Christ.

[Complete reading: Colossians 1:15–28]

GOSPEL *Luke 10:38–42*

Now as Jesus and his disciples went on their way, he entered a certain village, where a woman named Martha welcomed him into her home. She had a sister named Mary, who sat at the Lord's feet and listened to what he was saying. But Martha was distracted by her many tasks; so she came to Jesus and asked, "Lord, do you not care that my sister has left me to do all the work by myself? Tell her then to help me." But the Lord answered her, "Martha, Martha, you are worried and distracted by many things; there is need of only one thing. Mary has chosen the better part, which will not be taken away from her."

REFLECTION

Just as Abraham showed hospitality toward travelers, so too Martha received Jesus into her house and attended to his needs. We know from the Gospel of John that Martha and Mary are the sisters of Lazarus; Martha was the active one who confessed Jesus as the Messiah, and Mary anointed Jesus' feet with oil. In this gospel as well, Martha is active, apparently the older sister, while Mary assumes a more passive role, sitting at Jesus' feet and listening to him.

Martha's criticism of her sister for not helping with the preparation and serving of the food is understandable; anyone who has ever prepared a holiday meal for guests knows how much is involved. The centerpiece of the time spent together is often the communion shared in a common meal. It would certainly be considered inhospitable to have guests in one's home without offering refreshment or sustenance.

So the gentle rebuke of Martha by Jesus is somewhat troubling. We heard last week the story of the Good Samaritan, in which love is active. But here Martha is criticized for being active, for doing what was expected. The Gospel of Luke has consistently turned expectations upside down. In the story of the Good Samaritan, the Samaritan outsider shows how to live the Jewish law of love. Here, Mary is praised for *not* fulfilling her prescribed role in society.

The figures of Martha and Mary have long been identified with the different roles of the servants of God: Martha as the active minister and Mary as the contemplative. Indeed Mary, while praised for listening, is never given an active commission, never sent on the road with the other disciples who sit at Jesus' feet and learn.

What Mary does is offer a different type of hospitality. Rather than attending to the needs of the travelers and the many details involved in hosting guests, she offers her time to be present, to listen to Jesus. Being with another, regardless of the activity, is a way of welcoming, of caring, of loving.

■ Reflect on a time when you felt especially welcomed by someone else. What characterized the hospitality offered you?

■ Are you more like Martha or like Mary in your dealings with others?

PRACTICE OF FAITH

REUNION. "My heart burns within me; I long to see my Lord; I look for him, but I cannot find where they have put him." Echoes of Mary Magdalene's cry come to me in the joyful greeting of my three-year-old after a morning of preschool: "Mommy, here you are! I missed you. I thought I was losing you." As I rejoice in these thrice-weekly reunions, I wonder and inquire what she has done while I was away and how she has grown.

We, like Mary Magdalene, have an opportunity in reunion and in communion with the risen Lord, present in the assembly.

PRACTICE OF HOPE

SISTERS. I wonder how Martha and Mary got along before Jesus' visit. Was Martha always the workaholic control freak, and did Mary always shirk responsibility with posy-sniffing dreaminess? "Where is that report that was due yesterday?"

"I'm working on it, but I just *had* to go to that concert last night! I'm sure you understand?"

Sure. "You're fired!"

But, you see, Martha won't fire Mary even though she embarrassed her before the Lord himself. For Martha and Mary are sisters. They will stick it out together. So what happened after Jesus' visit? Martha is still careening in the kitchen, but perhaps she won't drown in her own efficiency anymore. Perhaps she'll listen to her sister's new song about that wonderful man who touched their lives. And Martha might say: "*There* is life. *There* is hope indeed."

PRACTICE OF CHARITY

MYSTERY MADE KNOWN. Annie Sullivan elicited from Helen Keller her first spoken word and opened up for our world one of the most fascinating and astonishing persons we have ever known. In the vine-covered pump house, Annie tapped the word on one of Helen's hands while water flowed on the other. Helen Keller, who had become blind and deaf at age two, came alive. She said the word "water." Annie, like Paul, completed what was lacking. Helen Keller, of course, went on to enlighten and instruct thousands by her spoken and written words. People with disabilities can thrive as persons when loved and treated fairly. The Americans with Disabilities Act, passed in 1990, seeks to assure rights of access and housing. Is your church or place of business in compliance?

WEEKDAY READINGS (Mo) Micah 6:1 – 8; (Tu) 7:14 – 20; (We) Jeremiah 1:1 – 10; (Th) 2:1 – 13; (Fr) 3:14 – 17; (Sa) 2 Corinthians 4:7 – 15

READING I *Genesis 18:20–32*

The LORD said, "How great is the outcry against Sodom and Gomorrah and how very grave their sin! I must go down and see whether they have done altogether according to the outcry that has come to me; and if not, I will know."

So the men turned from there, and went toward Sodom, while Abraham remained standing before the LORD. Then Abraham came near and said, "Will you indeed sweep away the righteous with the wicked? Suppose there are fifty righteous within the city; will you then sweep away the place and not forgive it for the fifty righteous who are in it? Far be it from you to do such a thing, to slay the righteous with the wicked, so that the righteous fare as the wicked! Far be that from you! Shall not the Judge of all the earth do what is just?" And the LORD said, "If I find at Sodom fifty righteous in the city, I will forgive the whole place for their sake." Abraham answered, "Let me take it upon myself to speak to the Lord, I who am but dust and ashes. Suppose five of the fifty righteous are lacking? Will you destroy the whole city for lack of five?" And the LORD said, "I will not destroy it if I find forty-five there." Again he spoke to the LORD, "Suppose forty are found there." The LORD answered, "For the sake of forty I will not do it." Then Abraham said, "Oh do not let the Lord be angry if I speak. Suppose thirty are found there." The LORD answered, "I will not do it, if I find thirty there." He said, "Let me take it upon myself to speak to the Lord. Suppose twenty are found there." The LORD answered, "For the sake of twenty I will not destroy it." Then Abraham said, "Oh do not let the Lord be angry if I speak just once more. Suppose ten are found there."

The LORD answered, "For the sake of ten I will not destroy it."

READING II *Colossians 2:12–14*

When you were buried with Christ in baptism, you were also raised with him through faith in the power of God, who raised him from the dead. And when you were dead in trespasses and the uncircumcision of your flesh, God made you alive together with Christ, having forgiven us all our trespasses, erasing the record that stood against us with its legal demands. God set this aside, nailing it to the cross. *[Complete reading: Colossians 2:6–19]*

GOSPEL *Luke 11:1–13*

Jesus was praying in a certain place, and after he had finished, one of his disciples said to him, "Lord, teach us to pray, as John taught his disciples." Jesus said to them, "When you pray, say:
Father, hallowed be your name.
  Let your dominion come.
  Give us each day our daily bread.
  And forgive us our sins,
  for we ourselves forgive
    everyone indebted to us.
  And do not bring us to the time of trial."

And Jesus said to them, "Suppose one of you has a friend, and you go to that friend at midnight and say, 'Friend, lend me three loaves of bread; for a friend of mine has arrived, and I have nothing to set out.' And the friend answers from within, 'Do not bother me; the door has already been locked, and my children are with me in bed; I cannot get up and give you anything.' I tell you, even though the friend will not get up and provide anything because of the friendship, at least because of the neighbor's persistence the friend will get up and provide whatever is needed.

"So I say to you, Ask, and it will be given you; search, and you will find; knock, and the door will be opened for you. For everyone who asks receives, and everyone who searches finds, and for everyone who knocks, the door will be opened. Is there anyone among you who, if your child asks for a fish, will give a snake instead of a fish? Or if the child asks for an egg, will give a scorpion? If you then, who are evil, know how to give good gifts to your children, how much more will the heavenly Father give the Holy Spirit to those who ask!"

REFLECTION

The Lord's prayer, that unifying and identifying prayer of Christians, was a response, we are told today, to a request that Jesus teach his disciples to pray in a manner that would identify them as his followers, over against the followers of John the Baptist. The prayer begins with a recognition of God's holiness and sovereignty, and moves on to express the requests of the community. This is not a private prayer; the petitions are expressed in the plural. This prayer is properly recited with others as an expression of common need and trust in God.

The requests in the prayer are threefold. First a request for bread is made, not for "this day," as in Matthew, but for "each day." Continual dependence on God's generosity is fitting in a land of famines and economic exploitation, and it is appropriate as well for itinerant preachers. The request for forgiveness is linked with the claim that "we" forgive others. The prayer to avoid trial may reflect the difficulties faced by the early Christian community that uttered this prayer; it can also be read as a desperate plea to avoid the impending trials to be faced by Jesus' disciples — and himself.

The teaching about prayer continues with the humorous account of the bothersome neighbor. If all else fails, persistence pays off, as it did in the similarly entertaining account of Abraham's argument with God. Beseeching God is appropriate; it acknowledges human dependence on the divine. But in both stories, it is not mere persistence but *chutzpah* which eventually achieves the desired response. The householder is won over not by friendship but by limited tolerance and by embarrassment for a neighbor in need.

Lest the emphasis on persistence be understood to mean that one need simply repeat "Gimme, gimme" in prayer to God, the story of the father and son clarifies that God desires what is good for petitioners. Need for the supreme gift — the Holy Spirit — must be acknowledged, but the gift is freely bestowed on all who request it.

■ Compare the Lord's prayer given here with the more familiar version in Matthew 6:9 – 13. Say each prayer slowly, preferably together with others. What does this prayer mean to you?

■ What does it mean to receive the gift of the Holy Spirit?

PRACTICE OF FAITH

DEVOTION. Martha of Bethany (July 29) was the sister of Mary and Lazarus, and a friend of Jesus. Martha was known for her devotion to Jesus. She went out to meet him with her grief at his absence from Lazarus's death, coupling regret ("if you had been here") with devotion and belief ("You are the Messiah, the Son of God").

She believed in the midst of disappointment because she believed in the essence of Jesus — not just mere appearances. She was devoted to the essence of Jesus but suffered the human emotion of missing his presence.

Remember in prayer those who are away from the table; let us pray for the return of their essence in their presence. We can hold their essence in prayer while we cannot have their presence.

PRACTICE OF HOPE

SCORPIONS AND FISHES. How little do I know my needs, yet how well do you provide for me, my God. In my foolishness I have asked you for scorpions and serpents. But you have given me eggs and fishes all the same. Night after night, I have knocked at your door. Year after year, I have chipped away at your doorpost, asking for rags. Your servants roll their eyes at my persistence. But now you have come down yourself in the middle of the night to clothe me in purple like a king. You have given me a white steed like a prince and a scepter like the ruler of the land. Your embrace has steadied my gaze. I ride into the rising sun with my head lifted high, and my eyes are bright with the light of the morning star.

PRACTICE OF CHARITY

PETITION. The Muslim men, heads capped for prayer, knelt as the loudspeakers amplified the chants for prayer at noon. As each man completed his prayer, he cupped his hands together, palms upward, and tenderly brushed his face, forehead to chin, in a touching, sacramental gesture. This motion, ending in briefly folded hands, seemed strange but also somehow familiar when I witnessed it a few years ago. Our prayers, like those of the Muslims, are not only private but in the presence of others, not only personal and spiritual but communal and physical, sacramental. Consider engaging your senses more fully in prayer this week. Sing, move about, pray aloud with a friend.

WEEKDAY READINGS (Mo) Jeremiah 13:1–11; (Tu) 14:17–22; (We) 15:10–21; (Th) 18:1–6; (Fr) 26:1–9; (Sa) 26:11–24

READING I *Ecclesiastes 1:2, 12–14; 2:18–23*

Vanity of vanities, says the Teacher,
  vanity of vanities! All is vanity.
I, the Teacher, when king over Israel in Jerusalem, applied my mind to seek and to search out by wisdom all that is done under heaven; it is an unhappy business that God has given to human beings to be busy with. I saw all the deeds that are done under the sun; and see, all is vanity and a chasing after wind.

I hated all my toil in which I had toiled under the sun, seeing that I must leave it to those who come after me — and who knows whether they will be wise or foolish? Yet they will be master of all for which I toiled and used my wisdom under the sun. This also is vanity. So I turned and gave my heart up to despair concerning all the toil of my labors under the sun, because sometimes one who has toiled with wisdom and knowledge and skill must leave all to be enjoyed by another who did not toil for it. This also is vanity and a great evil. What do mortals get from all the toil and strain with which they toil under the sun? For all their days are full of pain, and their work is a vexation; even at night their minds do not rest. This also is vanity.

READING II *Colossians 3:1–11*

So if you have been raised with Christ, seek the things that are above, where Christ is, seated at the right hand of God. Set your minds on things that are above, not on things that are on earth, for you have died, and your life is hidden with Christ in God. When Christ who is your life is revealed, then you also will be revealed with him in glory.

Put to death, therefore, whatever in you is earthly: fornication, impurity, passion, evil desire, and greed (which is idolatry). On account of these the wrath of God is coming on those who are disobedient. These are the ways you also once followed, when you were living that life. But now you must get rid of all such things — anger, wrath, malice, slander, and abusive language from your mouth. Do not lie to one another, seeing that you have stripped off the old self with its practices and have clothed yourselves with the new self, which is being renewed in knowledge according to the image of its creator. In that renewal there is no longer Greek and Jew, circumcised and uncircumcised, barbarian, Scythian, slave and free; but Christ is all and in all!

GOSPEL *Luke 12:13–21*

Someone in the crowd said to Jesus, "Teacher, tell my brother to divide the family inheritance with me." But Jesus replied, "Friend, who set me to be a judge or arbitrator over you?" And Jesus said to them, "Take care! Be on your guard against all kinds of greed; for one's life does not consist in the abundance of possessions." Then he told them a parable: "The land of a rich man produced abundantly. And he thought to himself, 'What should I do, for I have no place to store my crops?' Then he said, 'I will do this: I will pull down my barns and build larger ones, and there I will store all my grain and my goods. And I will say to my soul, 'Soul, you have ample goods laid up for many years; relax, eat, drink, be merry.' But God said to him, 'You fool! This very night your life is being demanded of you. And the things you have prepared, whose will they be?' So it is with those who store up treasures for themselves but are not rich toward God."

Thursday, August 6

THE TRANSFIGURATION OF THE LORD

Daniel 7:9–10, 13–14 *I saw the Man of Heaven on the clouds.*

2 Peter 1:16–19 *We are eyewitnesses to God's glory.*

Luke 9:28–36 *Who do the crowds say that I am?*

At the peak of the glory of summer, the Lord shines on the holy mountain. With the law and the prophets, we gaze on God face to face. Yet which mountain is it — Calvary or Tabor? Perhaps they are one and the same.

REFLECTION

Out of the blue, a question comes to Jesus concerning inheritance. Jesus responds by launching into a discussion of the dangers of wealth.

The story of the rich man strikes close to home for many of us. The man is blessed with a great abundance of crops and decides to devote his energies to enjoying his wealth; he assumes that he will have many years in which to concentrate on other aspects of his life. But his plans are interrupted when God announces that he will die, his wealth no longer to be enjoyed.

Inheritance laws are clearly not the real question here; the concern is not whether one should provide for one's children after death. Instead, Jesus deals with something more fundamental: the desire to possess.

What good do possessions do for one who is dead? The answer is obvious: nothing. But it is not only possessions themselves that are disparaged here. The rich man does not get the chance to build his larger barns and store his grain. It is the very thought of making his wealth his highest priority that results in his downfall. Jesus' criticism is of greed, the desire to have, to possess, to obtain.

For many of us, this desire can be consuming. We live in a society in which simple living is seen as odd. We compete to have the latest and best clothing, houses, cars, household equipment, even food; sometimes we even compete to be the most generous! Whether or not we ever obtain what our neighbors have, the very desire to have it can eat away at us. It can prevent us from being satisfied with what we have, from recognizing how richly we are blessed; it can also make us grasping and stingy, preventing us from seeing the real needs of others. And, as the Letter to the Colossians makes clear, it can prevent us from truly placing God first in our lives. Greed is a form of idolatry.

This is what the rich man in the parable did. He idolized what he had and lost sight of what he could be. How often do we fall into the same trap?

■ **Do you ever find yourself anxious to have a bigger or better house, car, etc.? What happens if you let go of that desire?**

■ **What characterizes true generosity?**

PRACTICE OF FAITH

SEEING. What changes how we look at someone? What light can help us to see someone in a different role in our lives? The Transfiguration of the Lord (August 6) cast the role of Jesus into a new light for the witnesses. They saw him in ways they had never seen him before, had not fully imagined or so vividly pictured.

Parents experience this light when a teacher describes their child in a role or behavior that they have not seen at home. The child is cast in a different light, and the vision of him is deepened in the praise or compliment.

Share with another parent a vision of their child which they may not have seen. Tell about the child's kindness or helpfulness in your presence.

PRACTICE OF HOPE

LIFESAVER. When the rich man heard what God had spoken, he was very afraid. He went quickly to sell all his land and possessions. Then he took the money from the sales and threw it about the streets of his town. By sunset, he had rid himself of everything. Exhausted, he sank down on a curbside and fell asleep. When midnight came, he was awakened by a dark figure who spoke to him.

"You fool! You have given away all your possessions in order to save your wretched life. Live now in poverty and dejection, and see what you have gained!" But God said to him: "Fear not the envy of death. From now on you will work the soil of the soul. In time it will produce abundantly, and you will build barns for crops that are never exhausted."

PRACTICE OF CHARITY

VANITY OF VANITIES. "I made it the old-fashioned way. I inherited it." Money enjoys a peculiar place in the lives of Americans. Decisions about life, school, where to live and what to wear are often based on money. But high in the Andes mountains, near Puno, Peru, the first consideration is how to help a neighboring family, how to contribute to the well-being of the community. In the United States, much striving seems to be toward increased income. What often results from this is that the possessions are merely "bigger" and "better": a better car, a more expensive watch, a finer house, more exotic vacations, a faster computer. Greed can be pervasive and elusive. Some Americans counter these tendencies by giving away, "giving back to God," ten percent of what they earn.

WEEKDAY READINGS (Mo) Jeremiah 28:1–17; (Tu) 30:1– 22; (We) 31:1–7; (Th) Transfiguration, see box; (Fr) Nahum 2:1–3; 3:1–7; (Sa) Habakkuk 1:12 — 2:4

AUGUST 9, 1998 Ninteenth Sunday in Ordinary Time
Tenth Sunday after Pentecost

READING I *Wisdom 18:6–9*

The night of the deliverance from Egypt was made known beforehand to our ancestors, so that they might rejoice in sure knowledge of the oaths in which they trusted. The deliverance of the righteous and the destruction of their enemies were expected by your people. For by the same means by which you punished our enemies you called us to yourself and glorified us.

For in secret the holy children of good people offered sacrifices, and with one accord agreed to the divine law, so that the saints would share alike the same things, both blessings and dangers; and already they were singing the praises of the ancestors.

READING II *Hebrews 11:1–3, 8–12*

Now faith is the assurance of things hoped for, the conviction of things not seen. Indeed, by faith our ancestors received approval. By faith we understand that the worlds were prepared by the word of God, so that what is seen was made from things that are not visible.

By faith Abraham obeyed when he was called to set out for a place that he was to receive as an inheritance; and he set out, not knowing where he was going. By faith he stayed for a time in the land he had been promised, as in a foreign land, living in tents, as did Isaac and Jacob, who were heirs with him of the same promise. For Abraham looked forward to the city that has foundations, whose architect and builder is God. By faith he received power of procreation, even though he was too old — and Sarah herself was barren — because he considered faithful the one who had promised. Therefore from one person, and this one as good as dead, descendants were born, "as many as the stars of heaven and as the innumerable grains of sand by the seashore." *[Complete reading: Hebrews 11:1–3, 8–19]*

GOSPEL *Luke 12:32–40*

Jesus said:

"Do not be afraid, little flock, for it is your Father's good pleasure to give the dominion to you. Sell your possessions, and give alms. Make purses for yourselves that do not wear out, an unfailing treasure in heaven, where no thief comes near and no moth destroys. For where your treasure is, there your heart will be also.

"Be dressed for action and have your lamps lit; be like those who are waiting for their master to return from the wedding banquet, so that they may open the door for him as soon as he comes and knocks. Blessed are those slaves whom the master finds alert when he comes; truly I tell you, he will fasten his belt and have them sit down to eat, and he will come and serve them. If the master comes during the middle of the night, or near dawn, and finds them so, blessed are those slaves.

"But know this: if the owner of the house had known at what hour the thief was coming, the owner would not have let the house be broken into. You also must be ready, for the Son-of-Man is coming at an unexpected hour."

Peter said, "Lord, are you telling this parable for us or for everyone?" And the Lord said, "Who then is the faithful and prudent manager whom his master will put in charge of his slaves, to give them their allowance of food at the proper time? Blessed is that slave whom his master will find at work when he arrives. Truly I tell you, he will put that one in charge of all his possessions. But if that slave says to himself, 'My master is delayed in coming,' and if he begins to beat the other slaves, men and women, and to eat and drink and get drunk, the master of that slave will come on a day when he does not expect him and at an hour that he does not know, and will cut him in pieces, and put him with the unfaithful.

"That slave who knew what his master wanted, but did not prepare himself or do what was wanted, will receive a severe beating. But the one who did not know and did what deserved a beating will receive a light beating. "From everyone to whom much has been given, much will be required; and from the one to whom much has been entrusted, even more will be demanded."

REFLECTION

Today's gospel begins by drawing a conclusion to the ideas presented last week. Material goods and the desire for them can become all-consuming, but there is a different type of wealth that is desirable. In fact, it is by freeing oneself of possessions and money that one can acquire a lasting treasure. The things to which people devote their energy and time indicate their values; one's heart needs to be centered on God and those most precious to God — those in need — rather than on oneself.

The rest of the gospel passage reflects questions that arose from the early Christian belief that Jesus would soon return in his glory and the delay that had already occurred. Written more than a half century after Jesus' death, this gospel needed to address concerns regarding laxity on the part of the members of the community who had already been waiting for Jesus' coming and were discouraged at his delay. The image of slaves awaiting their master conveys the message that Christians must always be waiting, alert. Even if there is a delay, the message is clear: Be ready!

Peter's question to Jesus provides the author an opportunity to direct some comments to leaders in the community. Again, slaves are symbolic of the servants of God. But these slaves are given greater responsibility than others. Of those who understand the master's desires, more is expected. All are to be prepared, for Christ's coming will not be announced; but those entrusted with leadership are held to a higher standard than others.

■ **The Second Coming has been delayed much longer now than the author of the gospel could ever have envisioned. In fact, our understanding of just what it means to reach the "end times" is significantly different from that of first-century Christians. Because we lack a sense of urgency regarding Christ's coming, we are especially prone to becoming complacent and inattentive. What can you do to remain alert and expectant?**

■ **What do you expect of leaders in your church or community? What does society expect of them? Can these be reconciled with the expectations of today's gospel?**

PRACTICE OF FAITH

SIMPLICITY. Living simply has become a theme of self-help guides and health and fitness fads. Living simply can be a means of improving many aspects of life. Simplicity is not a new idea for the church. Living simply was not *a* way of life for Saint Francis of Assisi, it was *the* way of life. Saint Clare (August 11) sought out Francis' support and his way of life and prayer. Clare chose poverty and service over a life of wealth and comfort. Francis and Clare chose this life not to make themselves feel better or healthier but to make others feel better and safer.

Consider supporting the work of the Poor Clares today. Simplify your wardrobe, simplify your eating habits and simplify all your consumption. Let others be the beneficiaries of your simplicity by giving out of your necessity and excess.

PRACTICE OF HOPE

BURNING LAMPS. Nothing worse than waiting for the Master after hours in a room with indifferent people, all lamps burning, and no pool table or television around. Conversation dies quickly after the usual platitudes. Do I have to go through this misery? Will this guy ever come home from his wedding party? Someone in the room begins to tell a story, a real yawner. Others start chiming in, and before you know it there is a whole pow-wow. Most embarrassing. Why are people beginning to look so gleeful while I'm so miserable? Why are they poking fun at me and teasing me? Don't you dare make me laugh! Here enters the Master: "Thank God y'all cheered up at last! I waited outside for the longest time. Couldn't possibly enter such a gloomy house! Now look at the cake I brought. Let's have a party!"

PRACTICE OF CHARITY

MUCH ENTRUSTED. MORE DEMANDED. Bill Lavery is an eye surgeon. Through technology and his own skills, he was able to restore sight to a man who had been blind for 40 years. Bill said it was the most satisfying thing he had ever done. To accomplish this modern miracle, Bill had to study for years, have faith in the talents he received, have the courage to master new technology and be willing to put those skills at the service of others. His treasure lies where his heart is: in the ability to help people in their need. Physicians for Social Responsibility provide medical treatment in a context of social justice. Learn about their worldwide efforts by contacting then at 1101 14th Street NW, Washington, D.C. 20005; 202-898-0150.

WEEKDAY READINGS (Mo) 2 Corinthians 9:6 – 10; (Tu) Ezekiel 2:8 — 3:4; (We) Ezekiel 9:1–7; 10:18 — 22; (Th) 12:1–12; (Fr) 16:59 – 63; (Sa) Assumption, see page 122

READING I *Jeremiah 38:4–6, 8–10*

Then the officials said to the king, "This man ought to be put to death, because he is discouraging the soldiers who are left in this city, and all the people, by speaking such words to them. For this man is not seeking the welfare of this people, but their harm." King Zedekiah said, "Here he is; he is in your hands; for the king is powerless against you." So they took Jeremiah and threw him into the cistern of Malchiah, the king's son, which was in the court of the guard, letting Jeremiah down by ropes. Now there was no water in the cistern, but only mud, and Jeremiah sank in the mud.

So Ebed-melech the Ethiopian, an officer in the king's house, left the king's house and spoke to the king, "My lord king, these men have acted wickedly in all they did to the prophet Jeremiah by throwing him into the cistern to die there of hunger, for there is no bread left in the city." Then the king commanded Ebed-melech the Ethiopian, "Take three men with you from here, and pull the prophet Jeremiah up from the cistern before he dies."

READING II *Hebrews 12:1–4*

Since we are surrounded by so great a cloud of witnesses, let us also lay aside every weight and the sin that clings so closely, and let us run with perseverance the race that is set before us, looking to Jesus the pioneer and perfecter of our faith, who for the sake of the joy that was set before him endured the cross, disregarding its shame, and is seated at the right hand of the throne of God.

Consider Jesus who endured such hostility against himself from sinners, so that you may not grow weary or lose heart.

In your struggle against sin you have not yet resisted to the point of shedding your blood.

GOSPEL *Luke 12:49–56*

Jesus said:

"I came to bring fire to the earth, and how I wish it were already kindled! I have a baptism with which to be baptized, and what stress I am under until it is completed! Do you think that I have come to bring peace to the earth? No, I tell you, but rather division! From now on five in one household will be divided, three against two and two against three; they will be divided: father against son and son against father, mother against daughter and daughter against mother, and in-laws against one another."

Jesus also said to the crowds, "When you see a cloud rising in the west, you immediately say, 'It is going to rain'; and so it happens. And when you see the south wind blowing, you say, 'There will be scorching heat'; and it happens. You hypocrites! You know how to interpret the appearance of earth and sky, but why do you not know how to interpret the present time?"

Saturday, August 15, 1998

ASSUMPTION OF THE VIRGIN MARY INTO HEAVEN

VIGIL

1 Chronicles 15:3–4, 15–16; 16:1–2 *David before the ark.*

1 Corinthians 15:54–57 *God gave us victory over death.*

Luke 11:27–28 *Blessed is the womb that bore you!*

DAY

Revelation 11:19; 12:1–6, 10 *A woman clothed in the sun.*

1 Corinthians 15:20–27 *Christ is the first fruits of the dead.*

Luke 1:39–56 *He has raised the lowly to the heights.*

Now we keep the festival of Mary's passover. In time, each one of us will be gathered into the reign of God, shining like the sun, with the moon at our feet.

REFLECTION

The one whom John the Baptist said would baptize with the Holy Spirit and with fire longs now for that fire and anticipates another baptism. This baptism is, indeed, a baptism of fire, an all-consuming, final, inexorable conflagration — it is Jesus' death.

Fire is often a sign of the final days, the judgment of God. Just as Jesus' death cannot be avoided, so too the Day of the Lord is inescapable. In the background today is the theme of last week's gospel: Be ready!

Elsewhere, Jesus is said to be the bearer of peace whose very birth inaugurates a new era of goodwill in the world. The present context, though, is anything but peaceful. Recall that we are accompanying Jesus on his path to the holy city Jerusalem, to his final hour. Jesus has been teaching what discipleship involves. It requires looking straight ahead, forsaking even family obligations; it means recognizing that all human beings, however lowly, are worthy and capable of love; it involves listening and sharing hospitality; it requires beseeching God and trusting in God's goodness. It is demanding, requiring total devotion and the surrender of money and possessions, even of the very desire to possess. It requires sharing resources with those in need. It means being always watchful, always ready, always "slave" to the teacher, the Master. It is not easy.

Given this understanding of discipleship, Jesus' words about bringing division are clearer. Following Jesus involves total commitment; there is no turning back. Such zeal is often difficult to understand and can cause conflict. No, it *will* cause conflict; the gospel is a burning fire that separates the committed from the half-hearted. To follow Jesus requires deciding on which side of the great divide one will stand.

■ **Have you ever experienced the division mentioned in today's gospel? Have you ever, or have you ever seen someone else, take an unpopular stand regarding a matter of principle? How did it feel? Was there a sense of inner peace despite the opposition?**

■ **What is your response to people who are exceptionally vocal about their faith, perhaps even proselytizing door to door? Does today's gospel selection help you to understand them better?**

PRACTICE OF FAITH

KNOWING. "Those who know God's love will love more easily." This is from Saint Bernard of Clairvaux (August 20). Children find it easy to know and love simultaneously. Adults sometimes need to know the difference and want to consider each aspect separately. Adults are easily consoled and impressed by knowing. Adults often dismiss loving and feeling as silly compared with knowledge. Bernard attempted a rejoinder of what some have separated. Bernard is inviting us to behave as children in holding the knowing and loving together.

Let the children in your life remind you that "to know me is to love me." Let the children in your life remind you that to know God is to love God, and to know God is to love others.

PRACTICE OF HOPE

WHAT FIRE? What is the fire like, my Lord, that you will cast upon the earth? Is it a raging brushfire, blazing through ancient forests, making space for new growth to come? Is it the sleeping fire of the earth that suddenly bursts forth and covers the land with flames and ashes, making fertile the very ground it torches? Is it the fire of some alchemist's furnace that melts down the old iron, divides metal from metal, and changes lead into gold? Or is it like the fire in my lover's eye that seeks to consume me, and consuming desires to be consumed? Lord, your fire is the fire of love — that mad love which, uniting, divides only to unite again. It is the flame within that bids me love my neighbor, the flame above that bids me love my enemy.

PRACTICE OF CHARITY

LIGHT THE FIRE OF DIVISION. St. Joseph's parish had a mix of workers from the army arsenal along with serious Catholic Worker peace demonstrators. Frequently, the security police at the arsenal were arresting protesters with whom they worshiped at St. Joe's. The pastor persuaded members of each faction to come together for the welfare of the people. The fire was about to be kindled. What took place, though, was an honest meeting of minds. The expert on Russian weapons listened to the advocate for nonviolence. Ideas and convictions were explored. No one "changed sides." No one capitulated — or compromised his or her integrity. But each grew in respect for the other, and lasting bonds of friendship formed. Each of us can persevere in the race, endure the suffering. Try reaching out in peace to someone with whom you disagree.

WEEKDAY READINGS (Mo) Ezekiel 24:15 – 24; (Tu) 28:1 – 10; (We) 34:1 – 11; (Th) 36:23 – 28; (Fr) 37:1 – 14; (Sa) 43:1 – 7

READING I *Isaiah 66:18–21*

"I know their works and their thoughts, and I am coming to gather all nations and tongues; and they shall come and shall see my glory, and I will set a sign among them. From them I will send survivors to the nations, to Tarshish, Put, and Lud — which draw the bow — to Tubal and Javan, to the coastlands far away that have not heard of my fame or seen my glory; and they shall declare my glory among the nations. They shall bring all your kindred from all the nations as an offering to the LORD, on horses, and in chariots, and in litters, and on mules, and on dromedaries, to my holy mountain Jerusalem, says the LORD, just as the Israelites bring a grain offering in a clean vessel to the house of the LORD. And I will also take some of them as priests and as Levites, says the LORD.

READING II *Hebrews 12:5–7, 11–13*

You have forgotten the exhortation that addresses you as children —

> "My child, do not regard lightly
>   the discipline of the Lord,
> or lose heart when you are
>   punished by God;
> for the Lord disciplines
>   those whom the Lord loves,
> and God chastises every child
>   whom God accepts."

Endure trials for the sake of discipline. God is treating you as children; for what child is there whom a parent does not discipline? Now, discipline always seems painful rather than pleasant at the time, but later it yields the peaceful fruit of righteousness to those who have been trained by it. Therefore lift your drooping hands and strengthen your weak knees, and make straight paths for your feet, so that what is lame may not be put out of joint, but rather be healed.

GOSPEL *Luke 13:22–30*

Jesus went through one town and village after another, teaching as he made his way to Jerusalem. Someone asked him, "Lord, will only a few be saved?" Jesus said to them, "Strive to enter through the narrow door; for many, I tell you, will try to enter and will not be able. When once the owner of the house has got up and shut the door, and you begin to stand outside and to knock at the door, saying, 'Lord, open to us,' then in reply he will say to you, 'I do not know where you come from.' Then you will begin to say, 'We ate and drank with you, and you taught in our streets.' But the Lord will say, 'I do not know where you come from; go away from me, all you evildoers!' There will be weeping and gnashing of teeth when you see Abraham and Isaac and Jacob and all the prophets in the kingdom of God, and you yourselves thrown out. Then people will come from east and west, from north and south, and will eat in the kingdom of God. Indeed, some are last who will be first, and some are first who will be last."

REFLECTION

The Gospel of Luke continually surprises and challenges. We have seen social categories inverted and misunderstandings abound, and we have met prodding when we wanted comfort. Within this gospel of inclusion and openness we meet today a claim that there is also reason for exclusion. In fact, those who rely most on the promise of partaking in the heavenly banquet will be "last," while latecomers will be welcomed. Recall the importance of meals for Jesus and his disciples, for the early Christian community and for us. No one wants to sit outside during Christmas dinner!

But Jesus makes further demands of his disciples in this passage. The path his followers walk is not easy; it involves striving, struggling. And it is not enough simply to know Jesus, to have feasted with him, to have heard his teachings. Those chosen for the heavenly banquet are those who have squeezed through the door, not those who got a foot in early but did not strive hard enough. The householder who closes the door does not recognize those pounding outside, despite their claims to have been present already. The message is clear: Being present is not enough. It is not simply knowing God that counts but being known by God.

It is not enough for us to be raised Christian, to attend church, to know the doctrines of the faith and to share in the eucharist. What is required is to be familiar to God, to be recognizable, to be known. Being known by another requires risk-taking, letting down defenses. Being known by God involves opening up to one who is able to bring fire as well as peace, one whose glance can be searing as well as kind. And it also involves action. Once the door has closed and the time has passed, it is too late. Entering by the narrow door is not something that can be put off until tomorrow; it must be done while the time is at hand. It must be done today.

■ **People usually gain familiarity with one another by spending time together and sharing activities and values. What can you do to make yourself better known to God?**

■ **Do you ever think that "tomorrow" you'll spend more time in prayer, learn more about your faith tradition or truly commit yourself to the values of the gospel? Does tomorrow ever come? Perhaps it is here — today.**

PRACTICE OF FAITH

HERALDING. This week the church remembers Saint Monica (August 27), Saint Augustine (August 28) and the beheading of John the Baptist (August 29). Many people have come to faith in Jesus and the church through these three people. Monica and John worked tirelessly to point others to the life of Jesus in the church. They met their own deaths with confidence in the mission of their lives.

Listen for a call to form, join or host a small faith community in your parish. Volunteer to help with the youth program. Bring a friend to a religious education class.

Recall John the Baptist: "I am not the Christ; I have been sent before him to prepare his way. He must increase, and I must decrease."

PRACTICE OF HOPE

DOORS AND LOCKS. That's it. I've had it. I'm going to bolt my front door for good. The only people who ever show up there are solicitors, investigators and missionaries. I don't want to see them. They can file a written complaint or send junk mail. As a matter of fact, I'll have a brick wall built behind the front door. I'll hang up a sign: "Depart from here, ye sons of b . . ." so that if they force the door open they'll be surprised, and they can gnash their teeth all they want. 'Cause, you see, all my *real* friends know the back way. They come through the alley, across a few narrow doorways and through the wintergarden right into the kitchen. That's where we sit and have a good time talking over coffee or tea. Seems like I'm crazy, because I always leave the back door unlocked. . . .

PRACTICE OF CHARITY

FRUIT OF RIGHTEOUSNESS. A Palestinian girl said, "I live across the street from the hospital in Jerusalem, where they take the bodies of the dead and dying after bombings. Sometimes they are Israelis, sometimes Palestinians. They all come in pieces. I don't want to see the blood flow. Maybe I can make a difference." For three weeks at a camp in Colorado, Israeli and Palestinian teens talked, shared meals and slept in the same tents. For the first time in their lives, the "enemy" became human. An Israeli girl said, "What the camp taught us about people is not to generalize but to seek out the human side, not the fearful and hating sides of our hearts." Learn how the group Seeking Common Ground accomplished this. Contact them at 51 Grape Street, Denver CO 80220; 303-388-4013.

WEEKDAY READINGS (Mo) Revelation 21:9 – 14; (Tu) 2 Thessalonians 2:1–17; (We) 3:6 – 18; (Th) 1 Corinthians 1:1– 9; (Fr) 1:17 – 25; (Sa) 1 Corinthians 1:26 – 31

READING I *Sirach 3:17–18, 20, 28–29*

My child, perform your tasks with humility;
then you will be loved
by those whom God accepts.
The greater you are,
the more you must humble yourself;
so you will find favor in the sight of the Lord.
For great is the might of the Lord;
but by the humble the Lord is glorified.
When calamity befalls the proud,
there is no healing,
for an evil plant has taken root in them.
The mind of the intelligent appreciates proverbs,
and an attentive ear is the desire of the wise.

READING II *Hebrews 12:18–19, 22–24*

You have not come to something that can be touched, a blazing fire, and darkness, and gloom, and a tempest, and the sound of a trumpet, and a voice whose words made the hearers beg that not another word be spoken to them. But you have come to Mount Zion and to the city of the living God, the heavenly Jerusalem, and to innumerable angels in festal gathering, and to the assembly of the firstborn who are enrolled in heaven, and to God the judge of all, and to the spirits of the righteous made perfect, and to Jesus, the mediator of a new covenant.

GOSPEL *Luke 14:1, 7–14*

On one occasion when Jesus was going to the house of a leader of the Pharisees to eat a meal on the sabbath, they were watching him closely. When he noticed how the guests chose the places of honor, he told them a parable. "When you are invited by someone to a wedding banquet, do not sit down at the place of honor, in case someone more distinguished than you has been invited by your host; and the host who invited both of you may come and say to you, 'Give this person your place,' and then in disgrace you would start to take the lowest place. But when you are invited, go and sit down at the lowest place, so that when your host comes, your host may say to you, 'Friend, move up higher'; then you will be honored in the presence of all who sit at the table with you. For all who exalt themselves will be humbled, and those who humble themselves will be exalted."

Jesus said also to the one who had invited him, "When you give a luncheon or a dinner, do not invite your friends or your brothers or your relatives or rich neighbors, in case they may invite you in return, and you would be repaid. But when you give a banquet, invite those who are poor, crippled, lame, and blind. And you will be blessed, because they cannot repay you, for you will be repaid at the resurrection of the righteous."

R E F L E C T I O N

The parable of the wedding feast uses social norms and the natural desire to be honored in order to make a point about humility. We all know the embarrassment of making a social blunder and having others notice. How especially unnerving it is for a guest to be told, "You are not as special as you think you are." Displaying a humble attitude in order to avoid such embarrassment and in the hope of greater honor is simply common sense. This would be especially true in the society reflected in the gospel, in which social status was clearly marked and determined one's behavior.

But Jesus indicates that he is not concerned with appearances. True humility is not simply taking a low seat in the hope of being honored. Instead, it is a matter of principle that those who exalt themselves will be humbled, while those who humble themselves will be exalted. The parable is no longer a lesson in etiquette but a statement of the reversal of the status quo, a theme we have seen brought to the fore repeatedly in this gospel.

After telling the parable, Jesus gives a lesson on hosting. Again, the normal social relationships are turned upside down. Rather than inviting friends and family, members of one's own social group, the host is instructed to invite those who cannot repay the favor. There is no generosity in offering hospitality to those who can repay it. Real generosity is being willing to give of oneself without ever receiving anything in return.

Although written for a different time and culture, these teachings have a timeless quality. How often we desire to be honored! Jesus tells us to seek humility with no thought of honor. How often we give gifts or extend invitations to those who do the same to us! This is simply an exchange of wealth, not true generosity. Jesus' words are demanding. They invite us to go beyond the norm, to a higher level of giving and of living.

■ **Our society often expects modesty and humility from women and boldness from men. Jesus does not differentiate. What are concrete ways in which people display genuine humility?**

■ **How often do you give gifts — material goods, money or your time — to those who will never repay you? Consider volunteering in a soup kitchen, hospital or homeless shelter or with another program that assists those in need.**

PRACTICE OF
FAITH

TEMPORAL AND ETERNAL. "You see, I dare not say to you, 'Give up everything.' Yet, if you will, you can give everything up even while keeping it, provided you handle temporal things in such a way that your whole mind is directed toward what is eternal" (Saint Gregory the Great, September 3).

The day of a funeral puts us right in the middle of the interplay of the ordinary things of our days and the extraordinary things of eternity. Eating, dressing and travel mingle with memories, thoughts and prayers for the dead and thoughts of our own lives and deaths.

Remember in prayer the dying and the dead. The last intercession each evening in Evening Prayer is always a prayer for the dead. Allow daily prayer for the dead to invite you to keep your "whole mind" on the eternal.

PRACTICE OF
HOPE

THE EXALTED. I don't know why I still get invited to dinner parties. I certainly blow it every time. I'm good at spotting the most important person in the room. Then I stalk them as they stand talking to other important people. At the right moment I leap forward and pounce. If I can drag away my prey, I hold it in conversation for as long as I can, no matter what. If the competition is too clingy, I try to make my kill right in their faces. What kills *me*, though, is that no one ever cares to prey on *me*. I've tried passive-aggressiveness. You know, humbling yourself in the hope of being exalted. It doesn't work. They just ignore you. What's the matter with me? What am I hoping for? Am I going to the wrong kinds of parties?

PRACTICE OF
CHARITY

FRIEND, MOVE UP HIGHER. Andy usually looked lonely, almost afraid. Melinda felt sorry for him. Then she happened to see him in the bandstand during the Summerfest. He was different: He was singing, in a clear, strong tenor voice. She would never have guessed he had such talent — hidden talent. Andy actually was quiet, uncomfortable with people. He found he could volunteer in a nursing home, where he was able to please and entertain his new friends. He used his talent — and he wasn't so lonely. Every person has talent, not earth-shaking talent, perhaps, but a gift of the spirit: a sense of humor, a gift of gab or gardening. Thank God today for your gifts. Share the talent, if you can. Find out about volunteer opportunities by looking under "Volunteer" in the Yellow Pages.

WEEKDAY READINGS (Mo) 1 Corinthians 2:1 – 5; (Tu) 2: 10 – 16; (We) 3:1 – 9; (Th) 3:18 – 23; (Fr) 4:1 – 5; (Sa) 4:6 – 15

READING I *Wisdom 9:13–18*

For who can learn the counsel of God?
Or who can discern what the Lord wills?
For the reasoning of mortals is worthless,
and our designs are likely to fail;
for a perishable body weighs down the soul,
and this earthy tent burdens the thoughtful mind.
We can hardly guess at what is on earth,
and what is at hand we find with labor;
but who has traced out what is in the heavens?
Who has learned your counsel,
unless you have given wisdom
and sent your holy spirit from on high?
And thus the paths of those on earth were set right,
and people were taught what pleases you,
and were saved by wisdom.

READING II *Philemon 8–17*

Though I am bold enough in Christ to command you to do your duty, yet I would rather appeal to you on the basis of love — and I, Paul, do this as an old man, and now also as a prisoner of Christ Jesus. I am appealing to you for my child, Onesimus, whose father I have become during my imprisonment. Formerly he was useless to you, but now he is indeed useful both to you and to me. I am sending him, that is, my own heart, back to you. I wanted to keep him with me, so that he might be of service to me in your place during my imprisonment for the gospel; but I preferred to do nothing without your consent, in order that your good deed might be voluntary and not something forced. Perhaps this is the reason Onesimus was separated from you for a while, so that you might have him back forever, no longer as a slave but more than a slave, a beloved brother — especially to me but how much more to you, both in the flesh and in the Lord.

So if you consider me your partner, welcome Onesimus as you would welcome me.
[Complete reading: Philemon 1–21]

GOSPEL *Luke 14:25–33*

Now large crowds were traveling with Jesus; and he turned and said to them, "Whoever comes to me and does not hate father and mother, spouse and children, brothers and sisters, yes, and even life itself, cannot be my disciple. Whoever does not carry the cross and follow me cannot be my disciple. For which of you, intending to build a tower, does not first sit down and estimate the cost, to see whether there is enough to complete it? Otherwise, when a foundation has been laid and the builder is not able to finish the building, all who see it will begin to ridicule the builder, saying, 'This person began to build and was not able to finish.' Or what king, going out to wage war against another king, will not sit down first and consider whether he is able with ten thousand to oppose the one who comes against him with twenty thousand? If he cannot, then, while the other is still far away, he sends a delegation and asks for the terms of peace. So therefore, none of you can become my disciple if you do not give up all your possessions."

Tuesday, September 8, 1998

BIRTH OF MARY

Micah 5:1–4 *She who is to give birth is born!*

Romans 8:28–30 *We share the image of Christ.*

Matthew 1:1–16, 18–23 *Of her, Jesus was born.*

The words mother — *mater* — and material — *matter* — are one and the same. In September, Mother Earth gives forth in fruitful abundance our material sustenance. And Mother Mary is born, who in her own fruitful body knit together earth and heaven.

REFLECTION

"Large crowds" were following Jesus, perhaps because of his teachings regarding the reversal of social positions. Such teachings would, of course, have been especially attractive to the poor and marginalized, and we can assume that the crowd consisted largely of people on the fringes of society. Here, rather than giving words of comfort, Jesus presents a bold challenge. To follow him requires "hating" one's family and even one's own life. This process of discipleship is certainly not easy!

The hatred mentioned in this gospel selection is not emotional hatred, the kind that is far too easy to adopt. Rather, it is the willingness to let go of these relationships, to relinquish them completely, in order to follow Jesus. The parallel reading in Matthew expresses it differently: "Whoever loves father or mother more than me is not worthy of me; and whoever loves son or daughter more than me is not worthy of me." But while the version in Matthew may clarify the meaning, let us not lose sight of the nature of Jesus' command: Discipleship requires absolute and total commitment. A primary challenge to this commitment comes not from the temptation to do what is clearly wrong but from the desire to be happy and comfortable. Jesus says that commitment is not comfortable. As we have seen before, it can create divisions. Commitment is never easy.

Discipleship requires prudent preparation and readiness, as the examples of Jesus illustrate. It cannot be a fad, something taken up lightly and then dropped when the going gets rough. It is always rough going. The message to the crowds following Jesus is that discipleship cannot be too popular. In fact, it can be spoken of in terms of a "cross," the Roman method of execution, comparable to the modern electric chair, and the method of torture that we know awaits Jesus. Finally, the cost of discipleship is financial as well. To journey with Jesus requires freedom to go where he goes. Possessions often get in the way of real freedom; they must be renounced.

■ **Do you have any possessions that would be difficult to relinquish? What relationships are important enough to you that they might interfere with the absolute demands of Jesus?**

■ **Can discipleship ever be reconciled with ordinary living?**

PRACTICE OF FAITH

SLAVE OF THE SLAVES. Saint Peter Claver (c. 1581 – 1654) spoke out, with actions and service, against the atrocity of racial hatred in his day. Peter Claver saw the affirmation or denial of personhood as an affirmation or denial of what already exists in each of us in Jesus Christ. In affirming personhood he was affirming the presence of Christ in the person.

There are big and small opportunities every day to either affirm or deny the personhood of others. We can start small with issues like not making fun of others from the safety of our homes and standing up for others who are being teased. Let us begin, in our homes, to watch our language and humor. Let us make sure our talk begins an affirmation, not a denial, of the personhood of others.

PRACTICE OF HOPE

THE ARCHITECT. My life is cluttered with unfinished building sites. Beautiful towers were meant to rise. I could see the pinnacles, the balconies, the flowered terraces, the gardens suspended in mid-air. People would wave at each other from one tower to the next, feeling lightness and love — a net of friendship extended through the air between all my beautiful towers. But alas, I failed. The ruins of limp elevations stand like decayed teeth, and flooded foundations scar the land. Maybe I'll build mud huts next. I'll ask my father and mother, my spouse and children and brothers and sisters — who all hate me — to help with the planning. Maybe we'll all move back together. Maybe a new net of friendship will form — this time on the earth, not in mid-air.

PRACTICE OF CHARITY

RENOUNCE ALL POSSESSIONS. A friend of mine switched careers late in life. His new social service position paid only half his previous salary. It irritated him. He saw younger, less experienced, less talented people making double what he made. It was quite vexing. He realized he had to make a decision: Either continue the painful comparative judgments or accept what he had chosen. He was startled when he made the adjustment and found that he was able to be at peace with himself. He could be content, not because he made more money or ceased improving at his work but because he altered his spirit, his attitude and his living habits. Shifting toward a simpler lifestyle made sense for him. Saint Elizabeth Seton said, "Let us live simply, that others may simply live."

WEEKDAY READINGS (Mo) 1 Corinthians 5:1 – 8; (Tu) Birth of Mary, see box; (We) 1 Corinthians 7:25 – 31; (Th) 8:1 – 13; (Fr) 9:16 – 27; (Sa) 10:14 – 22

READING I *Exodus 32:7–11, 13–14*

The LORD said to Moses, "Go down at once! Your people, whom you brought up out of the land of Egypt, have acted perversely; they have been quick to turn aside from the way that I commanded them; they have cast for themselves an image of a calf, and have worshiped it and sacrificed to it, and said, 'These are your gods, O Israel, who brought you up out of the land of Egypt!'" The LORD said to Moses, "I have seen this people, how stiff-necked they are. Now let me alone, so that my wrath may burn hot against them and I may consume them; and of you I will make a great nation."

But Moses implored the LORD his God, and said, "O LORD, why does your wrath burn hot against your people, whom you brought out of the land of Egypt with great power and with a mighty hand? Remember Abraham, Isaac, and Israel, your servants, how you swore to them by your own self, saying to them, 'I will multiply your descendants like the stars of heaven, and all this land that I have promised I will give to your descendants, and they shall inherit it forever.'" And the LORD relented concerning the disaster that had been planned for the chosen people.

[Complete reading: Exodus 32:7–14]

READING II *1 Timothy 1:12–17*

I am grateful to Christ Jesus our Lord, who has strengthened me, because he judged me faithful and appointed me to his service, even though I was formerly a blasphemer, a persecutor, and a man of violence. But I received mercy because I had acted ignorantly in unbelief, and the grace of our Lord overflowed for me with the faith and love that are in Christ Jesus. The saying is sure and worthy of full acceptance, that Christ Jesus came into the world to save sinners—of whom I am the foremost. But for that very reason I received mercy, so that in me, as the foremost, Jesus Christ might display the utmost patience, making me an example to those who would come to believe in him for eternal life. To the Sovereign of the ages, immortal, invisible, the only God, be honor and glory forever and ever. Amen.

GOSPEL *Luke 15:1–10*

Now all the tax collectors and sinners were coming near to listen to Jesus. And the Pharisees and the scribes were grumbling and saying, "This fellow welcomes sinners and eats with them."

So Jesus told them this parable: "Which man of you, having a hundred sheep and losing one of them, does not leave the ninety-nine in the wilderness and go after the one that is lost until he finds it? When he has found it, he lays it on his shoulders and rejoices. And when he comes home, he calls together his friends and neighbors, saying to them, 'Rejoice with me, for I have found my sheep that was lost.' Just so, I tell you, there will be more joy in heaven over one sinner who repents than over ninety-nine righteous persons who need no repentance.

"Or what woman of you having ten silver coins, if she loses one of them, does not light a lamp, sweep the house, and search carefully until she finds it? When she has found it, she calls together her friends and neighbors, saying, 'Rejoice with me, for I have found the coin that I had lost.' Just so, I tell you, there is joy in the presence of the angels of God over one sinner who repents."

[Complete reading: Luke 15:1–32]

Monday, September 14, 1998

HOLY CROSS

Numbers 21:4–9 *Whoever gazed on the serpent received life.*

Philippians 2:6–11 *He accepted death on a cross.*

John 3:13–17 *God so loved the world . . .*

As the darkness of another autumn lowers around us, we lift high the shining cross. The means of execution of a criminal has become the means of entering into eternal life. The wood of the cross is the ark that rescues us and the tree that feeds us.

REFLECTION

Today's gospel reading comments on value — the value of "sinners." For the Pharisees and scribes present, there is clearly no value to the others in Jesus' company: tax collectors, who are known as cheats and are despised for their role in "big government," and "sinners," presumably those unable or unwilling to abide by the commandments of Moses.

The parables of the lost sheep and the lost coin challenge the accepted value systems of Jesus' listeners. When one sheep is lost, the other ninety-nine are put at risk to save the wayward one. The woman searches diligently for her lost coin, perhaps creating chaos in the house in her efforts to find it. While the sheep and the coin themselves are of value, the process necessary to rescue or find them is great. Is it really worth it?

It is easy for us to acknowledge that all human beings have value. But it is far more pleasant and comfortable to spend time with people who do not make excessive demands on our time and resources. So often there is one child, one student, one colleague, one customer who requires an inordinate outlay of energy. It is easy to become resentful, to offer a rebuke or a plea for respite rather than a helping hand. But these are the lost sheep and the lost coins of the parables.

When one of the lost — the misguided, the sinners — repents, heaven rejoices. There is no cause for rejoicing in "converting" believers or in serving the undemanding. When an especially tough case proves successful, we, with the angels of God, rejoice.

The letter to Timothy expresses this truth regarding Paul. One who had persecuted the church, who was "foremost of sinners," was offered forgiveness and became an exceptional minister of the gospel.

■ **Are there people in your life who seem so needy, so demanding, that it is difficult to spend time with them? How do you deal with their demands?**

■ **Have you ever experienced a time when success followed an extreme amount of effort? Was your response similar to that of the shepherd and the woman, rejoicing far more over the outcome than you would over an easier success?**

PRACTICE OF FAITH

ORDINARY TIME. Parish and domestic faith communities can grow restless and inattentive during this long stretch of Ordinary Time. Often the people closest to the prayer and liturgy of the church speak of this as "down time." We try to invent ways to "liven things up." Actually, the beauty of this time is its duration, simplicity and exposition of the ordinary and everyday.

It is in paying attention to the rhythms and symbols of everyday life that we prepare to enter the extraordinary moments. Daily table prayer, repeated and ordinary, builds a memory bank to carry us into the special times in prayer and celebration. We form ourselves daily in the psalms so that our hearts and lips can readily proclaim them in the new light of Advent, Christmas, Lent or Easter.

PRACTICE OF HOPE

RESPONSORY. *God, come and help me. Lord hasten to rescue me.* For I am lost like a sheep in the wilderness. Night has fallen upon me, and the wolves have encircled me. Therefore I cry unto you: *God, come and help me.* I am alone in the midst of many people. I turn to my right, I turn to my left, and there is no one to hear my plea. Therefore I call unto you: *Lord, hasten to rescue me.* The sting of this loneliness I cannot bear any longer. My soul is like a hollow cave, and my body is chilled to the bone. Therefore I cry unto you: *God, come and help me. Lord hasten to rescue me.*

In the heart of darkness I seek for you, my beloved. In the dead of the night I will find you.

PRACTICE OF CHARITY

JOY IN HEAVEN. I was startled to see a little girl in her dance recital tutu in the parking lot outside my office window. Her mother was directing her to face the nearby building as she lifted her hands and twirled and dipped. She was dancing for her dad. He was watching from his jail-cell window. I do not know why her dad was in jail. Perhaps he, like Paul, was arrogant, or perhaps he was a man of violence. I do know that like most of us, he was the one sheep who strayed away from the ninety-nine. Our society currently jails more people than any other first-world country. Minority people are over-represented in jails. Consider visiting or teaching those who are imprisoned. It can be a rewarding experience.

WEEKDAY READINGS (Mo) Holy Cross, see box; (Tu) 1 Corinthians 12:12 – 31; (We) 12:31 — 13:13; (Th) 15:1 – 11; (Fr) 15:12 – 20; (Sa) 15:35 – 49

READING I *Amos 8:4–7*

Hear this, you that trample on the needy,
    and bring to ruin the poor of the land,
saying, "When will the new moon be over
    so that we may sell grain;
and the sabbath,
    so that we may offer wheat for sale?
We will make the ephah small and the shekel great,
    and practice deceit with false balances,
buying the poor for silver
    and the needy for a pair of sandals,
    and selling the sweepings of the wheat."
The LORD has sworn by the pride of Jacob:
Surely I will never forget any of their deeds.

READING II *1 Timothy 2:1–7*

First of all, then, I urge that supplications, prayers, intercessions, and thanksgivings be made for everyone, for rulers and all who are in high positions, so that we may lead a quiet and peaceable life in all godliness and dignity. This is right and is acceptable in the sight of God our Savior, who desires everyone to be saved and to come to the knowledge of the truth.

For there is one God; there is also one mediator between God and humankind, Christ Jesus, himself human, who gave himself a ransom for all—this was attested at the right time. For this I was appointed a herald and an apostle (I am telling the truth, I am not lying), a teacher of the Gentiles in faith and truth.

GOSPEL *Luke 16:1–13*

Then Jesus said to the disciples, "There was a rich man who had a manager, and charges were brought to him that this man was squandering his property. So the rich man summoned the manager and said to him, 'What is this that I hear about you? Give me an accounting of your management, because you cannot be my manager any longer.' Then the manager said to himself, 'What will I do, now that my master is taking the position away from me? I am not strong enough to dig, and I am ashamed to beg. I have decided what to do so that, when I am dismissed as manager, people may welcome me into their homes.' So, summoning his master's debtors one by one, the manager asked the first, 'How much do you owe my master?' The debtor answered, 'A hundred jugs of olive oil.' He said, 'Take your bill, sit down quickly, and make it fifty.' Then the manager asked another, 'And how much do you owe?' That debtor replied, 'A hundred containers of wheat.' He said, 'Take your bill and make it eighty.' And his master commended the dishonest manager because he had acted shrewdly; for the children of this age are more shrewd in dealing with their own generation than are the children of light. And I tell you, make friends for yourselves by means of dishonest wealth so that when it is gone, they may welcome you into the eternal homes.

"Whoever is faithful in a very little is faithful also in much; and whoever is dishonest in a very little is dishonest also in much. If then you have not been faithful with the dishonest wealth, who will entrust to you the true riches? And if you have not been faithful with what belongs to another, who will give you what is your own? No slave can serve two masters; for a slave will either hate the one and love the other, or be devoted to the one and despise the other. You cannot serve God and wealth."

REFLECTION

While today's selection from the prophet Amos is clear, the gospel reading is extremely difficult to understand. Amos criticizes business owners for their concentration, even during religious observances, on returning to work to make money. And it is not simply earning a living that is their goal; they intend to cheat their customers, taking advantage especially of the poor.

The gospel also discusses wealth, its use, misuse and ultimate (lack of) value. Jesus tells a story about a rich man, probably an absentee landlord, who leases his property to sharecroppers and hires a manager to oversee the operation, collect rent and distribute the proceeds from the crop. The owner learns that the manager is failing in his duties and fires him; the manager, concerned that he will be unable to find work, finds a way to provide for his future by rewriting the tenants' debts and thus securing their gratitude and favor. It is not clear exactly what is involved here; perhaps the owner had charged excessive fees or interest and the manager was correcting this, or perhaps the manager was relinquishing his right to his own commission.

The owner (or Jesus? — the term "master" could apply to either one) praises the manager for his shrewdness in securing his future, but it is unclear if the manager (called "manager of wickedness" or "dishonesty") did so through his own dishonesty or through setting right a wrong committed by the owner. Either way, Jesus uses him as a model and indicates that such dealings with money, shunned by "children of the light," are possible for the "children of this world."

The point is that wealth can be used shrewdly, probably by almsgiving, in order to "make friends" who will have a say in eternal matters. While possessions are tainted with "wickedness," they are also things people rely on (this is the meaning of "mammon") in order to live. Wealth can be used for good, but is not good in itself; as with human relationships and obligations, wealth is worthless when compared to commitment to God. Again, the gospel claims that one cannot be too devoted to possessions and remain devoted to God.

■ **Does today's gospel add anything to what has already been said about wealth?**

■ **Do you see any situations in the world today which resemble that illustrated by Amos?**

PRACTICE OF FAITH

FOLLOW ME. "Matthew got up and followed him." Matthew (September 21) found the gift of dignity in the act of following, of going behind another. He followed Jesus and in Jesus found his dignity.

Many children equate following with copying and find both undesirable. They gather from some of us adults that following is demeaning and that the goal should always be first place, not second. Children often become irritated with a younger one who, out of unabashed admiration, "copies everything I do." They find it embarrassing to be imitated.

Let us applaud and learn from the followers in our households. From the copy-ers let us learn the dignity in imitating something or someone good. Let us step back and say thank you to the people who lift us up by following or imitating us.

PRACTICE OF HOPE

CHILDREN OF THE LIGHT. It is hard to be faithful to the living, the children of this world. But I practice. I practice being faithful to the dead. I visit their graves and carry them in my heart and mind. I remember what gifts they brought to me before they crossed the threshold. Even now, the dead are giving their gifts. Ever loving, they reach out to me from beyond. They are the children of the light. They are the best teachers I have. From them I learn the lessons of life. When the time comes, they whisper into my ear: "You have been faithful in little. It is time now to be faithful in much. Remember the riches entrusted to you. Assume your stewardship. And remember what master you serve." The faithfulness of the dead can move me to tears.

PRACTICE OF CHARITY

TRAMPLE THE NEEDY. When Paul Blough was asked why he chose to continue his obstetrics practice in Haiti rather than enjoy his comfortable retirement, he said, "I guess I ran out of excuses. My family was raised, my wife had died, and I was still healthy. And I didn't have any reason not to go where help was so badly needed." Dr. Blough's "hospital" is one large room, windows open to a busy street, with one cold-water faucet. Why is Haiti so poor while the United States is so rich? Major corporations systematically relocate to areas of the world where labor is cheapest. The astute corporate manager of today must truly anguish about serving two masters. Catholic Relief Services seeks to help those in need around the globe. Contact them at 209 West Lafayette St., Baltimore MD 21021-3443; 800-736-3467.

WEEKDAY READINGS (Mo) Ephesians 4:1 – 13; (Tu) Proverbs 21:1 – 13; (We) 30:5 – 9; (Th) Ecclesiastes 1:2 – 11; (Fr) 3:1 – 11; (Sa) 11:9 — 12:8

AUTUMN ORDINARY TIME

Behold! The harvest!

The Lord brings us back to Zion,
we are like dreamers,
laughing, dancing,
with songs on our lips.

Other nations say,
"A new world of wonders!
The Lord is with them."
Yes, God works wonders.
Rejoice! Be glad!

Lord, bring us back
as water to thirsty land.
Those sowing in tears
reap, singing and laughing.

They left weeping, weeping,
casting the seed.
They come back singing, singing,
holding high the harvest.

— Psalm 126

What tears you cry,
sower God, over us all.
But how you laugh in amazement
and what songs you sing
when there is some harvest.
Your saints from Adam and Eve,
from Moses and Miriam,
from Mary and Joseph,
until our own grandparents and parents,
and we too,
need your tears
and long to hear your laughter.
Harvest us home to sing your praise
forever and ever.

— Prayer of the Season

READING I *Amos 6:1, 4–7*

Alas for those who are at ease in Zion,
   and for those who feel secure on Mount Samaria,
Alas for those who lie on beds of ivory,
   and lounge on their couches,
and eat lambs from the flock,
   and calves from the stall;
who sing idle songs to the sound of the harp,
   and like David improvise on instruments
      of music;
who drink wine from bowls,
   and anoint themselves with the finest oils,
      but are not grieved over the ruin of Joseph!
Therefore they shall now be the first to go into exile,
   and the revelry of the loungers shall pass away.

READING II *1 Timothy 6:11–16*

As for you, who are of God, pursue righteousness, godliness, faith, love, endurance, gentleness. Fight the good fight of the faith; take hold of the eternal life, to which you were called and for which you made the good confession in the presence of many witnesses. In the presence of God, who gives life to all things, and of Christ Jesus, who in his testimony before Pontius Pilate made the good confession, I charge you to keep the commandment without spot or blame until the manifestation of our Lord Jesus Christ, which God will bring about at the right time — God who is the blessed and only Sovereign, the Ruler of rulers and Lord of lords. It is God alone who has immortality and dwells in unapproachable light, whom no one has ever seen or can see; to God be honor and eternal dominion. Amen.
[Complete reading: 1 Timothy 6:6–19]

GOSPEL *Luke 16:19–31*

Jesus said: "There was a rich man who was dressed in purple and fine linen and who feasted sumptuously every day. And at his gate lay a poor man named Lazarus, covered with sores, who longed to satisfy his hunger with what fell from the rich man's table; even the dogs would come and lick his sores. The poor man died and was carried away by the angels to be with Abraham. The rich man also died and was buried. In Hades, where the rich man was being tormented, he looked up and saw Abraham far away with Lazarus by his side. He called out, 'Father Abraham, have mercy on me, and send Lazarus to dip the tip of his finger in water and cool my tongue; for I am in agony in these flames.' But Abraham said, 'Child, remember that during your lifetime you received your good things, and Lazarus in like manner evil things; but now he is comforted here, and you are in agony. Besides all this, between you and us a great chasm has been fixed, so that those who might want to pass from here to you cannot do so, and no one can cross from there to us.' The rich man said, 'Then, father, I beg you to send Lazarus to my father's house — for I have five brothers — that he may warn them, so that they will not also come into this place of torment.' Abraham replied, 'They have Moses and the prophets; your brothers should listen to them.' He said, 'No, father Abraham; but if someone goes to them from the dead, they will repent.' Abraham said to him, 'If they do not listen to Moses and the prophets, neither will they be convinced even if someone rises from the dead.'"

Tuesday, September 29, 1998

THE ARCHANGELS MICHAEL, GABRIEL AND RAPHAEL

Daniel 7:9–10, 13–14 *A thousand thousand wait upon God.*

Revelation 12:7–12 *The warrior Michael defeated the dragon.*

John 1:47–51 *You will see heaven open and angels descend.*

The transition from summer to autumn represents the battle of sin and death against the kingdom of heaven. Jesus himself uses this mythological language to describe the reality of his battle against evil. And Christ conquers: Michael defeats the dragon, Gabriel announces the kingdom, and Raphael heals the wounded.

R E F L E C T I O N

Just as our Jewish friends are preparing to bring to a close their High Holy Days with Wednesday's feast of Yom Kippur, so also we read a story of repentance — albeit delayed until after death. This story contrasts wealth and poverty, privilege and necessity, but also concentrates on the divisions among people, even those in close physical proximity. The wealthy man had all he needed, and he feasted daily with no regard for the desperate plight of the destitute man at the gate to his property. Surely the rich man knew of Lazarus but did not see it as his responsibility to be concerned with a lowly beggar for whom even the dogs had contempt. He placed a chasm between himself and Lazarus; because of his wealth and his social standing, he was unwilling to treat Lazarus as a human being deserving respect.

After death, the gulf between these two characters widens. But their status is reversed. The rich man had failed to exercise justice, failed to share his blessings. His appeal to Abraham, with whom Lazarus resides, is met with the response that he has already enjoyed blessings in abundance; it is now Lazarus's turn to have comfort. The rich man appears to regret his earlier life and implores Abraham for his brothers, but he still does not entirely understand where his concerns should lie. Abraham's response is telling: The law of Moses and the words of the prophets tell all that anyone needs in order to know how to live justly. With the Jewish people reside not only God's promises but complete instructions for right living.

The closing statements of the parable are a clear commentary on Jesus' death and resurrection and on the disbelief of many people, known to the community of the author, regarding the Christian claims about Jesus. Perhaps the tradition that Jesus had raised Lazarus from the dead, told only in the Gospel of John, was known to this author and influenced the choice of name for the poor man. At any rate, those who are unwilling to recognize the truths of the traditions of Moses and the prophets will be unwilling also to recognize the truth of life offered in Christ.

■ **Look around you. Are there people in your country, state or community, perhaps even your neighborhood, who are in desperate need? How can you narrow the chasm that exists between you and them? How can you share of your wealth and recognize them as God's children to be loved and respected?**

PRACTICE OF FAITH

SPIRITUAL CHILDHOOD. The youth of Saint Thérèse of the Child Jesus (October 1) yielded a gift of mature faith for the church. It was a faith that Thérèse always sustained in reading and in prayer. In her time of spiritual darkness she pinned a piece of paper with the words of the Creed on it inside her habit.

The faith and prayer lives of young people can still amaze us. We can provide the tools and opportunities for the nourishment of faith in our young people. Have available in your household the simplified formats of Morning and Evening Prayer, Catholic prayer books, individual Bibles for the bedrooms and books on the lives of the saints. Put a copy of the Creed near the baptismal candles or other places of prayer.

PRACTICE OF HOPE

DIVINE COMPASSION. If I were Lazarus and saw the rich man tormented in Hades, I wouldn't be able to bear it. I would wrest myself from Abraham's bosom and cry: "Father Abraham, I cannot rejoice, because I see my brother in torment in this fire!"

"But my child, don't you remember? He is the rich man who scoffed at you while you were lying in misery at his gates. He deserves this punishment."

"But Father, will his suffering end, as mine did?"

"No, my child, for no one may cross the chasm between him and us."

"Then, Father, this is not heaven to me. For what power could be more divine than compassion?"

"Lazarus, quit talking nonsense and tell me straight: Why should this wretch deserve a second chance?"

"Because, Father Abraham, he allowed me to feed on whatever fell from his table."

PRACTICE OF CHARITY

LAZARUS IN POVERTY. When Brian and Betsy married, they vowed to live simply. Fifteen years later, they persist. They and their two children live in a tiny Iowa town in the midst of farmers who struggle to stave off the encroachment of corporate farms. Brian and Betsy met while providing hospitality at the Catholic Worker House in Davenport. Their commitment seems to conform to Amos's call to counter the luxuries so many seek and to Paul's call to find a gentle spirit. The Catholic Worker movement fosters simplicity and hospitality and puts out an interesting newspaper. Subscribe to it for a penny a copy: The Catholic Worker, 36 East First Street, New York NY 10003.

WEEKDAY READINGS (Mo) Job 1:6 – 22; (Tu) Archangels, see box; (We) Job 9:1 – 16; (Th) 19:21 – 27; (Fr) 38:1, 12 – 21; 40:35; (Sa) 42:1 – 17

READING I *Habakkuk 1:1–4; 2:1–4*

The oracle that the prophet Habakkuk saw.
O LORD, how long shall I cry for help,
 and you will not listen?
Or cry to you "Violence!"
 and you will not save?
Why do you make me see wrong-doing
 and look at trouble?
Destruction and violence are before me;
 strife and contention arise.
So the law becomes slack
 and justice never prevails.
The wicked surround the righteous —
 therefore judgment comes forth perverted.
I will stand at my watchpost,
 and station myself on the rampart;
I will keep watch to see what the LORD
 will say to me,
 and what the LORD will answer
 concerning my complaint.
Then the LORD answered me and said:
Write the vision;
 make it plain on tablets,
 so that a runner may read it.
For there is still a vision for the appointed time;
 it speaks of the end, and does not lie.
If it seems to tarry, wait for it;
 it will surely come, it will not delay.
Look at the proud!
 Their spirit is not right in them,
 but the righteous live by their faith.

READING II *2 Timothy 1:6–14*

I remind you to rekindle the gift of God that is within you through the laying on of my hands; for God did not give us a spirit of cowardice, but rather a spirit of power and of love and of self-discipline.

Do not be ashamed, then, of the testimony about our Lord or of me his prisoner, but join with me in suffering for the gospel, relying on the power of God, who saved us and called us with a holy calling, not according to our works but according to God's own purpose and grace. This grace was given to us in Christ Jesus before the ages began, but it has now been revealed through the appearing of our Savior Christ Jesus, who abolished death and brought life and immortality to light through the gospel. For this gospel I was appointed a herald and an apostle and a teacher, and for this reason I suffer as I do. But I am not ashamed, for I know the one in whom I have put my trust. I am sure that God is able to guard until that day everything that I have entrusted to God. Hold to the standard of sound teaching that you have heard from me, in the faith and love that are in Christ Jesus. Guard the good treasure entrusted to you, with the help of the Holy Spirit living in us.
[Complete reading: 2 Timothy 1:1–14]

GOSPEL *Luke 17:5–10*

The apostles said to the Lord, "Increase our faith!" The Lord replied, "If you had faith the size of a mustard seed, you could say to this mulberry tree, 'Be uprooted and planted in the sea,' and it would obey you.

"Who among you would say to your slave who has just come in from plowing or tending sheep in the field, 'Come here at once and take your place at the table'? Would you not rather say, 'Prepare supper for me, put on your apron and serve me while I eat and drink; later you may eat and drink'? Do you thank the slave for doing what was commanded? So you also, when you have done all that you were ordered to do, say, 'We are worthless slaves; we have done only what we ought to have done!'"

REFLECTION

Jesus, or perhaps the author of the Gospel of Luke, often used earthy, familiar images to convey a message. In today's gospel passage, Jesus speaks about seeds that grow into trees and the social stratification of slavery, which was well-known in first-century Palestine. In the first instance, Jesus offers both reassurance and challenge to his disciples, who were seeking to increase their faith: Even a tiny amount of faith can do spectacular things. Surely they had enough for the challenges facing them, yet they would be able to do even more if their faith were to grow.

The second story is a clear lesson on discipleship. It is the responsibility of the follower of Jesus to serve others. No thanks are required or ought to be expected. Serving God's community should not entitle one to special treatment; service is required of one entrusted with the promises of life given by God.

The Second Letter to Timothy conveys further teachings on ministry. This letter purports to have been written by Paul to his friend and colleague Timothy, the leader of a local Christian community. To Timothy has been given the gift of the Spirit in the laying on of hands; the power of physical touch is recognized and advocated. This Spirit gives courage and love, but most of all this Spirit is dynamic, moving, powerful, able to move mountains. This is the "reward" of having faith and of serving God and God's people — the power of God's Spirit, active within a person.

What is troubling about today's readings is not the lack of thanks to be expected by disciples but rather the metaphor of slavery that is used to convey this message. The Gospel of Luke has no place for social hierarchy. It is odd that this author would present Jesus — the advocate of the poor and marginalized, the one who continually proclaims a reversal of social roles — as one who upholds the treatment of slaves. Although we can be assured that slavery was common, and we know that the metaphor expresses well the message of service for the sake of service, it makes us uncomfortable. From what we read in the rest of the gospel, it should.

■ **Have you ever witnessed the immense power of faith or the movement of the Spirit in your community? Share stories of this experience with others.**

■ **What do you think of the idea that serving God requires no gratitude?**

PRACTICE OF FAITH

CHERISH. The memorial of Our Lady of the Rosary on October 7 "invites all to meditate upon the mysteries of Christ." Through Mary we are brought into the full story of incarnation, passion and resurrection.

The invitation in Mary and the rosary is to meditate, reflect and slow down. One of the gifts of repetitive prayer is the invitation to pause and allow the words and rhythm to bring us closer to the mystery. Being open to growth in mystery requires patient listening. Lifting the words from memory to meditation requires patient listening.

Check the pace of your prayer. Determine if you need to slow down to hear the words and the story and mysteries behind them. Try to listen like Mary when she would "hear the word of God and cherish it in her heart."

PRACTICE OF HOPE

A MATTER OF FAITH. "This is just like the Master. 'Increase our faith,' we asked — straightforward enough. And he tells us about mustard seeds and uprooted trees! Honestly, I don't know what to make of it. But Bartholomew here has taken it literally. He's been sitting in front of this sycamore tree for days, trying to uproot it by the power of his faith. Nothing happens, of course, except that people come to stare at us. Who cares about stupid trees anyway? Do we need faith to attempt what is both impossible and absurd? C'mon, Bart, get off it. You're disgracing us all with this foolishness!"

"Hold it, Thomas, and listen to what I learned from the tree: What is more difficult — moving a sycamore tree or saying to the judgment and impatience of your heart, 'Be rooted up and be planted in the sea'?

PRACTICE OF CHARITY

VIOLENCE, STRIFE AND DISCORD. Nearly half the homeless families in this country have been victims of domestic violence. They plead in the words of Habakkuk: "I cry for help and you will not listen." Fortunately for people like Sandra, who rescued herself and her five children from an abusive partner, shelters are available. For others, the safety of a shelter is far away and filled to capacity. Sandra was able to obtain emergency housing, welfare benefits and job training so that she is now able to provide stability and support for her children. Her faith was an essential ingredient in her recovery, but if other women had not understood and supported her, her story would not have ended happily. Contact your local domestic violence coalition or volunteer at your local safehouse.

WEEKDAY READINGS (Mo) Galatians 1:6–12; (Tu) 1:13–24; (We) 2:1–14; (Th) 3:1–5; (Fr) 3:7–14; (Sa) 3:22–29

READING I *2 Kings 5:1–3, 7–17*

Naaman, commander of the army of the king of Aram, was a great man and in high favor with his master, because by him the LORD had given victory to Aram. The man, though a mighty warrior, suffered from leprosy. Now the Arameans on one of their raids had taken a young girl captive from the land of Israel, and she served Naaman's wife. She said to her mistress, "If only my lord were with the prophet who is in Samaria! He would cure him of his leprosy."

When the king of Israel read the letter, he tore his clothes and said, "Am I God, to give death or life, that this man sends word to me to cure a man of his leprosy? Just look and see how he is trying to pick a quarrel with me."

But when Elisha the man of God heard that the king of Israel had torn his clothes, he sent a message to the king, "Why have you torn your clothes? Let him come to me, that he may learn that there is a prophet in Israel." So Naaman came with his horses and chariots, and halted at the entrance of Elisha's house. Elisha sent a messenger to him, saying, "Go, wash in the Jordan seven times, and your flesh shall be restored and you shall be clean." But Naaman became angry and went away, saying, "I thought that for me he would surely come out, and stand and call on the name of the LORD his God, and would wave his hand over the spot, and cure the leprosy! Are not Abana and Pharpar, the rivers of Damascus, better than all the waters of Israel? Could I not wash in them, and be clean?" He turned and went away in a rage. But his servants approached and said to him, "Father, if the prophet had commanded you to do something difficult, would you not have done it? How much more, when all he said to you was, 'Wash, and be clean'?" So he went down and immersed himself seven times in the Jordan, according to the word of the man of God; his flesh was restored like the flesh of a little child, and he was clean.

Then Naaman returned to the man of God, he and all his company; he came and stood before Elisha and said, "Now I know that there is no God in all the earth except in Israel; please accept a present from your servant."

But Elisha said, "As the LORD lives, whom I serve, I will accept nothing!" Naaman urged Elisha to accept, but he refused. Then Naaman said, "If not, please let two mule-loads of earth be given to your servant; for your servant will no longer offer burnt offering or sacrifice to any god except the LORD."

READING II *2 Timothy 2:8–13*

Remember Jesus Christ, raised from the dead, a descendant of David—that is my gospel, for which I suffer hardship, even to the point of being chained like a criminal. But the word of God is not chained. Therefore I endure everything for the sake of the elect, so that they may also obtain the salvation that is in Christ Jesus, with eternal glory. The saying is sure:

If we have died with Christ,
    we will also live with Christ;
if we endure, we will also reign with Christ;
if we deny him, he will also deny us;
if we are faithless, he remains faithful—
for Christ cannot deny himself.

[Complete reading: 2 Timothy 2:8–15]

GOSPEL *Luke 17:11–19*

On the way to Jerusalem Jesus was going through the region between Samaria and Galilee. As he entered a village, ten people who had leprosy approached him. Keeping their distance, they called out, saying, "Jesus, Master, have mercy on us!" When he saw them, he said to them, "Go and show yourselves to the priests." And as they went, they were made clean. Then one of them, when he saw that he was healed, turned back, praising God with a loud voice. He prostrated himself at Jesus' feet and thanked him. And he was a Samaritan. Then Jesus asked, "Were not ten made clean? But the other nine, where are they? Was none of them found to return and give praise to God except this foreigner?" Then Jesus said to the Samaritan, "Get up and go on your way; your faith has made you well."

REFLECTION

Even though followers of Christ are not to expect gratitude for sharing the good news entrusted to them, as we saw last week, this does not mean that no gratitude is necessary. What is important in giving thanks is the recognition of the one from whom all things come; it is fitting to give thanks to God.

In the first reading, Elisha cures the foreigner Naaman of leprosy but refuses to accept a gift of gratitude. Elisha realizes that he has been acting as an agent for God and will not be compensated. What is most significant in this passage, however, is that it is one outside the bounds of faith that characterized Israel who was able to recognize the sovereignty and uniqueness of Israel's God.

So too, in the story of the ten lepers healed by Jesus, it was only the Samaritan who returned to thank Jesus for cleansing him. Jesus had given them all directions to follow the Mosaic law for the cleansing of leprosy; the nine were simply following his instructions. But the tenth one, the outsider, the member of a community despised by most Jews, recognized the hand of God in the healing and made obeisance at Jesus' feet in order to give thanks. The one from a community understood to be mistaken about God's relationship with the chosen people, the one who did not have the words of the prophets for instruction, who did not worship in the holy city of Jerusalem — this was the one who was able to see clearly the significance and origin of what had occurred and to give thanks. This, says Jesus, is faith.

Acknowledging the truth is not restricted to those who are highly educated or come from a particular religious or ethnic community. What matters is recognizing the truth and proclaiming it, regardless of one's background. Part of that truth is the knowledge of the source of all goodness and the willingness to express gratefulness to the one God.

■ **Can you recall an instance when someone you least expected was able to recognize and proclaim the truth? How can you be more open to the truth, wherever it is proclaimed?**

■ **Reread the second reading. What are the characteristics of faith? What would be involved in denying one's faith?**

PRACTICE OF FAITH

THE PATH. According to Saint Teresa of Avila (October 15), the path of truth is walked by placing oneself in "God's hands." To find this path, Saint Teresa says she "carefully considered the lives of some of the saints, the great contemplatives, and found that they took no other path: Francis, Anthony of Padua, Bernard, Catherine of Siena."

This is the path of a woman honored by the church with the title of Doctor. This Doctor of the Church learned by considering the example of others. Allow the names and stories of the saints to become household words by celebrating their days. Children are well versed in the names and stories of sports heroes because of their daily interaction and conversation about them. Let us enrich, in daily interaction and conversation, the circle of heroes to include the heroes of God and the church.

PRACTICE OF HOPE

LEPERS. In the face of decaying flesh, the voice of the poet grows husky. At the sight of failing eyes, the power of words wanes. Christ, where is your power now? Who walks among the lepers? Who touches the untouchable? Who will see nothing but their own fear and judgment, the revulsion of creeping death and inglorious suffering? Beware, my untouchable soul! The suffering you see is a poisonous mist that blinds you to the eye of the sufferer. There is light inside the failing body. There is a spirit in contest. There is a learner studying in cold sweat through sleepless nights. O Christ, make me bear the touch of the leper. Show forth your healing power in the agony of our meeting.

PRACTICE OF CHARITY

THE WORD OF GOD CANNOT BE CHAINED. A barber on a busy street in Denver has warned reformers that their efforts to gentrify the area will actually leave them lesser people, sheltered and protected from life's realities, impoverished in spirit by their desire to impose uniformity in the name of protecting their children. What happens, he insists, is that the children are raised in an unreal world and become ill-prepared to meet life's challenges. In today's reading, Naaman immerses himself seven times in order to be cured. The leper is a despised Samaritan. Diversity and understanding are as essential today as in biblical times. Suburbs and cities need to communicate. It could unchain the word of God and heal some of the leprosy of our society.

WEEKDAY READINGS (Mo) Galatians 4:22 — 5:1; (Tu) 5:1 – 6; (We) 5:18 – 25; (Th) Ephesians 1:1 – 10; (Fr) 1:11 – 14; (Sa) 1:15 – 23

READING I *Exodus 17:8–13*

Amalek came and fought with Israel at Rephidim. Moses said to Joshua, "Choose some men for us and go out, fight with Amalek. Tomorrow I will stand on the top of the hill with the staff of God in my hand." So Joshua did as Moses told him, and fought with Amalek, while Moses, Aaron, and Hur went up to the top of the hill. Whenever Moses held up his hand, Israel prevailed; and whenever he lowered his hand, Amalek prevailed. But Moses' hands grew weary; so they took a stone and put it under him, and he sat on it. Aaron and Hur held up his hands, one on one side, and the other on the other side; so his hands were steady until the sun set. And Joshua defeated Amalek and his people with the sword.

READING II *2 Timothy 3:14 — 4:5*

But as for you, continue in what you have learned and firmly believed, knowing from whom you learned it, and how from childhood you have known the sacred writings that are able to instruct you for salvation through faith in Christ Jesus. All scripture is inspired by God and is useful for teaching, for reproof, for correction, and for training in righteousness, so that everyone who belongs to God may be proficient, equipped for every good work.

In the presence of God and of Christ Jesus, who is to judge the living and the dead, and in view of Christ's appearing and his dominion, I solemnly urge you: proclaim the message; be persistent whether the time is favorable or unfavorable; convince, rebuke, and encourage, with the utmost patience in teaching. For the time is coming when people will not put up with sound doctrine, but having itching ears, they will accumulate for themselves teachers to suit their own desires, and will turn away from listening to the truth and wander away to myths. As for you, always be sober, endure suffering, do the work of an evangelist, carry out your ministry fully.

GOSPEL: *Luke 18:1–8*

Then Jesus told them a parable about their need to pray always and not to lose heart. He said, "In a certain city there was a judge who neither feared God nor had respect for people. In that city there was a widow who kept coming to him and saying, 'Grant me justice against my opponent.' For a while the judge refused; but later he said to himself, 'Though I have no fear of God and no respect for anyone, yet because this widow keeps bothering me, I will grant her justice, so that she may not wear me out by continually coming.'"

And the Lord said, "Listen to what the unjust judge says. And will not God grant justice to God's own elect who are crying out day and night? Will God delay long in helping them? I tell you, God will quickly grant justice to them. And yet, when the Son-of-Man comes, will he find faith on earth?"

R E F L E C T I O N

Today's gospel selection was written as a response to questions regarding the delay of the eagerly awaited return of Jesus to establish the final reign of God. Placed on Jesus' lips is an assurance that it is necessary to persist and never to give up hope. Preceding this passage are words of Jesus indicating that the reign of God cannot be readily observed; the coming of the Son of Humanity will be sudden, without warning.

The reading begins by telling us the meaning of the parable from the outset. Constant prayer and confidence in God's promises are necessary. The story unfolds to show us two figures. One is a widow, among the most vulnerable in society, who has been wronged and seeks justice. The other is a judge, powerful and respected, who has an obligation to protect "widows and orphans" and to dispense justice. The judge refuses to do his job, proclaiming respect neither for God nor for the community. It is only when he is embarrassed by the woman for all to see (literally, "given a black eye"!), and his status is threatened, that he relents.

Just as the widow persisted, so also are God's chosen ones to beseech God and to await God's justice. For the time is coming even though it may not have occurred yet.

Patience and persistence. These are at the heart of all the readings today. Patience and persistence were able to ensure victory for the Israelites at the hands of Joshua. In the second reading, the minister of the gospel is to persist in the faith, knowing what is true and refusing to be swayed by false teachers, while patience must be shown to members of the community.

Patience and persistence. They seem to be at odds with one another. One requires a certain inactivity, a waiting. The other involves active insistence, a righteous indignation at inaction. For the Christian the message is this: Wait for God. But don't stop asking, trusting that God hears.

■ **How would you characterize your personal prayer life? Of the various types of prayer — praise, thanksgiving, petition, contrition — which figures most prominently in your time with God? What do you think of the instruction to persist in beseeching God? For what do you pray?**

PRACTICE OF FAITH

THE LORD'S PRAYER. "If you study every word of the petitions of scripture, you will find, I think, nothing that is not contained and included in the Lord's Prayer." Saint Augustine in his letter to Proba speaks of prayer, petition and the Lord's Prayer. The Office of Readings from the Liturgy of the Hours this week invites us each day, in the second reading, which is taken from this letter, to grow in petition and the Lord's Prayer.

See if you can get your hands on Augustine's letter to Proba; consider it with household members who are old enough for the discussion. Include the Lord's Prayer in your daily family and table prayers. This is a prayer that travels well between your home and church communities.

PRACTICE OF HOPE

PERSISTENCE IN GRATITUDE. "I've had it with this beseeching business. I've done it for the longest time, and I'm sick of it. If I were the unrighteous judge, I would lean out my window and throw soda cans at that whining wretch on my doorstep until she gave up and my peace was restored."

Impressed with the violence of my imaginary outburst, I fixed a "no whining" sign on my rosary and tried to pray without asking for anything. It was very hard, but a remarkable thing happened. I began to feel *gratitude* for all kinds of things that had escaped me before: being alive, seeing a zebra-shaped cloud in the sky, having an adversary and an uncooperative judge who keep me on my toes. If I ever get whiny again, I'll know what to do so that I don't lose heart!

PRACTICE OF CHARITY

DON'T WEAR ME OUT. The image of Moses having his tired arms held aloft suggests that perhaps God has a sense of humor. Why else would God order a situation in which life depended on Moses' arms being elevated? The humor may not have occurred to those in the midst of the battle, but seeing the big picture helps. Humor is essential for a healthy life. Paul says to preach whether it's convenient or inconvenient. Don't you wish that sometimes he would lighten up? He says, "Proclaim with the utmost patience." There may be some humor there. Maybe Jesus' story includes a touch of irony, if not humor: "This widow is wearing me out." A follower of Christ could not be equipped for every good work without humor. Keep a healthy perspective, and look for signs of humor this week.

WEEKDAY READINGS (Mo) Ephesians 2:1–10; (Tu) 2:12–22; (We) 3:2–12; (Th) 3:14–21; (Fr) 4:1–6; (Sa) 4:7–16

READING I *Sirach 35:12–17*

Give to the Most High
    as the Most High has given to you,
  and as generously as you can afford.
For the Lord is the one who repays,
  and will repay you sevenfold.
Do not offer the Lord a bribe,
    for the Lord will not accept it;
  and do not rely on a dishonest sacrifice;
for the Lord is the judge,
  with whom there is no partiality.
The Lord will not show partiality to the poor,
  but will listen to the prayer
    of one who is wronged.
The Lord will not ignore the supplication
    of the orphan,
  or the widow when she pours out her complaint.

READING II *2 Timothy 4:6–8, 16–18*

As for me, I am already being poured out as a libation, and the time of my departure has come. I have fought the good fight, I have finished the race, I have kept the faith. From now on there is reserved for me the crown of righteousness, which the Lord, the righteous judge, will give me on that day, and not only to me but also to all who have longed for his appearing.

    At my first defense no one came to my support, but all deserted me. May it not be counted against them! But the Lord stood by me and gave me strength, so that through me the message might be fully proclaimed and all the Gentiles might hear it. So I was rescued from the lion's mouth. The Lord will rescue me from every evil attack and save me for the dominion of heaven. To the Lord be the glory forever and ever. Amen.

GOSPEL *Luke 18:9–14*

Jesus also told this parable to some who trusted in themselves that they were righteous and regarded others with contempt: "Two men went up to the temple to pray, one a Pharisee and the other a tax collector. The Pharisee, standing by himself, was praying thus, 'God, I thank you that I am not like other people: thieves, rogues, adulterers, or even like this tax collector. I fast twice a week; I give a tenth of all my income.' But the tax collector, standing far off, would not even look up to heaven, but was beating his breast and saying, 'God, be merciful to me, a sinner!' I tell you, this man went down to his home justified rather than the other; for all who exalt themselves will be humbled, but all who humble themselves will be exalted."

REFLECTION

Jesus' parable about a Pharisee and a tax collector tells us something about the stereotypes of these two professions in first-century Palestine. Tax collectors were known as rapacious cheats and were considered impure according to the Mosaic law. Pharisees were entrusted with the proper interpretation of that law; their occupation required an extensive education, and it afforded prestige and the assurance of righteousness. The author introduces the story with a description of Jesus' audience; they are depicted as people who think exactly as does the Pharisee in the tale.

Jesus does not indicate that the Pharisee is dishonest in his self-assessment. He may in fact be as righteous under the law as he claims. It is the *manner* of his prayer that is of most interest. Although he addresses his prayer to God, he is praying for himself, focusing his attention on his own glories by contrasting himself with such contemptible creatures as the tax collector. It is this contempt for others that signals to the reader that the Pharisee is not so righteous after all. The law and subsequent writings, such as the first reading, which comes from the Wisdom tradition, mandate concern for one's neighbor and provision for the lowly. And one of the recipients of the Pharisee's scorn, the tax collector, illustrates by his prayer that he is indeed "humble" and lowly.

By contrast with the Pharisee, the tax collector is not only honest but makes no claims of divine favor or forgiveness. He simply implores God's mercy. The characteristic Lukan reversal is already evident: The one thought to be righteous acts despicably while the perceived thief turns out to be honest.

Once again, the usual social, economic and religious categories are proved deficient in the face of Jesus' teaching. The theme set forth in the Magnificat and that recurs throughout the gospel is repeated: God has brought down the powerful from their thrones and lifted up the lowly. One is justified, set right with God, not by failing to sin but by honestly acknowledging sinfulness.

■ **It is easy to contrast oneself with others and either exalt oneself or wallow in self-blame. Resolve to concentrate on seeing yourself as God sees you: lovable and good, but also prone to error. Strive to assess yourself honestly. Be thankful and be contrite.**

PRACTICE OF FAITH

THE APPLE OF YOUR EYE. "Keep us, O Lord, as the apple of your eye." This common responsory in the Liturgy of the Hours has a wonderful simplicity. Its petition for affection and favor strikes us as almost naive. Perhaps it is embarrassing for adults to put themselves in an image best filled by a child seeking to be pleasing to a parent. It is also a petition for loving protection.

Listen to the prayers of petition from the "apples of your eye." We can hear in the petitions of children the trust and simplicity of this responsory prayer. Include time in household prayer for prayer of petition. Allow the prayers of children to be guidance in trusting and pleading for the protection and favor of the Lord.

PRACTICE OF HOPE

PHARISEES. "Hey! I'm doing things right. I'm working my butt off to earn an honest living. I hardly get to see my family, but guess what? We all go to church together. Yes sir, every Sunday. We have family values, I'm telling you. Not like those godless social and political activists who want to run the country. Nope, not like them. I'm doing things right."

Not far off: "God, be merciful to me, a sinner. Do not allow me to exalt myself over that reactionary cretin who comes strutting down the aisle. Do not make me cringe at the complacency of his ignorance. Do not make me feel superior because of the intolerance I expect from him. Infuse our hearts with a fire that would melt the armor of our judgment and free the light of our humanity."

PRACTICE OF CHARITY

THE HUMBLE SHALL BE EXALTED. A Chinese story illustrates beautifully the sentiments of Sirach, Timothy and Luke in today's readings. In the story, the scene in both heaven and hell is the same: an elegant, sumptuous feast, delightful to eat. In heaven all are happy and well fed. In hell all are gaunt, starving, hostile and bitter. The reason: The only way to eat is with chopsticks three feet long. No person can feed himself or herself but must be fed by someone else. Those in heaven have heard the cry of the oppressed, the orphan, the widow. They are delivered from the lion's mouth. They are the humble tax collector. They feed each other. Oxfam America is an organization that calls attention to those who hunger throughout the world. Contact them at 26 West Street, Boston MA 02111; 617-482-1211.

WEEKDAY READINGS (Mo) Ephesians 4:32 — 5:8; (Tu) 5:21 – 33; (We) 2:19 – 22; (Th) 6:10 – 20; (Fr) Philippians 1:1 – 11; (Sa) 1:18 – 26

READING I   *Revelation 7:2–4, 9–14*

I, John, saw another angel ascending from the rising of the sun, having the seal of the living God, and the angel called with a loud voice to the four angels who had been given power to damage earth and sea, saying, "Do not damage the earth or the sea or the trees, until we have marked the servants of our God with a seal on their foreheads." And I heard the number of those who were sealed, one hundred forty-four thousand, sealed out of every tribe of the people of Israel.

After this I looked, and there was a great multitude that no one could count, from every nation, from all tribes and peoples and languages, standing before the throne and before the Lamb, robed in white, with palm branches in their hands. They cried out in a loud voice, "Salvation belongs to our God who is seated on the throne, and to the Lamb!" And all the angels stood around the throne, around the elders and the four living creatures; they fell on their faces before the throne and worshiped God, singing,

"Amen! Blessing and glory and wisdom
and thanksgiving and honor
and power and might
be to our God forever and ever! Amen."

Then one of the elders addressed me, "Who are these, robed in white, and where have they come from?" I said to him, "Sir, you are the one that knows." Then he said to me, "These are they who have come out of the great ordeal; they have washed their robes and made them white in the blood of the Lamb."

READING II   *1 John 3:1–3*

See what love the Father has given us, that we should be called children of God; and that is what we are. The reason the world does not know us is that it did not know God. Beloved, we are God's children now; what we will be has not yet been revealed. What we do know is this: when it is revealed, we will be like God, for we will see God as God is. And all who have this hope in God purify themselves, just as the Son is pure.

GOSPEL   *Matthew 5:1–12*

When Jesus saw the crowds, he went up the mountain; and after he sat down, his disciples came to him. Then he began to speak, and taught them, saying:

"Blessed are the poor in spirit,
for theirs is the kingdom of heaven.
Blessed are those who mourn,
for they will be comforted.
Blessed are the meek,
for they will inherit the earth.
Blessed are those who hunger and thirst
for righteousness,
for they will be filled.
Blessed are the merciful,
for they will receive mercy.
Blessed are the pure in heart,
for they will see God.
Blessed are the peacemakers,
for they will be called children of God.
Blessed are those who are persecuted
for righteousness' sake,
for theirs is the kingdom of heaven.

Blessed are you when people revile you and persecute you and utter all kinds of evil against you falsely on my account. Rejoice and be glad, for your reward is great in heaven."

Monday, November 2, 1998

ALL SOULS

Daniel 12:1–3 *The dead will rise to shine like stars.*

Romans 6:3–9 *We shall be united with him in the resurrection.*

John 6:37–40 *I will not reject anyone who comes to me.*

In the Northern Hemisphere at this time of year, nature yields the awesome beauty of the harvest. Yesterday we rejoiced in the harvest of the saints. Today we reflect on what made this harvest possible: self-sacrifice, completed labors and death.

REFLECTION

We pause today and tomorrow to remember those members of our broad faith community who have run the race, who have endured to the end and now share in the promises of heaven. We think of the well-known holy ones whose stories inspire us; we think also of the saints from our own lives, real people with faults and failings as well as plenty of love and laughter, people whose lives we recall with pain and joy. We trust that these beloved children of God do indeed see God in truth, for to them have been revealed the truths that we know only in part.

In Revelation we read of a vision of the heavenly scene, a vision of salvation for members of the tribes of Israel and for multitudes from every nation. The inclusiveness of this vision results from the nature of the lives led by these holy ones; they are all those whose clothing has been washed in the blood of the Lamb. They have trusted in the saving power of Jesus' death and resurrection, even to the point of dying during persecution for the sake of their faith. To such as these and to us are addressed Matthew's beatitudes, words of encouragement and comfort despite the difficulties of life.

The beatitudes in this gospel do not have economic and social concerns as their central characteristics, as do the beatitudes in Luke. Here the message is personal, the concerns spiritual. A person's disposition is all-important in determining who receives these blessings. They are directed at the humble ones, the "poor in spirit" and the "meek"; those loath to make demands will be recipients of both heaven and earth. Likewise, the innocent, the "pure in heart," will enjoy the splendor of God's presence. Those who bestow mercy will be reciprocated, while others will be satisfied in their quests: Those who seek righteousness and who work for harmonious relationships will find satisfaction. The sense of aching that comes with sorrow and mourning will be eased. And finally, those persecuted for faith can rejoice in a heavenly reward.

As we reflect on all those Christians who have preceded us in death, we take comfort in knowing that they enjoy peace and have truly been blessed with the fulfillment of these promises for which we yet hope. We draw inspiration from their lives of faith and love, as we ourselves continue to struggle to be faithful and loving members of the Christian family.

PRACTICE OF FAITH

LITANY. Some of the books most recommended for very small children are texts with growing lists and repeated refrains. Children are captivated by naming things and by lyrical rhyming refrains. They find safety and accomplishment in the repeated refrain, and anticipation and excitement in hearing the new item added to the song or story. The Litany of Saints may not be as much fun as "Jesse Bear, Jesse Bear, What Will You Wear," but it offers us all the comfort of repetition and the anticipation of new things added on.

Bring home the Litany of the Saints. Sing it, chant it or speak it tonight. It can be found in many Catholic prayer books and in *Catholic Household Blessings and Prayers.* Many parishes make copies of the missal available for household prayer, and the litany can be found there also.

PRACTICE OF HOPE

BLESSINGS, TWO. Receive the blessings of the earth. Let its steadfastness give you reverence for what was before you and for what will be after you on your journey. Receive the blessings of rivers and oceans. Let their fertile waves increase your devotion for what moves in you and all about you on your journey.

Receive the blessings of the swift winds. Let the freedom of their play inspire your love for the unforseen on your journey. Receive the blessings of the sun, the stars and the fires below. Let their burning flames enkindle your desire to seek that which consumes and transforms you on your journey. And receive the blessings of the Son of Humanity. Let the power of his love shine forth at every crossing-point and receive you in his arms at the end of your journey.

PRACTICE OF CHARITY

INHERIT THE EARTH. In William Faulkner's story "The Man," torrential rainfall overwhelms even the mighty Mississippi River. At one point the water surges in three different directions at one time — the power, the energy! We are children of God, meant to inherit the earth. Revelation commands us not to damage the earth, the sea, the trees. As populations surge on like the torrents of a river, the balance between humankind and nature becomes delicate. Learn to treat our planet respectfully. Volunteer your group to clean a portion of a local roadway. Participate in protecting our environment by contacting the Sierra Club, 85 2nd Street, 2nd floor, San Francisco CA 94105; 415-977-5500.

WEEKDAY READINGS (Mo) All Souls, see box; (Tu) Philippians 2:5 – 11; (We) 2:12 – 18; (Th) 3:3 – 8; (Fr) 3:17 — 4:1; (Sa) 4:10 – 19

READING I *Daniel 7:1–3, 15–18*

In the first year of King Belshazzar of Babylon, Daniel had a dream and visions of his head as he lay in bed. Then he wrote down the dream: I, Daniel, saw in my vision by night the four winds of heaven stirring up the great sea, and four great beasts came up out of the sea, different from one another.

As for me, Daniel, my spirit was troubled within me, and the visions of my head terrified me. I approached one of the attendants to inquire concerning the truth of all this. So the attendant agreed to disclose to me the interpretation of the matter: "As for these four great beasts, four kings shall arise out of the earth. But the holy ones of the Most High shall receive the kingdom and possess the kingdom forever — forever and ever."

READING II *Ephesians 1:11–23*

In Christ we have also obtained an inheritance, having been destined according to the purpose of the one who accomplishes all things according to the divine counsel and will, so that we, who were the first to set our hope on Christ, might live for the praise of God's glory. In Christ you also, when you had heard the word of truth, the gospel of your salvation, and had believed in him, were marked with the seal of the promised Holy Spirit; this is the pledge of our inheritance toward redemption as God's own people, to the praise of God's glory.

I have heard of your faith in the Lord Jesus and your love toward all the saints, and for this reason I do not cease to give thanks for you as I remember you in my prayers. I pray that the God of our Lord Jesus Christ, the Father of glory, may give you a spirit of wisdom and revelation, as you come to know God, so that, with the eyes of your heart enlightened, you may know what is the hope to which God has called you, what are the riches of God's glorious inheritance among the saints, and what is the immeasurable greatness of God's power for us who believe, according to the working of God's great power.

God put this power to work in Christ when God raised him from the dead and seated him at the right hand of Power in the heavenly places, far above all rule and authority and power and dominion, and above every name that is named, not only in this age but also in the age to come. And God has put all things under the feet of Christ and has made him the head over all things for the church, which is the body of Christ, the fullness of the one who fills all in all.

GOSPEL *Luke 6:20–31*

Then Jesus looked up at his disciples and said:
"Blessed are you who are poor,
for yours is the kingdom of God.
"Blessed are you who are hungry now,
for you will be filled.
"Blessed are you who weep now,
for you will laugh.
"Blessed are you when people hate you, and when they exclude you, revile you, and defame you on account of the Son-of-Man. Rejoice in that day and leap for joy, for surely your reward is great in heaven; for that is what their ancestors did to the prophets.
"But woe to you who are rich,
for you have received your consolation.
"Woe to you who are full now,
for you will be hungry.
"Woe to you who are laughing now,
for you will mourn and weep.
"Woe to you when all speak well of you, for that is what their ancestors did to the false prophets.
"But I say to you that listen, Love your enemies, do good to those who hate you, bless those who curse you, pray for those who abuse you. If anyone strikes you on the cheek, offer the other also; and from anyone who takes away your coat do not withhold even your shirt. Give to everyone who begs from you; and if anyone takes away your goods, do not ask for them again. Do to others as you would have them do to you."

R E F L E C T I O N

Blessed, said Jesus, are the poor, the hungry, the down-trodden. Blessed are those who are hated and reviled for their faith. Rejoice!

It is an odd message, but it is fully in keeping with the upheaval so celebrated in the Gospel of Luke. Unlike those addressed in the Sermon on the Mount in Matthew, who are poor "in spirit," this gospel proclaims that the truly destitute — the homeless, those on welfare, those persecuted, tortured, perhaps killed for who they are and what they believe — are in fact blessed. They can take heart, knowing that society also reviled the prophets before them, and they can look forward to a day of reckoning.

But the day of reckoning is not joyful for everyone; woe to those who are well fed and comfortable in the midst of such suffering. For such as these, the judgment will be harsh.

These words could easily have been written for us, living in North America in the late twentieth century. Throughout the world, constant toil still results in starvation; wars rage; people lose their homes, their families; despots reign. Even in our own cities and towns, and scattered throughout our countryside, are those who struggle, who try to appear "normal," to work hard and contribute to society. It is a daunting task when the struggle to cook, to clean, to bathe and to do laundry without the benefit of running water consumes all one's time and energy. Jesus speaks words of comfort to such people and words of warning to those of us who are satisfied and complacent.

The challenge is before us: Pray for those who harm us; generously give to those who steal; love enemies. These are not simply pious words. They are a dare. Can we do it?

Yet we have, as the second reading assures us, the greatness of God's power acting in us. It is the same power that raised and exalted Christ. We are not challenged without also being given the strength to respond.

■ **These are hard words to hear and read. Imagine how different your life would have to be if we took the blessings and woes of this gospel text seriously.**

PRACTICE OF
FAITH
CHEEKS, COATS, SHIRTS. Most of us think of faith as something that shapes only our interior lives. Yet in the gospels, Jesus speaks words that deal not only with souls and minds but with the care of bodies, our own and those of others.

In our families we have opportunities to form Christian values in our children by teaching them not only to pray but also to help those in need. Complement the prayer life of your household with what we used to call the seven "corporal works of mercy": feeding the hungry, giving drink to the thirsty, clothing the naked, sheltering the homeless, visiting the sick, freeing the imprisoned and burying the dead. And if doing such works makes others exclude you and defame you, leap for joy: Your reward is great in heaven.

PRACTICE OF
HOPE
BLESSINGS, TWO. Receive the blessings of the earth. Let its steadfastness give you reverence for what was before you and for what will be after you on your journey. Receive the blessings of rivers and oceans. Let their fertile waves increase your devotion for what moves in you and all about you on your journey. Receive the blessings of the swift winds. Let the freedom of their play inspire your love for the unforeseen on your journey. Receive the blessings of the sun, the stars, and the fires below. Let their burning flames enkindle your desire to seek that which consumes and transforms you on your journey. And receive the blessings of the Son of Humanity. Let the power of his love shine forth at every crossing-point and receive you in his arms at the end of your journey.

PRACTICE OF
CHARITY
INHERIT THE EARTH. In William Faulkner's story "The Man," torrential rainfall overwhelms even the mighty Mississippi River. At one point the water surges in three different directions at one time — the power, the energy! We are children of God, meant to inherit the earth. Revelation commands us not to damage the earth, the sea, the trees. As populations surge on like the torrents of a river, the balance between humankind and nature becomes delicate. Learn to treat our planet respectfully. Volunteer your group to clean a portion of a local roadway. Participate in protecting our environment by contacting the Sierra Club, 85 2nd Street, 2nd floor, San Francisco CA 94105; 415-977-5500.

WEEKDAY READINGS (Mo) All Souls, see box; (Tu) Philippians 2:5 – 11; (We) 2:12 – 18; (Th) 3:3 – 8; (Fr) 3:17 — 4:1; (Sa) 4:10 – 19

NOVEMBER 8, 1998 Thirty-second Sunday in Ordinary Time
Twenty-third Sunday after Pentecost

READING I *2 Maccabees 7:1–2, 7, 9–14*

It happened that seven brothers and their mother were arrested and were being compelled by King Antiochus, under torture with whips and thongs, to partake of unlawful swine's flesh. One of the brothers, speaking for all, said, "What do you intend to ask and learn from us? For we are ready to die rather than transgress the laws of our ancestors."

After the first brother had died, they brought forward the second for their sport. And when he was at his last breath, he said, "You accursed wretch, you dismiss us from this present life, but the Sovereign of the universe will raise us up to an everlasting renewal of life, because we have for the laws of God."

After him, the third was the victim of their sport. When it was demanded, he quickly put out his tongue and courageously stretched forth his hands, and said nobly, "I got these from Heaven, and because of God's laws I disdain them, and from God I hope to get them back again." As a result the king himself and those with him were astonished at the young man's spirit, for he regarded his sufferings as nothing.

After the third brother too had died, they maltreated and tortured the fourth in the same way. When he was near death, he said to his torturers, "One cannot but choose to die at the hands of mortals and to cherish the hope God gives of being raised again by him. But for you there will be no resurrection to life!"

READING II *2 Thessalonians 2:16—3:5*

May our Lord Jesus Christ himself and God, our Father, who loved us and through grace gave us eternal comfort and good hope, comfort your hearts and strengthen them in every good work and word.

Brothers and sisters, pray for us, so that the word of the Lord may spread rapidly and be glorified everywhere, just as it is among you, and that we may be rescued from wicked and evil people; for not all have faith. But the Lord is faithful, and will strengthen you and guard you from the evil one. And we have confidence in the Lord concerning you, that you are doing and will go on doing the things that we command. May the Lord direct your hearts to the love of God and to the steadfastness of Christ.

GOSPEL *Luke 20:27–38*

Some Sadducees, those who say there is no resurrection, came to Jesus and asked him a question, "Teacher, Moses wrote for us that if a man's brother dies, leaving a wife but no children, the man shall marry the widow and raise up children for his brother. Now there were seven brothers; the first married, and died childless; then the second and the third married her, and so in the same way all seven died childless. Finally the woman also died. In the resurrection, therefore, whose wife will the woman be? For the seven had married her."

Jesus said to them, "Those who belong to this age marry and are given in marriage; but those who are considered worthy of a place in that age and in the resurrection from the dead neither marry nor are given in marriage. Indeed they cannot die anymore, because they are like angels and are children of God, being children of the resurrection. And the fact that the dead are raised Moses himself showed, in the story about the bush, where he speaks of the Lord as the God of Abraham, the God of Isaac, and the God of Jacob. Now God is God not of the dead, but of the living; for to God all of them are alive."

Monday, November 9, 1998

THE DEDICATION OF THE LATERAN BASILICA IN ROME

Ezekiel 47:1–2, 8—9, 12 *Saving water flowed from the temple.*

1 Corinthians 3:9–11, 16–17 *You are God's temple.*

John 2:13–22 *Consumed by zeal for God's house.*

Human flesh is God's dwelling place. In November, a season of ingathering, we assemble in the Spirit. Our own flesh and blood is becoming God's holy temple. All creation is becoming Jerusalem.

REFLECTION

The Jewish hope in the resurrection of the dead, so vividly recounted in the story of the brothers who held to their faith despite persecution, was a relatively late development. At the time of Jesus, the resurrection of the dead was still being debated. The party of the Sadducees took the traditional view that death was final, while the Pharisees proclaimed the newer teaching of an afterlife. The question posed to Jesus in today's gospel is set against the background of this debate and assumes the practice of levirate marriage, in which the brother of a man who had died childless would marry the widow in order to ensure that there would be heirs who would bear the name of the dead man.

The Sadducees' question is rather clever. Since no one can claim firsthand knowledge of the resurrection of the dead, they assumed that the order of the afterlife would resemble the order on earth. Human relationships would, they reasoned, continue. But the clever question is presented by means of a ridiculous example: A woman had married seven brothers, and the question of her true husband in the afterlife is intended to trip Jesus up and force him to deny the resurrection of the dead.

Jesus aligns himself with the Pharisees and produces a Pharisaic argument to support his position. First, he corrects the mistaken belief that the afterlife operates in the same way as life on earth; the righteous who die to eternal life are changed, transformed into heavenly beings. Resurrection is not the same as resuscitation. To make his point, Jesus appeals to the certain knowledge that the God of Abraham, Isaac and Jacob is a God of the living, thus "proving" that the patriarchs enjoy the resurrected life.

No words are here placed in Jesus' mouth predicting his own resurrection, but the concern about the afterlife may have stemmed from the early Christian community. Paul also addresses the claim that there was no resurrection from the dead, insisting that Christ's resurrection assures all that the afterlife is a reality for those Christians who have died.

■ **Do you ever wonder what life is like after death? How do you envision it? Does your view make any difference in your approach to life?**

PRACTICE OF FAITH

PARTING. Saint Martin of Tours (November 11) is remembered, in part, for knowing how to live well and how to die well. His deathbed story tells of his willingness to acept life or death as God desired. In his life and in his death, he kept his "eyes and hands raised to heaven."

Living well and dying well include learning how to part well in daily situations. Saying our daily good-byes gives us the basis of a parting ritual to be expanded upon when we have to part with someone permanently, because of either circumstances or death.

Take time to say good-bye when you leave home, work or school. In your household, expand that good-bye with a blessing. In our household this takes the form of "Good-bye and God bless you and remember who you are."

PRACTICE OF HOPE

GOD OF THE LIVING. Have you ever wondered where it is that you go when you're asleep? On what wondrous wings are you carried across expanses unknown, picking up dreams on the way to self-forgetfulness? And what more wondrous power yet allows you, after a voyage so uncertain, to return to yourself — still to yourself, still to those familiar hands and eyes and memories? Refreshed and replenished, you cry out: "Good morning, new world! I who was asleep greet you. I was dead to myself, yet all the while I was alive to God. Praise to the morning sun into whose glory I now rise!"

PRACTICE OF CHARITY

DIRECT YOUR HEARTS TO THE LOVE OF GOD. At the end of the wake, just before the casket was closed for the last time, Helen moved to say good-bye to her husband. She spoke to him as she always had, in the graceful movement of language signed by hands and fingers. Their mute world had been filled with loving communication in sign language. She touched Leonard's chest, sending him to God. The stillness suggested the eternal comfort with which Paul assured the Christians of Thessalonika. God is God of the living, and we are called to give thanks. As a sign of your love of God, prepare for your Thanksgiving celebration by planning to provide a meal at a homeless shelter or for a neighbor or family in crisis. Give signs of thanks for the everlasting renewal of life.

WEEKDAY READINGS (Mo) Dedication of the Lateran Basilica, see box; (Tu) Titus 2:1 – 14; (We) 3:1 – 7; (Th) Philemon 7 – 20; (Fr) 2 John 4 – 9; (Sa) 3 John 5 – 8

READING I *Malachi 4:1–2*

See, the day is coming, burning like an oven, when all the arrogant and all evildoers will be stubble; the day that comes shall burn them up, says the LORD of hosts, so that it will leave them neither root nor branch. But for you who revere my name the sun of righteousness shall rise, with healing in its wings.

READING II *2 Thessalonians 3:6–13*

Now we command you, beloved, in the name of our Lord Jesus Christ, to keep away from believers who are living in idleness and not according to the tradition that they received from us. For you yourselves know how you ought to imitate us; we were not idle when we were with you, and we did not eat anyone's bread without paying for it; but with toil and labor we worked night and day, so that we might not burden any of you. This was not because we do not have that right, but in order to give you an example to imitate. For even when we were with you, we gave you this command: Anyone unwilling to work should not eat. For we hear that some of you are living in idleness, mere busybodies, not doing any work. Now such persons we command and exhort in the Lord Jesus Christ to do their work quietly and to earn their own living. Brothers and sisters, do not be weary in doing what is right.

GOSPEL *Luke 21:5–19*

When some were speaking about the temple, how it was adorned with beautiful stones and gifts dedicated to God, Jesus said, "As for these things that you see, the days will come when not one stone will be left upon another; all will be thrown down."

They asked him, "Teacher, when will this be, and what will be the sign that this is about to take place?" And Jesus said, "Beware that you are not led astray; for many will come in my name and say, 'I am the one!' and, 'The time is near!' Do not go after them.

"When you hear of wars and insurrections, do not be terrified; for these things must take place first, but the end will not follow immediately." Then Jesus said to them, "Nation will rise against nation, and country against country; there will be great earthquakes, and in various places famines and plagues; and there will be dreadful portents and great signs from heaven.

"But before all this occurs, they will arrest you and persecute you; they will hand you over to synagogues and prisons, and you will be brought before rulers and governors because of my name. This will give you an opportunity to testify. So make up your minds not to prepare your defense in advance; for I will give you words and a wisdom that none of your opponents will be able to withstand or contradict. You will be betrayed even by parents and family, by relatives and friends; and they will put some of you to death. You will be hated by all because of my name. But not a hair of your head will perish. By your endurance you will gain your souls."

REFLECTION

On the journey to Jerusalem, Jesus taught his followers about discipleship, about what is involved in giving allegiance to him. Now, in Jerusalem, gazing upon the beauty of the Temple — the focal point of worship for Jesus and all the Jews, and the symbol of religious unity and the presence of God — Jesus gives a final exhortation to his followers.

Others in Jesus' presence noted the beauty of the Temple complex, leading to a prediction of the destruction of the Temple. The apocalyptic imagery used to describe the chaos and destruction characteristic of war is typical language used to describe dire events and especially times of persecution. Written after the Jewish revolt against the Romans, with its devastating conclusion including the fall of Jerusalem and the destruction of the Temple, these words placed on Jesus' lips give evidence to readers of this gospel that he was a prophet, that his word was true. Since Jesus is presented as trustworthy regarding the demise of the Temple, his words can also be trusted in other areas. And what he predicts is persecution of his followers.

The promise of trying times for Jesus' disciples can be understood on three levels. Jesus may indeed have been warning his earliest followers about the consequences of their choice to follow him. Surely the author of the gospel intended to warn the Christian community that they too may need to defend themselves against charges brought against them for their faith. Finally, we, as an extension of that early community, have the assurance that our faith is demanding. Sometimes, as we have seen before, it even causes divisions within families and brings hatred and contempt.

Jesus' final teaching on discipleship is how to respond to this onslaught of hatred and enmity. First, those who are persecuted are to trust that they will know how to respond to their accusers. And in addition, they are to withstand the trials with an endurance born of hope.

■ **Have you ever truly had to suffer for your faith? How did you respond? Or if you were to be faced with this challenge, how do you think you would respond?**

■ **In some areas of the world, those who live gospel values are regularly persecuted and literally tortured. How can you support them in their struggles for justice?**

PRACTICE OF FAITH

PRESENTATION. As we begin to turn toward Advent, we celebrate a memorial to Mary and her parents. The legend that is part of this celebration on November 21 is of Ann and Joachim, Mary's parents, bringing her to the temple at the age of three to dedicate and consecrate her to God's service.

Ritualizing certain moments shapes the memories and lives of the people involved. When parents present their children or adults present themselves for baptism, the definition and identity of the person, family and community are forever changed. "Now that you are here, we need you" is how one prayer describes this moment.

Recognize and welcome the new members presented and dedicated in your midst.

PRACTICE OF HOPE

MARTYRS. Martyrs intimidate me. I faint when I hear of their torments. Remember Laurentius's line (unpremeditated, I'm sure) when he got roasted? "This side's done. Time to flip me over." His *esprit* may have charmed the Romans. I am not convinced. I just shudder. Even Joan of Arc is hard to take. "Are you in the grace of God?" the inquisitors asked her. "If I am, may God keep me there. If I am not, may God receive me into it." Good girl, great line — but they burned her all the same. In my faintheartedness I turn to the non-martyr Martin of Tours. As an old man, longing to die after much labor and toil, he made the ultimate sacrifice, saying: "Lord, if I am still necessary to your people, I do not refuse to live. Thy will be done."

PRACTICE OF CHARITY

WORKING NIGHT AND DAY. The wallhanging pictured a stuffed Raggedy Ann doll squeezed half-way through a wringer. The formal biblical script said, "The truth will make you free, but first you'll be miserable." Jesus' assurances in the gospel seem to confirm this. So does Paul's insistence on his high moral example of working night and day. We do know and believe that idleness and arrogance are not productive. We also know the vital importance of extending help to others. The truth is that each year, Catholics throughout the country are asked to relieve the misery of others by contributing to the annual Campaign for Human Development. The campaign has provided social justice for many. Self-help projects have set many poor neighborhoods free. Plan to contribute generously this year.

WEEKDAY READINGS (Mo) Revelation 1:1 – 4; 2:1 – 5; (Tu) 3:1 – 22; (We) Revelation 4:1 – 11; (Th) 5:1 – 10; (Fr) 10:8 – 11; (Sa) 11:4 – 12

NOVEMBER 22, 1998
Christ the King
Twenty-fifth Sunday after Pentecost

READING I *2 Samuel 5:1–3*

All the tribes of Israel came to David in Hebron, and said, "Look, we are your bone and flesh. For some time, when Saul was king over us, it was you who led out Israel and brought it in. The LORD said to you: It is you who shall be shepherd of my people Israel, you who shall be ruler over Israel."

So all the elders of Israel came to David in Hebron; and King David made a covenant with them at Hebron before the LORD, and they anointed David king over Israel.

READING II *Colossians 1:11–20*

May you be made strong with all the strength that comes from God's glorious power, and may you be prepared to endure everything with patience, while joyfully giving thanks to the Father, who has enabled you to share in the inheritance of the saints in the light. God has rescued us from the power of darkness and transferred us into the dominion of the beloved Son of God, in whom we have redemption, the forgiveness of sins.

Christ is the image of the invisible God, the first-born of all creation; for in Christ all things in heaven and on earth were created, things visible and invisible, whether thrones or dominions or rulers or powers — all things have been created through him and for him. Christ himself is before all things, and in him all things hold together. Christ is the head of the body, the church; Christ is the beginning, the firstborn from the dead, so that he might come to have first place in everything. For in Christ all the fullness of God was pleased to dwell, and through Christ to reconcile to God's own self all things, whether on earth or in heaven, by making peace through the blood of his cross.

GOSPEL *Luke 23:33–43*

When they came to the place that is called The Skull, they crucified Jesus there with the criminals, one on his right and one on his left. Then Jesus said, "Father, forgive them; for they do not know what they are doing." And they cast lots to divide his clothing. And the people stood by, watching; but the leaders scoffed at him, saying, "He saved others; let him save himself if he is the Messiah of God, the chosen one!" The soldiers also mocked him, coming up and offering him sour wine, and saying, "If you are the King of the Jews, save yourself!" There was also an inscription over him, "This is the King of the Jews."

One of the criminals who were hanged there kept deriding Jesus and saying, "Are you not the Messiah? Save yourself and us!" But the other rebuked him, saying, "Do you not fear God, since you are under the same sentence of condemnation? And we indeed have been condemned justly, for we are getting what we deserve for our deeds, but this man has done nothing wrong." Then he said, "Jesus, remember me when you come into your kingdom." He replied, "Truly I tell you, today you will be with me in Paradise."

Thursday, November 26

THANKSGIVING DAY (UNITED STATES)

Sirach 50:22–24 *May the God of all grant you joy of heart.*

1 Corinthians 1:3–9 *I give thanks to my God always for you.*

Luke 17:11–19 *He fell at the feet of Jesus and thanked him.*

God has given us the earth, a land flowing with milk and honey. We show our thankfulness by being wise and selfless stewards of the earth and by sharing our gifts with one another.

REFLECTION

Through much of this liturgical year we have been traveling with Jesus on the road to Jerusalem and his death. Now, on the last Sunday before we begin again our spiral dance through the mysteries of our faith, we have arrived at our destination. We encounter Jesus at his last moment, on earth, tortured and bloody, reviled, hanging on the cross. In the central paradox of Christian belief, we celebrate today the feast of Christ as King, proclaiming as exalted the one who was executed. At the darkest moment we raise our hands and voices in praise of the one who is "making peace by the blood of his cross."

The idea of kingship is foreign to many of us. In the developed world, most of the monarchs who remain have largely ceremonial duties. It is hard to imagine society and the lives of the common people controlled by one person. When we do think of countries that operate on this model, we think of despots who rule with a heavy hand. This would have been much the same experience of Christians in the first century. It is difficult to apply this title to the defender of the powerless and the oppressed.

We know also the romantic concept, taught to us in childhood, of princes and princesses, of splendor and majesty. There is something foreign and yet familiar about the idea of royalty.

The Gospel of Luke, that paean to lowliness and humility, presents the exaltation of the Christ in terms of powerlessness. Our expectations have been turned upside down. It is the one who feasted with sinners who is righteous. It is the one despised who, throughout the gospel and in today's selection in particular, shows compassion. It is the one who suffered and died who gives life. And it is the one broken, lowly, powerless who is exalted. The gospel of reversal has come full circle.

■ How do you think Jesus would have responded to the claim that he is "king"? How do you understand the "kingship" of Jesus? Can you think of a better model for describing the honor to be given the risen Lord?

■ After following the Gospel of Luke for the past year, what theme has struck you most? What do you hope to carry with you into the new liturgical year?

PRACTICE OF FAITH

CALENDAR. We live a good deal of our lives by the scrawling on a large calendar posted on the wall of the kitchen. Each new month reveals blank spaces that with a few invitations, phone calls and schedules distributed are soon darkened. But more importantly, we live by another calendar that comes already filled in with invitations. This is the calendar of the liturgical year. The invitations on that calendar are invitations in colors and names of saints and days and Sundays and seasons. They are invitations to enter into and celebrate the rhythm and cycle of the church's life. The challenge for our family is to keep the calendar in the kitchen auxiliary to the one on the dining room wall.

Hang a poster of the Year of Grace, the Liturgical Year, near your family table.

PRACTICE OF HOPE

FEAR. *Save yourself!* Hear this dark litany, piercing like the cold reflection of a saw-toothed blade.

Save yourself, for that's what I did. We're on our own in this game, so get with it or go under!

Save yourself, for no one has thought of saving *me.* And who should be more deserving of compassion than I?

Save yourself, for you have failed me bitterly. All my hopes were invested in you, and they came to naught. Do not expect any help from me!

Save yourself, if you can, for I no longer need you. We were like cat and mouse, and it was good fun while you squeaked in my claws. But now you're getting weak, and I will finish you off.

Behold the love that could face this blade. Behold the warm blood of hope trickling from the cross.

PRACTICE OF CHARITY

SEAMLESS GARMENT. The soldiers at the cross cast lots for the garment of Christ the King. Tradition tells us that it was a seamless garment. The fully woven fabric has become a metaphor for the reverence for all human life that should characterize members of Christ's kingdom. Neither abortion nor mercy killing, neither capital punishment nor killing in battle should mar Christian conduct. Human life is sacred from beginning to end, from conception to final breath. In Christ was absolute fullness of life. Christians have been rescued from darkness and share the lot of the saints. A new year of grace is about to renew Christ's followers — a new seamless garment, year to year, life to life.

WEEKDAY READINGS (Mo) Revelation 14:1 – 5; (Tu) 14: 14 – 19; (We) 15:1 – 4; (Th) Thanksgiving, see box; (Fr) 20: 1 — 21:2; (Sa) 22:1 – 7

Information on the License to Reprint from
At Home with the Word 1998

The low bulk-rate prices of *At Home with the Word 1998* are intended to make quantities of the book affordable. Single copies are $7.00 each; 5–99 copies, $5.00 each; 100–499 copies, $4.00 each; 500 or more copies, $3.00 each. We encourage parishes to buy quantities of this book.

However, Liturgy Training Publications makes a simple reprint license available to parishes that would find it more practical to reproduce some parts of this book. Reflections (and questions), Practices, Prayers of the Season, and/or the holy day boxes can be duplicated for the parish bulletin or reproduced in other formats. These can be used every week or as often as the license-holder chooses. The page size of *At Home with the Word 1998* is 8 x 10 inches.

The license granted is for the period beginning with the First Sunday of Advent — November 30, 1997 — through the solemnity of Christ the King — November 22, 1998.

Note also that the license does *not* cover the scriptures, psalms, or morning, evening and night prayer texts. See the acknowledgments page at the beginning of this book for the names and addresses of these copyright owners. Directions for obtaining permission to use these texts are given there.

The materials reprinted under license from LTP may not be sold and may be used only among the members of the community obtaining the license. The license may not be purchased by a diocese for use in its parishes.

No reprinting may be done by the parish until the license is signed by both parties and the fee is paid. Copies of the license agreement will be sent on request. The fee varies with the number of copies to be reproduced on a regular basis:

Up to 100 copies: $100
101 to 500 copies: $300
501 to 1000 copies: $500
More than 1000 copies: $800

For further information, call the reprint permissions department at 773-486-8970, ext. 268, or fax your request to 773-486-7094, att: reprint permissions.

GIFTS OF PRAYER-INSTRUMENTS OF PEACE

Use this series of pocket-sized prayer books to pray for and with those who are in need or to celebrate ministry of care in our lives. LTP's prayer books have a distinctive design that reflects the dignity of prayer and provides a means for family ritual and group prayer. These prayer books make excellent gifts and fit easily into most greeting cards. Give the enduring gift of prayer to yourself and loved ones.

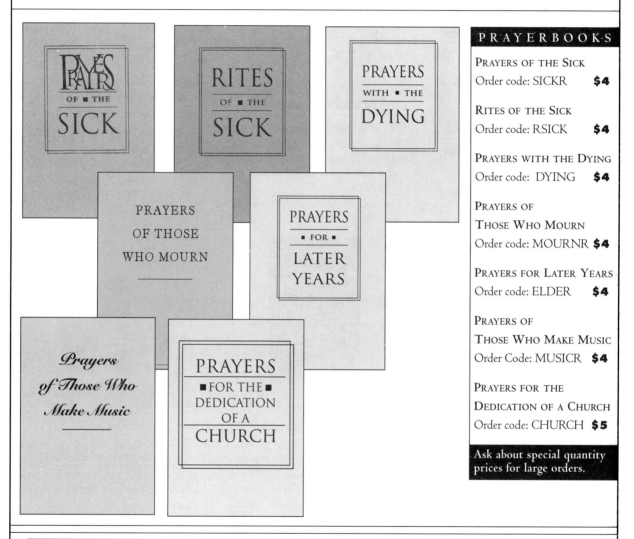

PRAYERBOOKS

PRAYERS OF THE SICK
Order code: SICKR **$4**

RITES OF THE SICK
Order code: RSICK **$4**

PRAYERS WITH THE DYING
Order code: DYING **$4**

PRAYERS OF THOSE WHO MOURN
Order code: MOURNR **$4**

PRAYERS FOR LATER YEARS
Order code: ELDER **$4**

PRAYERS OF THOSE WHO MAKE MUSIC
Order Code: MUSICR **$4**

PRAYERS FOR THE DEDICATION OF A CHURCH
Order code: CHURCH **$5**

Ask about special quantity prices for large orders.

FOR THE SEASONS

KEEPING ADVENT AND CHRISTMASTIME
Order code: KAC3 **$3** each

KEEPING LENT, TRIDUUM AND EASTERTIME
Order code: KLTE2 **$3** each

ORDER FROM YOUR RELIGIOUS BOOKSTORE OR FROM:

LTP

LITURGY TRAINING PUBLICATIONS

Blessed Be God

A book of special prayers, psalms and blessings. For use during the various seasons of the year, for use in the school or the home. Includes images that can be colored by the child. Paperback, Order code: BBGSIN **$2** each

Order code for pack: BBGCDP

Pack of 10 for **$15**

Fling Wide the Doors
A Calendar for Advent and Christmastime

A spectacular six-sided tower that has doors that open to reveal the special days of preparation during Advent and the celebrations of the Christmas season. Some days have more than one door! A delight for children young and old. Includes a daily prayer book.

Family size: (12 inches high)
Order code: ADCAL **$10**

Community size: (18 inches tall)
Order code: ADCAL2 **$17**

Forty Days and Forty Nights
A Lenten Ark Moving toward Easter

Here's an "advent calendar" for Lent! There are windows and doors for every day of Lent and the Triduum. Discover the animals that are on board and their biblical significance. A prayer book is included.

One size only.

Order code: ARK **$15**

Let the Children Sing

A wonderful listening tape of 15 selections representing a cross-section of music styles used at Sunday Mass. Listen and learn common hymns from Mass. Cassette.

Order code: PRECAS **$9.95**

Let the Children Sing II

Additional songs from various times that remain alive and relevant today in the church's liturgy. Introduce the child to this treasury of common song. Cassette.

Order code: PRECA2 **$9.95**

Bible Stories for the 40 Days

Tales from the Bible for each day of Lent that bring to life the characters we all need to know. With wonderful illustrations to ignite the imagination of very young children. Used with the *Lenten Ark* it provides a first look at the meaning of Lent. Paperback.

Order code: ARKBK **$15**

Winter
Celebrating the Season in a Christian Home

A colorful, easy-to-use, do-it-yourself book to support the Christian traditions and holidays in the home. Delightful adventures into some great doings: St. Nicholas Day, tree trimming, Epiphany cake, card sending, house blessing and all the days of Christmastime. Paperback.

Order code: WINTER **$15**

ORDER FROM
YOUR RELIGIOUS
BOOKSTORE
OR FROM:

LITURGY
TRAINING
PUBLICATIONS

Listening to God's Word

by Eileen Drilling and Judy Rothfork

Initiation into the Christian life is fundamentally a sharing of faith. Whether passed from parent to child or from teacher to student, faith involves the whole family of God. The authors have put together an exciting approach to faith sharing. Children will enjoy the time spent talking about God with an adult, and adults will be inspired by their child's growth in faith. This is an easy way to support our children in their relaionship with God and for them to interiorize the gospel. It is an easy way for families to express verbally and ritually their experience of God and to strengthen their life together by sharing experiences, prayers and blessings. Although *Listening to God's Word* is designed for 8-12 year-olds, younger children will enjoy the stories and activities, and older children may use the Adult Journal or assist younger children.

Listening to God's Word is:
- intergenerational faith-sharing
- based in the Sunday gospels
- comprised of three resources
- activities with scripture and ritual

Use ***Listening to God's Word*** as a resource for:
- children's catechumenate
- sacramental preparation
- parish family programs
- faith formation in the home
- religion class
- vacation Bible school
- children's liturgy of the Word

YEAR C:

Activities and Stories
Order code: LCATC **$15**

Child's Journal
Order code: CJORNC **$5**

Adult's Journal
Order code: AJORNC **$5**

Year A available Fall 1998

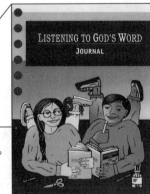

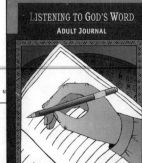

Above: pages 84 & 85 from *Activities and Stories, Year B*

ORDER FROM YOUR RELIGIOUS BOOKSTORE OR FROM:
LITURGY TRAINING PUBLICATIONS